All should stop to ponder the magnitude of God's "amazing grace" to us. As one preacher said, "I knew I was saved, but I didn't know I was saved like this!"

—Tom Grady, President
Grace Ministries International

A wonderfully personal look at what it means to walk with Jesus as a member of the family of grace!

—Robert E. Naylor
President Emeritus
Southwestern Baptist Theological Seminary

Right on target ... a badly needed work.

—M. Dale Allen
Professor of Bible
Missouri Baptist College

Tried, biblical, and spiritually revolutionary insights about the Christian life. Apply the concepts in this book and you'll be changed forever.

—Larry W. Poland, Ph.D.
Chairman and CEO
Mastermedia International

This book is a tremendous tool for understanding the truth of our identity in Christ. It's written in a personal, down-home style using everyday analogies that make the ideas applicable in the real world.

—Lamar C. Smith
Chairman and CEO
USPA&IRA

WHAT GOD WISHES CHRISTIANS KNEW ABOUT CHRISTIANITY

BILL GILLHAM

HARVEST HOUSE PUBLISHERS
Eugene, Oregon 97402

Cover by Koechel Peterson & Associates, Minneapolis, Minnesota

WHAT GOD WISHES CHRISTIANS KNEW ABOUT CHRISTIANITY
Copyright © 1998 by Bill Gillham
Published by Harvest House Publishers
Eugene, Oregon 97402

Library of Congress Cataloging-in-Publication Data
    Gillham, Bill, 1927–
        What God wishes Christians knew about Christianity / Bill Gillham.
          p. cm.
        Includes bibliographical references.
        ISBN 1-56507-557-9
        1. Christian life.   I. Title.
        BV4501.2.G51125   1998
        230—dc21   98-3536
                                                             CIP

Printed in the United States of America

            99 00 01 02 03 /BC/ 10 9 8 7 6 5 4 3 2

Dedicated to Jesus Christ, my Hero

Contents

INTRODUCTION

I SHUDDER AT THE TITLE I've given to this book! How presumptuous! But I rest in God's grace that He's confident of my purpose. I selected this title partly in hopes that it would prompt you to glance through the Contents pages. I also chose it because I'm that comfortable with the truths in the pages that follow—not *my* truths, you understand, but those found in the Bible you love.

What you *perceive* as truth greatly influences your beliefs. To illustrate this, try to connect these four dots by making three straight lines through them (the possible solutions are on the last page of this section).

A second factor the devil uses to block us from God's truth is our emotions. Let me illustrate. Lay the book down, extend your arms forward and clasp your hands. Notice which thumb is on top. Now unclasp your hands and then reclasp them, interlacing them with the other thumb in the topmost position. Now rotate your clasped hands back and forth a bit. Feels weird doesn't it? You've programmed your brain to *feel* more comfortable in the first position. The second doesn't *feel* right. A wise Christian will guard against discerning truth via his emotions. Folks, they're not trustworthy! We've programmed them in this world.

If your perceptual mind-set and conditioned emotions dictated that all potential solutions must be *boxlike*, they limited your ability to discern truth. If you've fallen into the trap of *feeling* that teaching that doesn't *feel* right is error, your ability to receive God's truth has been limited. Satan uses this same principle to blind you in spiritual matters. We create a perceptual/emotional filter screen that we call "truth" and automatically delete or misconstrue all teaching that sticks in its web. A. W. Tozer said that nothing so twists the soul of man as a distorted view of God. I urge you to pray: "Sir, if there's any *biblically documented* truth in this book that will enhance my relationship with Jesus and the Father, teach it to me. You alone can show me how to eat the meat, but throw away any bones that Bill may have included inadvertently." Test your religious tradition, and my teaching as well, by trusting *only the Holy Spirit and the Bible* as you read, not your own opinion or emotions.

Someone has wisely said that the Bible is the best commentary on the Bible. I have sought to document the teachings in this manuscript by the Word of God, not by human opinion. I have not documented each point by referencing the works of honored scholars, as in my doctoral dissertation at Oklahoma State University (which makes for tedious, laborious reading). I have written primarily as layman to laymen, although seminary-trained theologians are certainly encouraged to study and critique the work. It came from years of Bible study, listening to mentors, checking Christian readings, hearing sermons, doing counseling, brainstorming in the shower and while mowing my lawn, *always testing ideas by biblical documentation and the inner witness of the Holy Spirit*. Although the book is not intended as a theological cousin to the "For Dummies" software manuals, my purpose is to produce a simple (not simplistic) explanation of certain profound truths from God. My target audience is all disciples who have a passion to walk in vital union with Jesus Christ.

Although the topics covered do not comprise an exhaustive list, they cover a wide spectrum of problem areas for many Christians. My prayer is that understanding the topics and "lifting them out" will bring you the inner peace that it has brought to me and to the thousands of folks whose testimonies have graced my mailbox over the years.

Note: I will depict the time dimension as God's freeway upon which man travels. We will visit "rest stops"—refreshing oases—for pilgrims who long to experience that elusive place which the Bible calls "God's rest."

Two possible solutions to the puzzle:

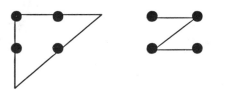

Resting in Sweet Jesus,
Bill Gillham

1   THAT THERE IS MORE TO THE CROSS THAN FORGIVENESS

BACK WHEN I PLAYED FOOTBALL, most teams ran the "single-wing formation." The tailback lined up six yards or so behind the center. He was the team's skill player, taking most of the center's snaps and running to his left or right, cutting back to hit the hole or sweeping the ends with blockers clearing the way. I was one of those blockers, only instead of *clearing* the way, the back of my legs looked like I was frequently *in* the way. Some teams were fortunate enough to have a tailback who was not only a good runner, but who also posed a second threat to the defense by his ability to pass. He would appear to be running the ball, but would suddenly either pass on the run or pull up and throw with his feet planted.

And then a few teams were blessed with what was called a triple-threat tailback. His third talent was his ability to take the snap while rocking back on his kicking foot, then quick-kicking the ball over the heads of the surprised defensive secondary, all in the twinkling of an eye. It was a great offensive maneuver that caught the defenders by surprise and often netted a college or professional team 70 yards or so in improved field position.

Wilbur Williams was a coach's dream come true—a 190-pound tailback who could run with the ball like water down a mountain stream and leave defensive players tackling nothing but air. "Double W," as the sportswriters nicknamed him, could run a 9.3 hundred! When he broke through the line of scrimmage, it was time to sing, "Turn Out the Lights, the Party's Over."

Wilbur was an early bloomer who, at age 14, shaved daily. On the football field, he was recognized as a man among boys. In middle school, it was not uncommon for him to score nine out of ten times that he carried the ball. The high school coach salivated like Pavlov's dog when he thought about Double W entering high school.

And sure enough, the Pirate varsity football team blasted through their schedule in Double W's freshman year as he shattered the school rushing and scoring records. They finally lost in the semifinals of the state play-offs to the ultimate state champions. "Wait till next year!" became the Pirates' battle cry till the following autumn.

But history kept repeating itself throughout Wilbur's career. The Pirates, with Wilbur breaking his old rushing records each new season, destroyed all opponents until they met the state's best teams in the play-offs. One of them invariably had enough good players and the coaching staff needed to design a defense that slowed Wilbur's running. Sad to say, the Pirates not only failed to sweep four state titles, they didn't capture a single one.

Sadder yet was the fact that, unknown to the town, the players, the coach, or Wilbur, they could have easily had four state championship trophies in their showcase had they known more about the talents Wilbur possessed. God had given Wilbur Williams the ability to become the greatest *triple-threat* tailback in the history of the game! Dormant within his body lay the ability to be an outstanding passer and kicker! Double W was a triple-threat tailback just waiting to be discovered.

You see, the entire community was so focused on *one* of Wilbur's world-class skills that no one suspected that he possessed these two additional talents. Although Wilbur's running ability was fabulous, the combination of these *three* skills would have placed him in a class by himself.

So what does this have to do with Christianity? I'm convinced that many Christians focus on one gracious facet of what our magnificent Champion, Jesus Christ, accomplished for us: the forgiveness of our sins. God forbid that I am minimizing our forgiveness! But Jesus accomplished two additional miracles for us that I was unaware of for years: *He had changed my identity from sinner-man to saint-man and had crucified my old Adamic life and given me His life.* You might say that Jesus is a triple-threat Savior who has given us *three* glorious weapons which enable us to do a good job of "laying aside every encumbrance, and the sin which so easily entangles us, [so we can] run with endurance the race that is set before us" (Hebrews 12:1). As new creatures in Christ, we

- are forgiven of all our sins
- have undergone a change in our identity from sinner to saint
- have received new life—Christ *as* life—to replace our former life.

Someone may say, "Bill, I've never thought of it that way. When I came to Christ, all I understood was that by the shed blood of Jesus I would be saved. Are you saying that when I asked Jesus to come into me and forgive me of all my sins, that I didn't really get saved? Are you saying that I must come back to Jesus and ask Him to accomplish these two additional miracles for me: change my identity from sinner to saint and give me His life in exchange for my old one?" Great day, no, I'm not saying any such thing! When you were physically born, you were given more than skin. You got eyes, stomach, kidneys, bladder, and so on. As I came to Christ, I understood one fact: I was forgiven of all my sins. I was "saved to the uttermost." But as in the football

13

illustration, in addition to my forgiveness there were benefits which came to me through Jesus Christ that I was unaware of.

Look at it this way. The Lord led a friend of our ministry to purchase computers for all of us. I received mine. It now resides in my office. I don't check five times a day to see if it's still mine. I thank God for its word-processor function. But I find that there is something going on among our staff that distresses me. These Christians receive more benefit from their computers than I do. This makes me feel like a second-class citizen. They try to ease my pain by telling me that my computer has the same abilities as theirs. They testify that life will be easier for me if I'll simply study the manufacturer's handbook to learn how much more I received in addition to a word processor. Folks, I *have* the same computer that they have. I am a citizen of computer heaven, just like they are. *But I don't enjoy the power that they do.* I don't embrace all the functions that my colleagues benefit from.

I believe multitudes of Christians are in a similar boat. Although they have all the components which make up the salvation package when they came to the Savior, they benefit from only one: the forgiveness of their sins. What a marvelous, gracious gift! But isn't it just like God to give us even more! He changed our identity and gave us new life.

The gospel of Christ details that through the finished work of Jesus we can be forgiven, transformed, experience intimate fellowship with God and the body of Christ, bring honor to Christ on earth by our godly obedience, and finally reign with Him forever.

Every new creature in Christ embraces the wondrous, liberating truth of forgiveness through the blood of Christ (Romans 5:9). But life on earth is far more complex than being forgiven of our sins. For example, the wife whose Christian husband mistreats her finds no comfort in knowing that he's forgiven! She wishes he would treat her like Christ treats His bride. Such a husband desperately needs to understand that he already possesses the key to victory over his ungodly behavior. The power of a changed life came into this man at his salvation, but because he fails to comprehend this, he does not experience it. He continues to be dominated by his old, fleshly ways.

⁄ "Christ Who Is Our Life"

One Person alone has lived an overcoming life on earth: Jesus Christ. That one Person said, "I am the vine, you are the branches; he who abides in Me, and I in him, he bears much fruit; for apart from Me you can do nothing" (John 15:5). Christ is the vine in this metaphor; we Christians are the branches. Branches have *no independent life*. Branches "live and move and have their being" by the *life* of the vine. So long as branches abide (draw their life from the vine), they experience a fruitful existence. Branches never *produce* fruit; branches *bear* the fruit that is produced by the *life* of the vine *through* them. Should they try to live independently, they will die. Without vine life, they "can do nothing." Jesus said that without His life flowing through us, we are impotent, powerless.

Let me pose some questions. What if our salvation encompasses *a new kind of life* in addition to the forgiveness of sins? What if eternal life is not a mere extension of our old life, but a literal, new life? What if eternal life is actually the life of Jesus Christ? That may be a new concept to you, but just because you may not understand it, please don't stop reading. My intention is not to be confrontational or argumentative. I love you. Let's reason together from the Scriptures, trusting the Holy Spirit to reveal truth. What if the Spirit of Christ who indwells us is *intended* to express life through us? And what if it is *His* life *through* us that gives us power over the world, our own flesh, and the devil? If this were the case and a Christian husband understood how to

15

let Christ live through him to minister *agape* love to his wife, would this make a huge difference in their marriage? Would Christ through him treat his wife like a precious gift from God? Would the fruit of the Spirit begin to become evident in this man behind the closed doors of his home as well as publicly? That's a no-brainer. Christ living through this man would radically change his behavior for the better. Folks would want to find out more about the secret to such power.

— Are you aware that the terms *eternal life* and *everlasting life* are not synonyms? Whereas *everlasting* describes something which has a beginning but no end, *eternal* describes something which has neither beginning nor end. The natural man has *everlasting* life. His life began at birth and extends forever into infinity—dwelling in hell by his own choice.

Although a *translation* of the Bible may mistakenly say that Christians have *everlasting* life, this is not supported by the Greek or Hebrew. We Christians have *eternal* life. Eternal life is not a phenomenon, nor an *it*, but a Person, Jesus Christ. *Eternal Life* should best be capitalized because this is another name for Jesus Christ. The Bible documents this: "What was from the beginning, what we have heard, what we have seen with our eyes, what we beheld and our hands handled, concerning the Word of Life—and the life was manifested, and we have seen and bear witness and proclaim to you *the eternal life*, which was with the Father and was manifested to us" (1 John 1:1-2). This passage reveals that Christ and Eternal Life are one and the same. Jesus said, "I am ... the life" (John 14:6). "In Him was life" (John 1:4). "When Christ, who is our life, is revealed ..." (Colossians 3:4). Eternal Life is a Person, Jesus Christ. When you came to Jesus, He did not "come into *your* life"; He exchanged *His* powerful, obedient life, for your old rebellious, independent, self-serving life. Jesus Christ is *our life*, folks, and we have the glorious privilege of cooperating with

Him by trusting Him to express His life through us on earth. What a magnificent difference that makes!

Christians are individually members of the body of Christ on earth. Metaphorically speaking, I'm a toe, you're a thumb. Although we're different, we each have the same life: Christ. This is puzzling; it's a mystery (Colossians 1:27) which is to be believed and acted upon, not necessarily understood.

God's intent is that as Christ lives through the husband, the husband will love his wife like Christ loves *His* wife, the church. If, however, the husband never comprehends this, is there additional help for his wife? Did Jesus Christ accomplish anything at her salvation which will comfort her? By all means!

Our Identity Was Changed in Christ

Since Christ is *her* life, the good news is that *she* no longer has to live with this husband who acts like such a hammerhead. Christ is to live with him *through* her, by faith. Through faith, she is to cast the burden of living with this man onto Jesus. It is Christ's responsibility to express life through her to her husband. And as if this marvelous truth were not enough, she must also understand and embrace the fact that she was crucified in Christ as who she was by her natural birth and then reborn as who she now is in Christ (Romans 6:6; 2 Corinthians 5:17). She was changed from a sinner to a saint through this glorious spiritual process—not a sinner saved by grace, but a saint who has the capability to sin, but who longs to overcome it. As a saint, she can rest in her total, unconditional acceptance by God.

Christians who understand only that they are forgiven mistakenly see themselves as forgiven sinners on their way to heaven. Not understanding that Jesus has already changed their identity from sinner to saint (holy one) leads them to the mistaken belief that they will be changed into holy people at their physical death. My friend Peter Lord says,

"What you are here, you'll be there. Most Christians think that *death* is going to complete what Jesus couldn't do; that when you die, you'll suddenly be zapped into holiness. But death is an enemy! There's something wrong with a theology that says that our enemy is going to do what Jesus is impotent to do." We've *already been* changed into holy people (saints) in Christ's death and resurrection, so we're *already* "qualified" to live with God. If we were not, God's Holy Spirit could not dwell within us now! Mother Teresa didn't become a saint by committee vote based upon her performance. A person can only be changed from sinner to saint by crucifixion/rebirth in Christ. You're already as much of a saint as you'll ever be. You're the same person you'll be in eternity after you shed your earthsuit at death. You say, "Well, great day, if this is true, then why don't I *act* like a saint?" Good question. Hold onto your ticket stub; we'll cover this later.

A Suit of Clay—Our Temporary Dwelling

Second Corinthians 5:1,2,8 reveals what transpires at our physical death:

> For we know that if the earthly tent [body] which is our house is torn down, we have a building from God, a house not made with hands, eternal in the heavens. For indeed in this house we groan, longing to be clothed with our dwelling from heaven.... We are of good courage, I say, and prefer rather to be absent from the body and to be at home with the Lord.

Notice that God differentiates between you and the earthsuit in which you live. He is revealing that the earthsuit is *not who you are*. He says, "If the earthly tent *which is our house* is torn down, *we* have a building from God ... in the heavens." God breaks you out from your *house*. The house

18

is not your identity. Just to be sure we get it, He repeats it: "In this house *we* groan." Does the house groan or do *we* groan? *We* groan. The house is not *you; you* temporarily indwell it. Notice that the person who is "absent from the body and present with the Lord" is the same person who indwelt the body on earth. His identity is unchanged by death. Although the *body* will indeed be changed in the future (1 Corinthians 14:42-44), you and I will not be changed from a sinner to a saint at our physical death, because God has already accomplished this through Christ. God, through Paul, addresses this letter to all the "saints" (2 Corinthians 1:1). He never speaks to "sinners saved by grace." That's man's religious opinion, which is not supported by Scripture. By teaching that Christians have already been changed into the glorious people that we'll be eternally, I'm not teaching Gnosticism (negating the importance of the body). I'm simply saying what the Bible says—that the true you is *not* the body in which you live. Your personality (soul) and spirit comprise the saint who indwells your dying, earthbound body.

The passage which speaks about your being changed in the twinkling of an eye is not speaking about changing you, but about changing your *body*. God says: "I tell you a mystery; we shall not all sleep, but we shall all be changed.... For this perishable [earthly body] must put on the imperishable [supernatural heavenly *body*] and this mortal [physical *body*] must put on immortality [heavenly *body*]" (1 Corinthians 15:51,53). Your soul and spirit have already been changed at salvation. Folks, the only change we will experience through death is liberation from the earthsuit. When we eject from the body, the devil can no longer hassle us. Although we will live forever in God's presence, and had to experience an identity change in order to qualify for such a glorious future, the Bible teaches that this change *has already taken place* in Christ at salvation. That's why God calls us saints.

↗ The Christian who believes he is a sinner saved by grace is either uninstructed or is ignoring a significant portion of what Jesus accomplished for us as revealed through God's secretary, Paul. Such a Christian faces life in much the same manner as the faithful Old Testament Jew. That unregenerate man *correctly* saw himself as a sinner who must regularly travel to the Temple and strive to fulfill all of the requirements of the Law in order to acquire God's forgiveness and blessing. In addition to that burden, experiencing the Spirit of Christ living through him to give him victory over the world, the flesh, and the devil was unavailable to him (even in his wildest dreams!). Nor was it possible for him to have his identity changed from sinner to saint. Do you see that this describes the mentality of many born-again saints of God today? Do you experience consistent victory over "the sin which so easily entangles us" (Hebrews 12:1)? Although *no man can ever attain sinless perfection*, you can experience the victorious life. But you must embrace more of the gospel than your blessed forgiveness.

More Than Forgiven

Chaim was consumed with guilt. He simply could not understand how he could have stooped low enough to be unfaithful to his dear wife, but he had done it and had lived with the guilt of his sin ever since. It was three months ago this week that it happened. What could have come over him? He couldn't even remember her name, for heaven's sake. He had met her at the village well, and she had begun talking to him about her life as a prostitute in a pagan temple and ... arrrgh! One thing led to another and arrrgh! Dear God, what he would give to erase his foolish act of passion!

Today he arrived at the Temple in Jerusalem where the high priest would offer sacrifices and prayers to YHWH (Yahweh) for the sins of the people. Chaim made the 40-mile journey to stand with the others while the priest offered prayers and offerings for sins. He had brought the most-prized animal in his flock as his offering, praying each step of the way that Yahweh would accept it and forgive him; and now he stood in silence, waiting for the priest to emerge from behind the veil and so reveal that Yahweh was pleased with the sacrifices and prayers for forgiveness for the people. The curtain rustled a bit, there was movement behind it! There! The high priest came forth! *Forgiven! Praise Yahweh, I'm forgiven!*

Chaim's heart swelled with gratitude. *Never* did he believe that he would feel so clean again! Praise Yahweh! He danced for joy as he skipped like a child toward the city gate which led toward home. Then he moved to the side, away from the others, and fell on his face in gratitude, thanking Yahweh again. His heart welled up within his breast. On impulse, he turned and ran back toward the Temple compound. He simply *had* to do more to express his gratitude to Yahweh! On he ran, darting through the throng which was still streaming from the Temple. He dashed through the gate into the outer court, now abandoned by the crowds, intent on going behind the veil to fall on the ark and embrace the presence of Yahweh, expressing the fervor of his gratitude for his forgiveness.

This story could not have a happy ending. If Chaim had tried to go behind that veil and into the Holy of Holies, he would have become a crispy critter. Knowing the difference between you and Chaim is pivotal. If you had to give a specific reason why Chaim would have been struck dead, what would you say? "Well, Bill, he wasn't as forgiven as we are through Christ." Oh, but he was; forgiven is forgiven. God gets to make the rules. Chaim looked to God in faith via the

21

revelation available to man at that time. Was Chaim not one of God's chosen? Sure—he was a Hebrew. Was he not committed to God? Of course. If sincerity and repentance were measured by personal effort, the man was making an 80-mile round-trip on foot, half of it driving or pulling an animal sacrifice. You've gotta wonder how many Christians are that repentant about their sins. Chaim was as serious as a heart attack about his faith.

The difference which sets you apart from Chaim is a critical "rest stop" on God's freeway, so let's pull in for a closer examination. What is it about you, a new person in Christ, that not only exempts you from needing to get behind God's veil, but also enabled God to move in behind *your* "veil"? His Holy Spirit indwells you! Although Jesus' sacrifice paid for all your sins, whereas Chaim's forgiveness was meted out to him on a sacrifice-by-sacrifice basis, the difference between the two of you goes beyond forgiveness. *You have experienced a change in your identity!* Chaim remained a sinner-man; new creatures in Christ are saints (holy ones).

A New Spiritual Identity

Although faithful Old Testament Jews were forgiven, had they attempted to enter into God's holy presence—behind the Temple veil—they would have died instantly due to their spiritual identity by natural birth: sinner-men. The high priest, on the other hand, had been granted a grace-exemption as God's intercessor on behalf of the people. What is it that exempts you from needing such a *human* priest/intercessor? *You have literally been cleansed via being crucified in Christ and then reborn in His resurrection!* "[You] are the temple of the living God" (2 Corinthians 6:16b)! How can this be? It's because you are not only permanently forgiven via Jesus' blood, but you are so permanently holy that the Spirit of Christ permanently indwells you. It was through

Christ's beloved body that He accomplished this change in your identity, dear one. Hold on, now; stay with me as I reason with you from the Word. Of course, you should praise God that your sins are forgiven by His precious blood. What a fantastic gift from God! But, gang, you received even more than that! My point is that you should give equal praise to God that your spirit identity was changed from sinner to saint by being crucified and then reborn in Jesus' precious body. Both are mandatory before a person can host the Holy Spirit of God, and this has already been done for you. "The temple of God is holy, and that is *what you are*" (1 Corinthians 3:17). Forgiveness alone won't give you the privilege of hosting God's Spirit. Do you see that? Although the Old Testament believer like Chaim had forgiveness, he could not enter into the presence of God like you do. Although it's not mandatory that you embrace this truth to be saved, it *is* mandatory that you embrace it in order to experience victory over the world, your flesh, and the devil.

The Temple veil was torn in two at Christ's death, exposing the Holy of Holies, and thus revealing that God would no longer dwell in a "temple made with hands." He now dwells in another kind of temple that is "made without hands." "We heard Him say, 'I will destroy this temple made with hands, and in three days I will build another made without hands' " (Mark 14:58). *Born-again people are the new Holy of Holies of whom Jesus spoke!* God no longer dwells in a stone temple. We're now "living stones ... being built up as a spiritual house for a holy priesthood" (1 Peter 2:5b). There could be no such living stones till Jesus was raised from the dead to become our spiritual progenitor. " 'The first man, Adam, became a living soul.' The last Adam [Christ] became a life-giving spirit" (1 Corinthians 15:45).

Even if God still dwelt in a gilded wooden box, we could, *because of the magnificent, gracious effectiveness of*

Jesus' sacrifice, throw ourselves upon that box in love and gratitude. We could open it and reach inside—no problem! God has vacated the premises and left a forwarding address. The movie *Raiders of the Lost Ark* depicts God as frying the bad guys who dared to touch the ark—a typical Hollywood spin on reality. Great Scott! We've got it much better than having God in a wooden box! God's presence among men is no longer in a building in your city, nor in a box made with human hands. He lives in the spirit of every person who is born again. And as these saints (holy ones), we don't have to travel to some Mecca-type geographic locale to visit God. *We live in "vital union with Him" inside our earthsuits!* Holy God cannot reside in an unholy dwelling, and there's no way any person can cleanse himself of his old unholy identity: sinner-man. Yet, "nothing [is] impossible with God" (Luke 1:37). *He* purged us and *He* cleaned us up by co-crucifying us and then rebirthing us in Christ. We have a new spirit. You and I are now holy dwellings: "For the temple of God is holy, and *that is what you are*" (1 Corinthians 3:17). The Greek for temple here is *naos,* meaning "holy of holies" where the Holy Spirit dwells, as opposed to *hieron,* that part of the temple to which all of the people had access. Christians are the holy place where the Spirit of God now dwells on earth! What a magnificent Savior! What marvelous grace!

Sinner or Saint?

For years I partook of the bread at the Lord's table and thanked God for my forgiveness. Then one day as the elements were being served in my church, the Holy Spirit popped a revelation-type question into my head: If, as we celebrate the Lord's Supper we only commemorate our forgiveness, why did Christ ordain that there be *two* elements—the wine and the bread? Why the bread to remember His broken body? After all, it is through the blood of Christ that

we are forgiven, so why not celebrate with a single element—
the cup?

Gratitude for our forgiveness of sins is appropriate as we
commemorate the shedding of Christ's *blood*, and such gratitude is to be expressed when we partake of the cup. It was
in Jesus' *body*, however, that we were crucified as sinners
and reborn as holy, righteous children of God. Folks, we
were not crucified in Jesus' blood, but in His precious body.
I realize that if we try to assign specific roles to Christ's
blood and His body, we run into trouble because Christ is
One, not compartmentalized. It took all of Jesus to save all
of us. Christ felt the physical pain of the crucifixion via His
body. His precious blood, on the other hand, issued from its
wounds. We are on safe theological ground to believe that it
was in Christ's body that we were crucified and then reborn.
God says it this way: "Therefore, my brethren, you also were
made to die to the Law through *the body* of Christ, that you
might be joined to another, to Him who was raised from the
dead, that we might bear fruit for God" (Romans 7:4). The
old spirit-you died in Christ's *body* before the new spirit-you
was born in His resurrection! "We have been sanctified
through the offering of *the body* of Jesus Christ once for all"
(Hebrews 10:10). "A new and living way which He inaugu-
rated for us through the veil, that is, His *flesh [body]*" (Hebrews 10:20). God is showing us the importance of Jesus'
physical body here and its function for us. Just as Jesus' shed
blood is necessary for the forgiveness of sin, *His crucified
and resurrected body is the means by which our identity was
changed from rejected sinners into acceptable saints.* Gang,
in addition to Jesus' blood, Jesus' *body* was heavily involved
in satisfying the requirement that we must possess the "holiness, without which no man shall see the Lord" (Hebrews
12:14 KJV). *We* (drumroll with trumpets) *are* (drumroll with
trumpets and tambourines) *holy new creatures in Christ*, and
His precious *body* was a vital factor in effecting this change

in our spirit *identity*. I find the Lord's table even more mean-ingful as I worship and adore Christ for my forgiveness as I partake of the cup, and *for my new identity as I partake of the bread.*

The Christian who believes he is first and foremost a "sinner saved by grace" tacitly denies that his change of identity through the crucified and resurrected body of Christ is a factor in our salvation that is just as vital as the forgive-ness of our sins through the shed blood of Christ. Folks, that statement is not blasphemy. The blasphemy is that for years I was ignorant of the miracle that Jesus Christ accomplished for me via His precious body: the changing of my spirit identity from sinner to saint. I didn't learn that until 22 years after salvation. Whereas Jesus' blood was shed to change our guilt to forgiveness, Jesus' body was sacrificed to change our identity from sinner to saint. Understanding your true identity as a saint is crucial to your experiencing the abun-dant life Jesus spoke of, because you will "life out" whatever you believe about yourself to avoid feeling like a phony. Believe you are a "sinner saved by grace," and you'll act like one; believe you are a holy, purified saint who admittedly sins at times, but who hates that life-style, and you'll be highly motivated to act like such a saint. It's just that simple.

You can no more be a sinner saved by grace than you can be a married single person. The instant a single person marries, you might say that he "dies" as a single person and is "re-created" as a married person. *Birth* always determines identity. When you came to Christ, you instantly died as a sinner (Galatians 2:20). You were then reborn with a new identity; you are now a saint of God (Romans 1:7). As a saint, you've been cleansed, and you now house the Holy Spirit of God in your new spirit (1 Corinthians 6:17; Romans 8:9). And let me caution you. God is not "playing like" you are now a saint when, in fact, you are a grubby wretch. A dramatic inner change transpired when you got saved. You are *literally* a saint, or God wouldn't call you a saint 60 times *after the cross*. Paul addresses his epistles to "all the saints," never to "all the sinners saved by grace." Will you believe and walk in these 60 references, or cling to one verse (1 Timothy 1:15) in which Paul refers to himself as "chief of sinners"? There are many things in the Bible that I do not understand, and that's one of them. I try to walk by what I *do* understand and trust the Lord to fill in the gaps. But when I do the math on that 60 to 1 ratio, plus all the verses which say that Christians are righteous, it's a no-brainer. We're saints, gang.

Yet Another Miracle

Although I knew that "Christ in you, [is] the hope of glory" (Colossians 1:27), Christ may as well have been living on Mars for all the benefit I used to experience from His presence. What about you? Do you fellowship with Him? Trust Him as your Teacher? Read His love letter in His presence and trust Him to touch your heart through it? Marvel together at the beauty and majesty of His creation? Cry in His arms when you're hurting? Stand amazed by His blessing at the birth of a child? Marvel at His power during a crashing thunderstorm? Someone asked why the apostle John was the only one who got to lay his head on Jesus' breast, and the answer was given, "Because he was the only one who tried it." The miracle of Christ indwelling you does not involve the blood of Christ nor the *body* of Christ, but the *Spirit* of Christ, the Holy Spirit, who came into you to share intimate fellowship with you.

Christ, Your Life

In addition to His deep desire for fellowship with you, there is a second glorious reason why Christ indwells you via His Spirit: to express His life through you. *You presently*

*trust Him to take you to a future heaven, but do you use that
same identical faith to trust Him to face each day through
you?* In other words, are you trusting Him for *living* as well
as for *dying*? You can do the latter and ignore the former,
but it's far short of God's grace to you. When you discern
that a lost friend is trusting in his own merit to stand before
God one day, you are saddened because you know what an
affront it is to God for him to ignore the gracious sacrifice of
Christ on the cross. Tell me: Do you live life as if God's forgiveness through Christ is all you need—that you are doing
pretty well without "bothering" with these other truths that
I've pointed out? I mean this kindly: Is this not also an affront to God's grace? Is this not behaving as if you believe
you are so strong that you need not embrace all of what
Christ accomplished for you in order to make it through
each day?

The Spirit of Christ

"You are not in the flesh but in the Spirit, if indeed the
Spirit of God dwells in you. But if anyone does not have the
Spirit of Christ, he does not belong to Him" (Romans 8:9).
When juxtaposed in this manner, the phrases "in the flesh"
versus "in the Spirit" differentiate between the lost and the
saved. The verse states two things: Anyone who isn't indwelt
by the Holy Spirit is lost, and to get the Holy Spirit you must
"belong to [Christ]" (be born again). It also indicates that the
Spirit of Christ and the *Holy Spirit* may be used interchange-
ably—they are synonyms.

"And if Christ is in you, though the body is dead because
of sin, yet the spirit is alive because of righteousness" (Romans 8:10). The "Spirit of Christ" in verse 9 (above) is the
One who gives this life to your spirit. Your *physical body*
was not regenerated (born again) at salvation. This is obvious as you observe the once-youthful, vibrant bodies of
Christians degenerating toward death daily. (No one contacts

me to pose for bathing-suit commercials since my earthsuit looks like it needs ironing.) But such is not the case with the *spirit* of the new creature. "The one who joins himself to the Lord is one spirit with Him" (1 Corinthians 6:17). Your spirit is alive and righteous. Your spirit is the seat of life in you. The Spirit of Christ who indwells your spirit is now your life, just as He said, "I am the way, and the truth, and *the life*" (John 14:6).

Do you know Jesus Christ as the "triple-threat" Savior that He is? Are you enjoying the earthly benefit from the accomplishments of Jesus' blood for your forgiveness, Jesus' body for your identity change, and Jesus' Spirit as your life? God wishes that you would.

29

2 THAT THE NORMAL CHRISTIAN'S EXPERIENCE IS NOT THE NORMAL CHRISTIAN LIFE

MY FRIEND FRANK WAS DRIVING me from the airport to the church he pastors in Baton Rouge, where I was to conduct a seminar. He exited from the hectic chaos of the freeway, then turned onto a quiet street bordered by relatively unde- veloped land. The change of pace was welcome. Some im- pressive, modern buildings appeared in the distance to play visual tag with us through the trees. It seemed as though we were approaching an area of considerable activity, but I saw that I was mistaken. The road evolved into four lanes divided by a median, but there was no traffic. We had the broad avenue to ourselves, traveling between what appeared to be empty dorms, vacant classroom buildings, and ambient structures. Then it dawned on me: This is what is left of Jimmy Swaggart University—built to bring glory to Christ, but now a hollow reminder of the weakness of one man's flesh!

The silence of the abandoned campus produced its mirror image inside our car as Frank picked up on my pen- sive mood. To our left we passed a picturesque walkway lined with dozens of tall silver flagpoles, most of which pointed empty fingers at the sky—a somber reminder that their once-proud service of displaying the multinational flags of a worldwide ministry had collapsed in shame. I felt a deep sadness in my spirit because of the black eye that Jesus had received due to Brother Jimmy's moral failure.

I imagined the thousands of students, visitors, supporters, and staff who once graced this marvelous facility. Anonymous faces of thousands of young Christians flashed through my mind—faces glowing with the excitement of becoming a part of this godly campus ministry where Jesus Christ was lifted up as a testimony to this dark world. Then their dreams were shattered by a devastating blow. Their human champion, their charismatic leader who had led tens of thousands to Christ, had been exposed as a moral failure and then as a rebellious brother, unwilling to submit to the discipline of the church. Not many things are sadder than a fallen Christian leader.

Perhaps you may have the attitude that Jimmy Swaggart is yesteryear's news, or there may even be someone who's asking "Jimmy who?" "C'mon, Bill, give us a fresh, new story." While it's true that Brother Jimmy's saga is now relegated to the archives, his struggle is as old as Samson's and as contemporary as "Good Morning, America." Every denomination has skeletons of fallen former champions in its closets; hey, many churches do. Perhaps the problem has even touched your family. Of course, Christ does not depend upon man to defend His reputation. We can, however, enhance or degrade His reputation among men by the way we live. Fallen Christians doubtless never set out to be an embarrassment to Jesus or serve as Exhibit A to many of us that "there, but for the grace of God, go I. . . ." But haven't you asked yourself (as well as God) if there isn't a biblical answer to the accelerating problem of powerless lives which are common to pew and pulpit? We would agree that this is a far cry from the abundant, victorious life over the world, the flesh, and the devil that Jesus promised.

A 1991 survey of pastors, conducted by the Fuller Institute of Church Growth, revealed the following information about the professional and personal lives of the clergy:

- 80% believe pastoral ministry has affected their families negatively.

- 33% say being in the ministry is an outright hazard to their family.

- 75% report a significant stress-related crisis at least once in their ministry.

- 50% feel unable to meet the needs of the job.

- 90% feel they were inadequately trained to cope with ministry.

- 70% say they have a lower self-image than when they started.

- 40% report a serious conflict with a parishioner at least once a month.

- 37% confess having been involved in inappropriate sexual behavior with someone in the church.

- 70% do not have someone they consider a close friend.

Have we taken a wrong exit off the freeway somewhere along the centuries of Christian tradition? And if so, can we identify it and get back on the overcoming path? I believe the answer to both questions is yes.

Most of us can't identify with Brother Jimmy's voyeurism. But when you generalize from the temptation which is unique to his flesh and substitute your own besetting sin, you thank God that you don't have to "work out your salvation" before a worldwide television audience. If you've never experienced it or witnessed it firsthand, it's difficult to imagine how power, once attained, can become treasured, especially to a male. When that power is on a roll, it's a heady narcotic that can make a person, saved or unsaved, feel that he is due special privileges. He thinks, *God is blessing me. What is one little sin like this going to hurt? It's not as if it's hurting anyone. Besides, God will forgive me and, what the heck, we all sin.* Or if such power is lost, it can spiral him into the depths where he'll be more vulnerable to the temporal salve of using a coping mechanism to ease the pain, to feel better through substitute gratification. This can take on as many forms as there are human appetites, whether these be physical, psychological, or spiritual.

— A county judge, ostensibly a Christian, lived down the block from us years ago. He must have ordered his suits from the Southern County Judge uniform factory because as he drove by our house in his big Caddy wearing his white suit, he looked like Colonel Sanders with a cowboy hat. This guy didn't *walk* into a room, he swept into it! The most dangerous place to stand in our town was between His Honor and a potential vote. It's a shame that he was born a hundred years too late to ride a white horse and wear a cape. Attorneys were realizing large American dollars from their fees, and I always wondered why the judge would not only forego getting in on that action, but would spend significant sums of his own money seeking reelection to an office that paid a fraction of what he could have acquired in private practice.

Then one day I received an invitation from the county. They invited me to attend a party called "jury duty," so of course I "felt led" to attend. When I had the chance to watch the judge in action in his natural habitat, my questions were answered about why this man served at such financial sacrifice. He was "god" in that courthouse. It was "Judge" this and "Judge" that. "Yes, Judge" and "No, Judge." Men and women alike jumped when he said, "Frog." And I mean he ate it up like a man coming off a 40-day fast; he gloried in the power of public office. The good judge had surrounded himself with underlings and was loving the role of overling.

I had the impression that he would have served without salary. Believe it—he *loved* wielding that gavel.

Such a narcotic can take on many manifestations. Even pastors are vulnerable. The flesh being what it is, if a man happens to be a pastor who receives multi-accolades from both brothers and sisters in Christ, it's tough to avoid believing that they're right! The devil has gotten more than one godly man to slide down into disgrace by savoring his own press clippings.

I know a man—a bi-vocational pastor/politician—who fell. He's with the Lord now, but since he repented and then was very transparent about his moral failure, I don't think he would mind my discussing his flesh with you. He showed great promise of becoming a godly man even as a teenager. He was the type of kid that every mother and dad would wish to have as a son or son-in-law someday. He was handsome, humble, intelligent, pure of heart, winsome, athletic, and best of all, totally committed to becoming all that God intended for him to be. He could have had women lining up for him like a rock star, but he retained his purity. What a package! He had the personality skills to become whatever he desired. He decided on a career in politics, and the people in his home area hailed his ascent to high public office with joy, as all of us would have.

You're bound to have heard of him. He actually encouraged folks to call him by his first name—David. After a glorious career, King David began to get sort of "long in the tooth." Even though Nolan Ryan, the great right-hander for the Texas Rangers, still had enough mustard on his fastball to pitch a strong game at age 44, he finally had to hang up his spikes. Today's baseball players report for spring training when the daffodils begin to bloom, but in David's day the macho guys marched off to war. David had celebrated his forty-seventh birthday, and the old sword arm just wasn't what it used to be, so he stayed behind and watched as the army marched off to fight the current bad guys.

How do you suppose David felt about his masculinity as he went into the locker room to hang out with the soldiers who were laughing, joking, and polishing up their weapons? Do you suppose he felt left out? What would he feel as he saw one of his own sons getting some advice on swordsmanship from his commander instead of asking Dad? Do you suppose he stood before his mirror after his shower and disapproved of what he saw? Do you think he made mental comparison of his physique with those of the young warriors who were now singing as they marched out the gates toward the battlefields?

I don't think it's a stretch to believe that David was not exactly doing cartwheels after the gates to the city had closed and he had gone up on the palace roof to listen to the last weak strains of the band as it marched over the hill. Do you suppose the devil tried to use this downer to slip notions into David's thought-life—perhaps even thoughts of resentment toward God for not enabling David to remain physically fit as a reward for his years of meritorious service. Did David think, *You let Moses remain fit till he was 120. Why not me? I belong with my men!* Do you suppose David may have had a pity party with an invitation list of one? Would this make him feel even more dejected and lonely? Of course, to all of this.

It's evening and he had read every scroll in the house. He's frustrated, a bit depressed, bored. . . . *Man, I've got to get some air*, David may have thought. And as he walked out onto his rooftop, he may have moved slowly to the edge to place his hands on the solid mass of the rail and looked down. *Man, it's quiet. So quiet with all of my men gone.* Splash, swish. *What's that? Who is that? Wow! Oh, my!* Folks, he was the king. He had the power. All he had to do was say the word, and Bathsheba was his for the night! *It's not that I'm going to do anything. Her husband, Uriah, is gone. She's probably as bored as I am. I'll have her over for dinner. We'll just talk. What's it going to hurt?*

— What do *you* do to break monotony, to ease frustrations, to relax, to escape from responsibility, or whatever? Some men are highly tempted to do what David did, and if they fall and they're Christians, they hate themselves for their weakness. Some men who have been given the stewardship of power often use that power to sate their flesh. Sad to say, many of these men are born-again, yet many have no knowledge of how Jesus Christ holds the secret to their victory over the flesh. The Spirit of Christ living through them can overcome their flesh.

There is nothing quite so sad as the tale of an effective Christian whose ministry was launched with the spiritual equivalent of a Super Bowl half-time show only to blow its fuses and leave the "spectators" choking on the smoke. Gang, moment-by-moment victory over evil is not a reality for many sincere Christians with a heart to glorify Christ. Their actions fall far short of their desires due to having no knowledge of how to let Christ express His overcoming life through them.

Although this is the normal experience of many Christians, it's a far cry from the normal Christian life that the Bible describes. I would guess that most Christians believe it's inevitable for us to sin hundreds of times per day (when you include the sins of the thought-life), and they've settled into this fatalistic mode until they die or Jesus comes. The Bible does not teach that our physical death is God's provision for our freedom. It teaches that Jesus Christ's death, resurrection, ascension, and sending of the Holy Spirit is God's provision for our freedom. Since that is so, then why is the body of Christ not enjoying this freedom? What's the problem? Did some significant truth that is able to empower us to victory either fall on deaf ears or fall instead through the cracks and leave many of us crippling along with dirty spark plugs? This was certainly my case. I never dreamed that God had a solution already installed in me. Perhaps this is the case with you as well. If so, let's open God's love letter to us and trust the only One who can teach us the mind of the Lord—the Holy Spirit—to give understanding of how to appropriate the victory that is ours in Christ.

3   THAT ONLY CHRIST CAN LIVE THE CHRISTIAN LIFE THROUGH US

Self-reliance: Reliance on one's own ability, judgment, or resources—Webster.

AMONG THE THOUSANDS OF modern conveniences we enjoy are the cordless devices: cordless drills to cordless sanders, self-contained devices to slice your roast or trim your whiskers, portable telephones, rechargeable flashlights, *ad infinitum.* The principle is: Use it till its power is exhausted, return it to its "base station" for recharging, then repeat the cycle. When it's finally called home to gadget heaven, you give it a decent burial and pick up a new one. Ya' gotta love 'em!

But, gang, God never intended for us to apply the effectiveness of such self-empowered devices to our day-to-day personal walk with Him. Christians who approach life via the "cordless" method live in the power of their own personality and/or body. Their source for living life is themselves, and they are vulnerable to slowly losing their cutting edge and finally grinding to a halt. God calls this trusting in the "arm of flesh" (2 Chronicles 32:8). "Thus says the Lord, 'Cursed is the man who trusts in mankind and makes flesh his strength . . .' " (Jeremiah 17:5). If Christians with this self-reliant philosophy of the Christian life were expendable tools, they would be ready for the trash bin, but with God they're ready for the fresh revelation of how to trust Christ within them as even more than Savior and Lord; Christ is to express *His* life *through* them. I wonder if Christ could live an overcoming life through you if you knew how to cooperate with Him to do so? Of course. That's what experiencing Christ as life through us is all about.

Cordless Christianity

The secret to an overcoming life lies in understanding how to stay "plugged into Christ" moment-by-moment, as opposed to operating as if we had a rechargeable battery. Jesus called this "abiding" in Him (John 15:4). We must trash the unbiblical belief that an independent, self-reliant life is worthy of our pursuit—even noble and virtuous—and learn how to live in total dependence upon Christ within us to express His life through us. Continuous dependence upon Christ both now and forever is the message of the gospel. But somehow the Deceiver has managed to sweep this truth through the cracks. He's convinced us that we're to "live our lives for Jesus" (as if He were so impotent that He needed our help), instead of allowing Jesus Christ to express His own life through His own body—the individual members of His corporate church.

/ What if each part of your body acted independently of the head? You get a small sample of the adverse effect that such independence can have when your head tells your body to get out of bed to go to the bathroom at 3:00 A.M., only to discover that one foot has chosen to stay asleep. It's like it's saying, "Y'all go on. I *feel* like staying here." Each individual Christian as a part in the body of Christ is to "life out" his unique identity by being totally dependent upon the Head, Jesus Christ, as his life. Independent living is not Christianity; it is a man-made caricature of Christianity. The Christian life is accomplished just like it was acquired: by faith; we are to simply believe that Christ is our life because God says so (John 14:6; 15:5; Romans 15:18; Colossians 3:3-4), and then

act like it's true. As we will see, there is a huge difference
between trying to live our lives *for* Christ versus Christ living
His life *through* us—the difference between failure and
overcoming.

As a cordless Christian, I gave life the ol' college try all
week as the pressures of the world volleyed me off its walls
like a racquetball. Then, praise God, it was 5:00 P.M. Friday; I
had made it through another workweek. I saw Sunday as
the opportunity to plug into my "spiritual base station." (I
even spoke of church attendance as "getting my battery
recharged to face another week.") Then I repeated the cycle.
Folks, do you see that this approach is very little different
from that of the pre-cross Jew? He depended on himself,
calling upon God in times of need, and often feeling like his
calls were being forwarded to God's voice mail. This
approach to life pretty much parallels the way I lived for the
first 13 years of my Christian life. Oh, I was at the church
every time the doors were open, and Jesus was definitely
the *focal point* of my life, but *He was not my LIFE.* If God
had somehow removed the power of my own flesh (what I
called *my* life), I would have collapsed like a punctured balloon because that was my only source. I hadn't the faintest
idea that Christ was to live His life through me while I rested
in His sufficiency instead of in the power of my own personality.

As time rolls by for the Christian who lives that way, the
joy of the Lord he knew early on is often supplanted by
wearisome religious duty. He rests in the knowledge that
he's going to heaven when he *dies*, but he knows nothing of
resting in Christ on earth as he *lives.* "While a *promise* remains of entering [God's] rest, [he seems] to have come short
of it" (Hebrews 4:1). For most of us, that describes the only
approach we've known since we got saved. I'm certainly not
saying that the world is to be our Disneyland, but I am
saying there is much more to the Christian life than what

many believers experience. Regardless of my opinion, the important thing to recognize is that God says there is more to the Christian life than the cordless variety offers. He calls it *abundant* life.

Normal Christianity Is Not the Norm for Many Christians

The key to living the victorious Christian life is not a new spin on the old, old story; it's *normal* Christianity. It's as old as the New Testament. Experiencing *normal* Christianity through the week yields such a sweet, intimate, obedient relationship with God that we don't attend the worship service to get recharged; we attend the services to discharge our worship and praise to the Lord because we're overflowing with love and gratitude (Psalm 23:5).

By letting Christ express His life through us on a moment-by-moment basis, we experience the overcoming, abundant life that Jesus spoke of (John 10:10). Many Christians have taken the independent, do-it-yourself exit off God's "freeway." Cordless Christianity explains why many Christians experience unexciting or perhaps defeated lives. It explains everything from the so-called male mid-life crisis to depression, sheer boredom to anxiety attacks, passivity to dominance, abrasiveness to "wimping out," the workaholic to the sofa spud, legalism to license, perfectionism to slovenliness, etc. These are all manifestations of living in the power of human flesh. Jesus Christ is the only One who ever lived the Christian life, and I have found that by letting Him express His life through us, by faith, we experience the Christian life as God intends.

How Much Faith Is Required?

How much faith did you place in yourself to acquire salvation? None. Then why do you trust in *your* ability, *your* talent, *your* strength, *your* charisma, *your* education, *your* intellect, *your* beautiful earthsuit, even *your* spiritual gifts, to *live* the life that you acquired by faith? Oh, the folly of such independent living! Jesus said, "I am the way, and the truth, and the life" (John 14:6). Jesus is not *a* life. He didn't give you a *type* of life, nor did He set the curve for a life-style, leaving you some principles by which to live. Christ (drumroll) *is* (drumroll) *your* (drumroll and crashing cymbals) *life*. "For you have died and *your life is hidden* with Christ in God. When Christ, *who is our life*, is revealed, then you also will be revealed with Him in glory. Therefore consider the members of your earthly body as dead to [sin]" (Colossians 3:3-5). Eternal life is not a mere extension of your old, sinful Adamic life. Here is God's definition of eternal life: "What was from the beginning, what we have heard, what we have seen with our eyes, what we beheld and our hands handled, concerning the Word of Life—and *the life* was manifested, and we have seen and bear witness and proclaim to you *the eternal life*, which was with the Father and was manifested to us" (1 John 1:1-2). Christ *is the eternal life* you signed up to acquire if you are born anew. Eternal Life is a *Person*, not an extension of your old Adamic life, not an "it," not a phenomenon or a set of values. And this Person, who is Himself Eternal Life, is to express life through you, by faith, as you present yourself to God as a living sacrifice (Romans 12:1). This is not to be *understood* so much as to be *believed* and *acted* upon.

⌐ There is so much more to your salvation than a one-time experience which guarantees heaven. Living the Christian life is experienced via using the same faith by which you got saved. It is experiencing a moment-by-moment, intimate, personal relationship with Christ who indwells you—living "in vital union with [Him]" (Colossians 2:6 TLB). In addition to trusting Christ as Savior and Lord, God wishes that you would trust Christ as life *through* you to face each day *for* you. God says it like this in Galatians 3:1,3: "You foolish [Christians], who has bewitched you? ... Having *begun* by the Spirit [God's power and grace, by faith], are you now being perfected by the *flesh* [depending upon your own resources—human effort]?"

"For you have died and your life is hidden with Christ in God. When Christ, who is our life . . ." (Colossians 3:3-4) does not record Paul's ideas, gang. This is God speaking to you. Admittedly, God Himself is the Source at work through the speaker, Paul (Romans 15:18).

/ God says in the verses above that your life is "hidden." This means that you must see this via your spiritual eyes, by faith. It's fine if you understand it, but you can obey it regardless of whether you understand it or not. If you need more understanding, you can address God: "Sir, if there is something here that I need to understand, show it to me. I'm not simply curious. I want to know so I can have a better relationship with You." Paul writes, "The life which I now live in the flesh [in the body] I live by faith in the Son of God, who loved me, and delivered Himself up for me" (Galatians 2:20). For years I knew I would *die* embracing my faith in Christ, but I never knew I was to *live* by that same faith in Him. Jesus said, "I am the vine, you are the branches; he who abides in Me, and I in him, he bears much fruit; for apart from Me you can do nothing" (John 15:5). Somehow the key is to live like the branch on a vine lives, depending upon the life of that vine. Now hold that thought.

Is There More Benefit in Salvation Than a Future Heaven?

Consider Paul's statement, "For if while we were enemies, we were reconciled to God through the *death* of His Son, much more, *having been reconciled*, we shall be saved by His *life*" (Romans 5:10).

There was a time in my pilgrimage when I breezed by this verse, assuming that it referred to my future in heaven. You see, I concentrated solely on the *death* of Jesus as the payment for my sins, never realizing that He accomplished much more for me than that glorious act. The phrase I just used—"much more"—came right out of the verse. I was unintentionally minimizing a significant part of Jesus' finished work. I believed that the reference to His life related only to a future heaven instead of our life on earth as well. I put all my doctrinal weight on His death and none on His life, and I believe that many Christians are making that same mistake.

You'll agree that the first half of this verse—"reconciled to God through the death of His Son"—references Christ's death as the way God saved you from everlasting hell. Then Paul writes, "much more . . ." You've gotta love those two words. God is not given to superlatives. After all, if you've never told a lie and you're incapable of ever doing so (Titus 1:2), your yes means yes and your no means no. So when God uses words or phrases like "much more," we ought to get ready for an important announcement. Here it is: "Much more, having been reconciled [a guarantee of heaven], we shall be saved by His *life*." Saved by His *life*? Saved from what? We are already saved from hell by the *death* of Christ in the first part of the verse, so what is this "much more" we get saved from by the *life* of Christ?

His life *through you* saved you from bearing the circumstances of living on earth! That's right. Christ's death saved you from hell *below* the earth; Christ's life saves you from hell *upon* the earth. Here's how it works: The boss buzzed you on the intercom and told you to come to his office. He said that the report you had submitted for the quarter was unacceptable, and he gave you one week to rewrite it. That's the sort of hell on earth that Christ has saved you from. As you're sitting there with your heart in your throat, you're to think, *Lord Jesus, I'm so glad that I don't have to do this rewrite. You are my life and this is Your baby. Thank You for saving me from this.* You think that concept in a microsecond. Then you say, "Yes, sir, Mr. Mulligan. I'll do my best. The problem will be fixed. You can count on it." Then you think, *Whew, Lord! You really do have a problem here. I'm so glad that I don't have to do this rewrite.* Yes! The burden is the Lord's!

— Afterward, *you* burn the midnight oil, highly motivated as your hands sometimes fly over, sometimes labor over the keyboard of your computer, trusting that *Christ* is doing this report *for* you, *through* you on a moment-by-moment basis. Yes! You don't go fishing and wait till you feel the Spirit of Christ take over and carry you to the computer terminal. *You* go sit at the keyboard. *You* save the document to a working file and then begin the rewrite job. However, your faith is saying, *"OK, Lord, where do we begin? I don't have a clue."* This, my friend, is trusting Christ as life through you, by faith. Have you missed this piece in the salvation equation? Christ as life comes right along with the package that you acquired when you got saved. Many of us have trusted Jesus as Savior; we've trusted Him as Lord, but may have never trusted Him as life until we meet something which is absolutely beyond our ability. Trusting Christ as life is "[casting] your burden upon the Lord" (Psalm 55:22)—a command, not an option. God commands you to shove the burden of living on earth squarely onto the broad shoulders of your Savior and to keep piling it on Him moment-by-moment. Gang, this may sound like a cop-out to you, but it's normal. You were not saved to "carry your own weight." That is the devil's idea. Not only is this not noble, it is sin to carry your own weight! It's independence. God says, "Whatever [as in breathing God's air] is not from faith is sin" (Romans 14:23b).

Or let's say that you have to get a fan fastened to the small frame on the ceiling by inserting three small bolts, using one hand to hold the screw and the fan, holding the screwdriver in your other hand, and the two other bolts in your lips, while standing on a ladder wearing high heels (just kidding). As you trust Christ as life, the first bolt lines up in the hole, but when you bring the screwdriver to bear, it slips off the bolt head, and you drop everything as you grab the fan with both hands. You think, *Whew, Lord, we had tough luck on that one, but thank You for catching the fan. OK, let's try again.* And the two of you go at it again. Perhaps it takes five or six tries to do the job, but you are having a time of camaraderie with Jesus Christ as the two of you work together to install a ceiling fan! That's pleasing to Him. That's a *spiritual* exercise. He longs for this sort of fellowship with you. He longs to build meaningful memories with you—just the two of you. This is the way you build a relationship with Christ! You and He can share some chuckles together over the battle that was won over those tiny holes in that crazy fan as you drive to work together the next day. Gang, this is the way you get to *know* Jesus Christ. You don't have to wear a sandwich board proclaiming the end of the world in order to achieve this. This is the "normal Christian life" as author Watchman Nee called it. This is "lifing out" the metaphor of Jesus being the vine and you being a branch. You experienced Vine-life while hanging a fan, by faith.

Forgive me for getting personal, but we all know that testosterone produces a higher sexual appetite than estrogen. Sometimes the farthest thing from a wife's mind is to respond to her husband's sexual overtures. This can be a burden to both spouses, which Christ can deal with. The husband can think: *Lord, I'd like to fulfill my desire, but if You want me to back off, that's OK. I leave this up to You, Jesus. You are my life, and You won't make demands through me.* On the other hand, let's say that the wife is thinking: *Lord, You know that I am not the least bit interested*

*in this, but Your Word says that my body is not my own. I
realize that my husband needs me to respond to him. So I
trust You as my life, even in this.* And she begins to *act* interested, believing that Christ is her life. Obviously, it may work
the other way around, with the Lord giving the husband the
message that he is to wait till a more appropriate time.

Hey, we don't hang Jesus on a hook in the hall when
we enter the marriage bedroom. Sex is God's invention, not
Satan's. Look at it this way: The electricity is the life of my
electric sander. The electricity doesn't sand the board. It is
the enabler which allows the *sander* to sand the board. I'm
certainly not teaching a *ménage à trois*, that Christ is having
sex with us! Christ is the Enabler here. Christ as life through
both husband and wife is God's solution to all relational
problems, including marital sex.[1]

You can see that the Christian who fellowships with
Christ as I've illustrated in these anecdotes will soon become
fast friends with Him. Wouldn't it be highly unlikely that a
person who lives like this would snap at the kids or rag on
his spouse? Of course. The developing, intimate relationship
with Christ would so strengthen this person that he would
want to *habitually* practice letting Christ express life through
him to do God's will on earth. Isn't that great? You wouldn't
be controlled by a bunch of rules and regulations, but by the
inner *life* of Jesus Christ. This is what God means by saying
that He has written His laws on our hearts and minds (Hebrews 10:16).

Christ As Life in Daily Living

"If anyone does not have the Spirit of Christ, he does not
belong to Him" (Romans 8:9b). When you became a Christian, the "Spirit of Christ" (Holy Spirit) entered into you. Why
did Jesus come into you? Why didn't Jesus come *before* you
so He could lead you (some say that's His function); or *beside* you so you could lean on Him when you grow weary

(some say this is His function); or *behind* you to give you a jump start when you need help (others claim this is His job), or perhaps *under* you to carry you when you can't make it on your own (as the poem "In His Steps" teaches)? *It's because Jesus is the only One who ever has or who ever will live the life which is pleasing to the Father, and He is to express His life through you on a moment-by-moment basis.* Christ's life alone gets God's Good Housekeeping Seal of Approval. Everything else is trashed.

It's presumptuous of any person to think he can emulate the life of Christ. God doesn't want to "help" you live on earth any more than He wanted to "help" you get saved. He did it all for you then: He wants to do it all for you now. This way God, not you, gets the honor (glory). Salvation is all of God, nothing of man. Folks, the Christian life is to be experienced in exactly the same way it's begun. He wants to *do it all for* you, *through* you. In this way He gets just as much glory (credit) for saving you from the hell of life as He does for saving you from the hell of death, and He gets to build the intimate relationship with you which He longs for. He *died* to attain this relationship with you! Please don't continue in your independent self-sufficiency, naïvely believing that this is pleasing to the Father, that He is proud of your strength. He's covered this in His love letter: "They will be held guilty, they whose strength is their god" (Habakkuk 1:11).

Independence was Adam's original sin. He, in effect, said, "I'll do it *my* way! I don't like *your* way! I insist on being in control of my life!" God hates independence. You please God through dependence by offering yourself as a living sacrifice through whom Christ can express life to the world. He wants to express His life through you, a part of His body, the church. You were re-created in Christ to be a unique, precious vessel through whom he reveals Himself to the world. The Father accomplished this by rebirthing you as

49

a brand-new creation in Christ's resurrection (1 Peter 1:3)—a fantastic, life-changing truth we'll study in a later chapter.

And folks, this is not limited to "church" activities, but also treating your spouse and kids in a Christlike manner, being friendly in the elevator, courteous at the four-way stop, patient in the checkout line, etc. He's talking about living a godly *life*.

If you're familiar with our ministry, you know that part of my testimony is that I disgraced the name of Christ for years by the way I treated my precious wife, Anabel—and I was a deeply committed Christian! But God turned it around for me by revealing that Christ expressing His life through me would treat her like a queen if I would just *act* like He was doing so, by faith. It turned our marriage around![2] Christ will replicate the same *agape* life-style through us today that He expressed 2000 years ago when He was limited to one earthsuit. (The Greek word *agape* connotes action and means "doing the most constructive, redemptive thing for another.") Christ's sacrificial death for us is the epitome of *agape* love. By His life through our many earthsuits, we can bring honor to His name (reputation) on earth, which is what every born-again person desires. Jesus said it this way: "He who believes in Me, the works that I do, he will do also; and greater works than these he will do; because I go to the Father" (John 14:12). One Vine (Christ) with millions of branches (saints who trust Christ as life, by faith) can "bear much fruit" and do "greater works than these."

God wishes Christians knew that they were never intended to live the Christian life. He wishes we knew that Christ is to live the Christian life through His body of volunteers, the church, and that as such we will experience consistent victory over the world, the flesh, and the devil. Such a person is not a cordless Christian; he's plugged into a Source that's more powerful than an atomic generator!

4 THAT AT SALVATION CHRIST BECAME THEIR LIFE

"WELL, I HATE TO TELL YOU this, but the engine in this car has had it. And it's not worth the money it would take to get it up and running. You've got to have a new engine."

If those are not some of the saddest, most depressing words in the English language, they're contenders. When a second opinion validates the original diagnosis, you've got limited options: Either trade cars, or install a new or rebuilt engine—and neither option makes you feel like Dorothy skipping along the yellow brick road.

That diagnosis could have been given to my spiritual "engine" once. I thought it was normal Christianity to keep patching up my same old engine. And boy, did I work at it! You tie the average Christian to me, and I would have dragged him to death. I took courses in how to change my own Christian spark plugs. I learned how to tinker with my Christian distributor so I could make all my Christian cylinders fire on time. I ground my teeth at my poor Christian gas mileage and ordered a special Christian gadget that was guaranteed to save me so much Christian gas that I would have to make regular stops to drain the excess out onto the highway—but it was a scam. Double drat.

After about 13 years of this, I pulled into the "Emergency Stop Only" space with my engine smoking. I wasn't experiencing the abundant life Jesus promised, and if any of my friends were, they weren't telling me about it. Most of us never discover that Jesus is all we need until Jesus is all we have. I reached that point. I think I'm no different than many

Christians in that God had to let me experience personal failure trying to live life before He could share His diagnosis and treatment with me. My motto was, "If it ain't broke, don't fix it." Well, as they say in Oklahoma, "I was broker 'n Granny's hip," and I needed fixin'.

Independence Is the Mother of All Sin

His diagnosis? My theology on victorious living was wrong. And I don't mean that the fine tuner needed tweaking; it needed a major overhaul. I was practicing "cordless Christianity." My philosophy was expressed in the poem "Footprints in the Sand." You recall how it goes: As the Christian looks back over the footprints in the sand of his life, he sees Jesus' footprints alongside his. Sometimes he sees only one set of footprints and asks Jesus what that signifies, to which He responds, "Oh, that's where I had to carry you." Well, that may sell lots of wall plaques, but it's mighty bad theology because it implies that the better I can live *independently*, the less I'll need to trust Christ to do it *all* for me. I didn't see the obvious fallacy that, if I can improve enough, I can function without Christ. The only time I'll need Him is to take me to heaven. This way, Jesus can spend His time helping the weak. In fact, if I'm dedicated enough and can become capable enough at living independently, I can help Him help the weak, which is what I had been trying to do. I was living as though independence were a virtue, when it was in fact a sin. God said, "They will be held guilty, they whose strength is their god" (Habakkuk 1:11). I was naïvely committing the same sin as Adam, who made the first declaration of personal independence—remember? He did it *his* way, and his offspring have been hard at it ever since.

You Were Crucified with Christ in A.D. 33

One of the things you learned at Sunday school is that two thieves were crucified with Jesus on Calvary. And if you weren't in Sunday school as a kid, suffice it to say that you got the message. But there is much more biblical ink dedicated to the fact that *you* were crucified with Christ than there is to document the deaths of those two thieves.

This truth has been skipped over more times than an elementary-school sidewalk. It's been buried, denied, scoffed at, explained away, rationalized, or simply misunderstood by most modern theologians. Do I claim to have the market cornered on truth? Hardly. But God has revealed *one* truth to me: He tells the truth. And when He puts together a chain of 12 verses, 9 of which say that we died in Christ, it's a no-brainer that He's telling it like it is (Romans 6:2-13). But, I would like to see a George Gallup poll among Christians on how many believe they were literally crucified with Christ. I would say the number of affirmative responses would be quite low. Had you asked me that question years ago, I would have philosophized about it, saying that God saw me *as if* I were crucified, but it "obviously" didn't *literally* happen. Although I wouldn't have verbalized it this way, I supposed that God merely "played like" I was crucified in Christ for some reason known only to Him. I considered my crucifixion with Christ to be a mere "paper transaction" in the mind of God, and had no idea that it had anything to do with my victory over the world, the flesh, and the devil.

Romans chapter 6 is the most complete treatise of this event in the Bible. Most of us mark up our personal Bibles, but like a friend of mine said, "Before the Holy Spirit opened my eyes to the reality of our crucifixion with Christ, Romans 6 was the cleanest page in my Bible." Even though the Bible clearly states that we were crucified in Christ, the overt or tacit denial of the literality of this truth by most theologians is often explained away as "positional truth." The bare bones of positional truth is much like an insurance policy. It teaches that we Christians must *physically* die before we can collect the benefits. The Bible does indeed speak of experiences that will be actualized only after we leave our earthsuits, but the language in such instances carries the future tense to indicate that this is the case. Our crucifixion in Christ is *exactly the opposite*. It is conveyed in past-tense verbs: *"Knowing this, that our old [man] was crucified with Him"*; *"I have been crucified with Christ"* (Romans 6:6; Galatians 2:20). It's a done deal.

The Christian who treats this teaching as if it were not present-day reality is misinterpreting God's word. The verbs don't lie. And we're not dealing with an insignificant issue, such as whether you will get to name your white horse in heaven (Revelation 19:14). We're dealing with the key to experiencing an overcoming life. God had no plan for making something beautiful of *your* life—that do-it-yourself life inherited from Adam. God's plan is to kill that life and re-create you with an overcoming, *obedient* life—Christ *as life*. Christ is more than Savior and Lord; He is our *life*: "Jesus said, 'I am the way, and the truth, and *the life*'" (John 14:6). God did not *change* your life, He *exchanged* your life—your old life for Christ *as* life.

I believe Jesus might say it this way:

> The kingdom of heaven is like electricity, which went virtually unnoticed by man until Ben Franklin tried to get in touch with it. Electricity would largely go unnoticed were it not for the vehicles through which it expresses itself; things ranging from cars to carousels, coffeemakers to circuit breakers, lightning to lighting, etc. All of these are expressions of the same life: electricity. I, who created electricity (John 1:3) have chosen to function in a similar manner via My Spirit. Christians are members of My body on earth, each designed to be a unique expression of My life through them. The Father's plan is for people to be drawn to Me by observing My *agape* servant-life being expressed through Christians. This will enable the Holy Spirit to contrast *Me* against a world system driven by Satan.

This will prepare people's hearts to understand, as I explain to them through Christians "this mystery . . . which is Christ in you, the hope of glory" (Colossians 1:27).

The Christian life is like an infant in the womb. Although the child is *in* the mother, yet the mother is life *in* the child. Without the mother's life flowing through the umbilical cord, the child would have no life. "For in Him we live and move and exist" (Acts 17:28). The child lives, moves, and exists in its mother. Mom is the baby's source. The baby in the womb is an expression of its mother's life.[1]

Perhaps you're asking, "If Christ is the life of all Christians, do I lose my identity? Am I an automaton?" Not at all. Consider again the analogy of the electric tools plugged into the wall socket at my workbench. Such tools have no independent life. *Each tool depends upon a life which is in it, but which is not of it.* That is a metaphor of each Christian. So long as each tool "abides" (stays plugged into the wall outlet), it manifests its identity (functions as its creator intended). I'll tell you when the tools lose their individuality, their *identity*. It's when I unplug them. They all become paperweights! It's the *life* in the tool which gives it its unique identity. Without its life, it "can do nothing." Notice the similarity in what Jesus said about us: "I am the vine, you are the branches; he who abides in Me, and I in him, he bears much fruit; for apart from Me you *can do nothing*" (John 15:5). The Christian who stays plugged into Jesus Christ as life, by faith, experiences his true identity. Although he is unique among the millions of Christians, he enjoys the same life as they: Christ. On the other hand, the Christian who believes that he expresses his own individuality (lives independently) manifests a *false* identity; he never experiences his true identity one single time on earth! Although this Christian will never *lose* his biblical identity, he spends his entire life at a masquerade ball, naïvely posing as someone he is not. And although he believes he is making his mark, in reality he "can do nothing" (Jesus Christ, A.D. 33).

God's View

"But, Bill, how can I have been crucified in Christ? Jesus was crucified 2,000 years before I was born! How could I possibly have been crucified in Him?"

We must understand that God is not obligated to make sure that we understand everything about the Christian life. His concern is that we believe what He says about it. At times we just have to believe Him even though we don't understand. Let's see if we can gain insight into our crucifixion with a simple illustration.

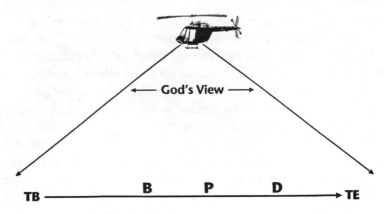

Figure 4A

The space between TB (time begins) and TE (time ends) in Figure 4A represents the time dimension. Since time is God's creation, it follows that God Himself cannot be time-dimensional; if He were, He is subject to or controlled by His own creation ... time. Can't be. You and I, however, are time-bound. Let's depict your earthwalk in the time line. *B* represents your physical birth and *D* your physical death.

The letter *P* on the line represents the present. You con-sider everything from the *P* backward as "past" because you're a time-conscious critter; everything from *P* forward is the "future." But God sees your entire time line from *B* to *D* as "present." He is like a man in a helicopter hovering above your line. Not only this, but He sees *forever* into what you call "future." This is how He dictated all of those prophecies in the Bible. They are not future tense from the helicopter view; they are present tense. Second Peter 3:8 says, "With the Lord one day is as a thousand years." And you think, *Hmmm, God has a lot of time on His hands.* But the rest of the verse says, "And a thousand years is as one day." *Uh-oh, it's not saying God has lots of time; it's saying, "Time, schmime."* Time is meaningless from the helicopter view-point. God's entire view is present tense!

In addition to seeing forever into the future, God sees forever into the past. In Figure 4B, I've added Adam and the cross. *Everything that is required for you to experience victory over the world, the flesh, and the devil happened during those marvelous days encompassing Jesus' sacrificial death, burial, resurrection, and ascension.* "His works were finished from the foundation of the world" from the helicopter view (He-brews 4:3).

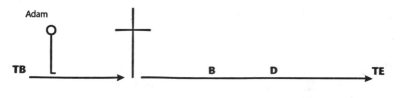

Figure 4B

Let me now address the question, "How could I possibly have been crucified in Christ before I was even born?" by asking a question. How many of your sins did Christ take to the cross 2000 years ago? All of them, of course. How many of your sins had you committed 2000 years ago? None of them; you were yet to be born. Then how could God have possibly laid your sins on Christ at the cross? Answer: the helicopter illustration! *God is not limited by the time dimension.* He is omniscient (all-knowing). From His helicopter view, God "sees" the entire time dimension as present tense. He sees forever into both future and past.

Just as you have enough faith to believe the Bible when it says that your sins were laid on Christ 2000 years ago for your forgiveness even though you would not commit them until centuries later, you must also believe that you were crucified in Christ, purged of your old identity, as well as reborn with a new identity and new life—Christ! Hey, believing this is no more outlandish than believing Christ carried your sins 2000 years before you were born! If you can believe that, you can believe this! Same Christ, same Bible, same faith, same salvation, but perhaps two fantastic treasures which you had never realized that you have: your new identity in Christ, and Christ as life. These parts of the salvation package (which must be just as important as your blessed forgiveness, or God wouldn't have effected them) must also be accepted by faith. Of course, you can be saved without understanding everything that you gained through Christ, but you will be handicapped in both spiritual warfare and spiritual development. The thief on the cross alongside Jesus had very little understanding of what the salvation package contained, yet he was given the complete benefit through coming to Christ by faith.

William R. Newell, the esteemed former assistant to the president of Moody Bible Institute and their Bible teacher at large, has this to say about our literal crucifixion in Christ:

> These words are addressed to faith only. Emotions
> deny them. To reason, they are foolishness. [But] this
> crucifixion was a thing *definitely done by God at the*

cross, just as really as our sins were laid upon Christ. It is addressed to faith as a revelation from God. Reason is blind. The "word of the cross" is "foolishness" to it. All the work consummated at the cross seems folly, if we attempt to subject it to man's understanding. But, just as the wonder of creation is understood only by faith (*"By faith* we understand that the worlds were prepared by the Word of God" [Hebrews 11:3]), so the eternal results accomplished at the cross are entered into by simple faith in the testimony of God about them.

It is no light thing that this is announced to you and me, that all we were and are from Adam has been rejected by God. Scripture is not now dealing with what we have done, but with what we *are*. No one by nature will be ready to count himself so incorrigibly bad as to have to be *crucified!*

This is the opposite of [those] who set you to crucifying yourself. You must "die out" to this, and that. But God says our old man, all that we were, has already been dealt with—and that by *crucifixion with Christ*. And the very words "with Him" show that it was done back at the cross; and that our task is to *believe* the good news, rather than to seek to bring about this crucifixion ourselves.[2]

Gang, that was the party line in one of the leading evangelical institutions in America in 1938! Would you say that Satan has been effective in stuffing the truth of our crucifixion in Christ between the cracks in modern Christianity?

Look at these words from one of the most highly acclaimed Bible teachers of this century, A.W. Tozer:

The cross is a symbol of death. It stands for the abrupt, violent end of a human being. In Roman times, the man who took up his cross and started down the road was not coming back. He was not going out to have his life redirected: he was going out

59

to have it ended! It struck cruel and hard and when it had finished its work, the man was no more!

In coming to Christ we do not bring our old life up onto a higher plane; we leave it at the cross. Thus God salvages the individual by liquidating him and then raising him up again to newness of life![3]

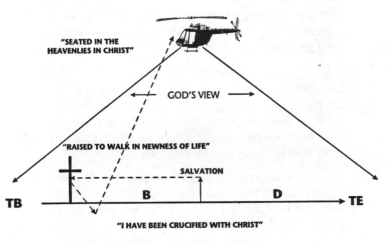

Figure 4C

/ Look at Figure 4C. "Christ was made to *be sin* [a sinner] [for you] that [you] might become the righteousness of God in Him" (2 Corinthians 5:21). The *old you* was crucified *in* Christ at the cross. "Knowing this, that our old self was crucified with Him, that our body of sin might be done away with, that we should no longer be slaves to sin" (Romans 6:6). You were subsequently buried and then reborn in His resurrection: "Therefore we have been buried with Him through baptism into death, in order that as Christ was raised from the dead through the glory of the Father, so we too might walk in newness of life" (Romans 6:4). "We are His workmanship, *created in* Christ Jesus" (Ephesians 2:10). After this you ascended to heaven in Christ. "And raised us up with Him, and seated us with Him in the heavenly places, in Christ Jesus" (Ephesians 2:6). Notice the verbs; they're all past tense! This is yours to embrace by faith just as you embraced your forgiveness by faith.

Lift Off!

— Step out of your car and climb up into God's helicopter over there on the landing pad. He's got it all revved up. You're in for the ride of your life. I'm going to stay here in the rest stop and wait for you. You're lifting off and going clear back down the freeway to the crucifixion. Higher, higher. Look down below as you read the following verses, giving special attention to the verb tenses. God worked a miracle in you down there. These verses are all from God's tour-guide book—Romans. The numerals represent verses that are taken from chapter 6. All of them say that you died as the person you once were.

- How shall we who *died* to sin still live in it? (2)

- Or do you not know that all of us who have been baptized into Christ Jesus have been baptized into His *death*? (3)

- We have been buried through baptism into *death*. (4)

- We have become united with Him in the likeness of His *death*. (5)

- Knowing this, that our old self was *crucified* with Him ... (6)

- He who has *died* is freed from sin. (7)

- Now if we have *died* with Christ ... (8)

- Consider yourselves to be *dead* to sin. (11)

- Present yourselves to God as those alive from the *dead*. (13)

Listen! God is speaking to you:

> Turn your head to the left and look over here at Me.
> No. Right into My eyes. Look at Me. Who did you see
> being crucified down there *in My Son*? That's right.
> *You* died in My Son, Jesus! I crucified everything
> about you that I could not tolerate in My holy pres-
> ence. Now move your eyes up the freeway three
> days. What do you see? That's right! That's you being
> reborn as a new, righteous child in My Son's resurrec-
> tion (2 Corinthians 5:17,21)! I gave spiritual birth to
> you! You're now My child! I am so proud of you! And
> look at that—only *one life* arose from that grave. My
> Son *is* your *life* Yes! Anyone born of His Spirit has
> Christ *as* life. "For you *have died* and *your life is
> hidden with Christ* in God. When Christ, *who is our
> life*, is revealed, then you also will be revealed with
> Him in glory" (Colossians 3:3-4). Christ is now *your*
> life. You're a *brand-new spirit being*, and you're
> *equipped with My Son as life*. Is that great or what!
> That, along with your forgiveness, is how I bridged
> the separation between you and Me. And we're al-
> ways going to be together, just like this!
>
> Now, I'm going to take you back to the rest stop.
> Much of what I have shown you, you must continue
> to believe by faith. My promise and my trustworthi-
> ness will be your lifetime guarantee of these things.
> Treasure them. I prepared them to take you through
> the deep-water days of life on earth. I have given you
> My Holy Spirit as an "earnest" that I will never back
> out on My promises (2 Corinthians 5:5). Ah, here we
> are. I'll always treasure this ride with you. And I'll
> always love you. Be faithful to Me. My son is coming
> back for you soon.

Wow. That was some ride, wasn't it? What a God! That
view you got of your crucifixion in Christ was real, you
know. If a card were to be placed in a book, everything the

book was subjected to would be experienced by the card. Leave the book in the rain, and the card gets wet. Throw the book in the fire, and the card burns. Nail the book to a tree, and the card is pierced. "He chose us *in Him* before the foundation of the world, that we should be holy and blameless before Him" (Ephesians 1:4). So, you were *in Jesus* as He walked up Calvary. You were *in Him* when He was nailed to the cross. Just like the card in the book, you were crucified *in Him*. This was a physical phenomenon for Jesus; it was a spiritual phenomenon for you. Like God told you, He killed everything about you, spiritually, that He could not tolerate in His holy presence. This was the first step as He was preparing to re-create you as a clean vessel so He could cohabit in your spirit with you once you became a saint! This is part of your salvation through your new birth. This is not a feeling any more than being an American is a feeling; it's a fact, like your U.S. citizenship is a fact. All you did to become an American was be born here. All you did to become a new creature in Christ was to be first crucified as who you were and then reborn in Christ's resurrection.

D. Martyn Lloyd-Jones left his career as a physician and became one of the world's most respected theologians. He wrote an entire book about chapter 6 of Romans. Look what he says about our crucifixion in Christ:

> The old man is the man I was in Adam; that is the man that has died once and forever. This is, to me, one of the most comforting and assuring and glorious aspects of our faith. We are never called on to crucify our old man. Why? Because it has already happened— the old man was crucified with Christ on the cross. Not to realize this is to allow the devil to fool you and to delude you. What you and I are called upon to do is to cease to live as if we were still in Adam. Understand that the "old man" is not there. The only way to stop living as if he were still there is to realize that he is not there. If you are a Christian, the man you used

to be has gone out of existence; he has no reality at
all; you are in Christ. If we but saw this as we should,
we would really begin to live as Christians. We would
all hold up our heads, we would defy sin and Satan,
we would rejoice in Christ as we ought.[4]

— Had God not fixed it so you would die in Christ, when
you were reborn as a Christian you would be spiritual
Siamese twins, one evil, one good, who constantly fought
for the upper hand—a spiritual schizophrenic, a "house divided against [yourself]" (Matthew 12:25). Do you remember
what Jesus said about such a house? "Any ... house divided
against itself [can never] stand" (Matthew 12:25)! I don't intend to be ugly about this, but this two-headed monster is
precisely what we Christians are taught that we are by most
well-meaning Bible teachers. The Greek text does not support this. If we are, in fact, creations with two spirit natures,
one good, the other evil, then we are a "house divided
against itself." And what did Jesus say? "Any kingdom divided against itself is laid waste; and any city or house divided against itself will not stand" (Matthew 12:25). That's
precisely the reason that God had you crucified in Christ
before He caused you to be reborn—so you would never be
a house divided against yourself! Tragically, despite what
Jesus said, and despite what men and women like those
saintly old giants taught tens of thousands of Bible teachers
in the first three quarters of the twentieth century, modern
Christians have been and are being taught that we have *two*
spirit natures one good and one evil—that each Christian
warrior is indeed a "house divided against himself." Is it any
wonder that we see the fulfillment of Jesus' prophecy? Many,
many deceived Christians collapse each day. As long as the
church continues to believe and teach this untruth about our
identity, we'll continue to be a defeated group of warriors
who sound pretty brave as we praise the Lord in the

assembly, but get picked off by snipers as soon as we hit the parking lot.

"But, Bill! That's exactly the way I *feel!* I *feel* like the good me fights against the bad me. I see that the Bible says that I was crucified in Christ. You've convinced me. But I can't deny the reality that I live with."

We'll get there, but we're going to have to continue to build our case on Scripture, not on your experience. This is going to take the remainder of the book. When we finish, we'll be better able to compare what God says is reality against what your feelings and your experience say is reality. Let's both trust God that you'll have received enough revelation by then to choose against your feelings and your experience in favor of God's Word. We've got to go by the definition of *reality* in *His* dictionary, not ours.

Simply *believing* in the literality of our crucifixion with Christ however, won't guarantee that you'll not wind up in the motel room like Brother Jimmy did, but I'll tell you this: *Walking* in it will keep you out of that motel room. How would a dead man react to the idea of propositioning a prostitute? He wouldn't. He's dead to such plans. This is not to be *felt*, but *believed*, gang!

Beginning Again

It's going to take some doing to change your lifelong habit of living independently into depending upon Christ to express His life through you. Too often our *feelings*—rather than God's Word—become the controlling factor in our lives. We must count the facts about ourselves as true as declared by *God*, not as declared by our feelings and the world-system programming of the thoughts we process. As we consistently walk in the "light" (truth of God's Word) and by the life of the Spirit of Christ through us, God will begin to develop a sense of reality within us of what is already true about our identity—that we are literally new creations in Christ.

In addition to the fallacy that our identity in Christ is merely positional, not literal, another common deception Satan may plant in your mind is that claiming Christ as life is simply a method for handling emergencies, that you should continue on as is until you face a crisis, and then call on Jesus to handle it through you. That won't work. How does this differ from your present method of operation? Most Christians do the best that they can and then call on Christ to help them when they hit a snag, don't they? That's not God's plan, gang. The fact from God's Word remains: Christ is your life. "For you have died and your life is hidden with Christ in God. When Christ, who is our life, is revealed, then you also will be revealed with Him in glory" (Colossians 3:3-4). This is to be the new fact of life for how you face each moment of each day, and it's going to require *practice*. The more you practice Christ as life through you, the more you will *experience* His overcoming the world, the flesh, and the devil through you (Hebrews 5:14). You're going to love this new way to face life!

5 THAT BIRTH, NOT PERFORMANCE, DETERMINES IDENTITY

⎯The cheetah's initial burst of speed in the chase
reaches approximately 60 miles per hour! His sleek,
aerodynamic lines have evolved over millions of years
to enable him to attain such speed.

But the prey is no easy mark. The deer uses its agility
to quickly change directions just as the cheetah seems
certain to overtake him. The cheetah has developed
nostrils which flare for maximum air intake to cool his
body; but even so, he must snare his prey rapidly as
he can only sustain such speeds for a short time before his body overheats.

AND, SURE ENOUGH, THE CHEETAH abandons the chase.
The narrator on the educational channel assures us that he'll
have better luck next time. But I'm cringing from this educated man's explanation of how God's critters evolved from
zero. As my Sunday-school teacher says, "Nothing plus
nothing equals *something?* Give me a break."

Our Creator God

God's Word says, "All things came into being [through
Christ], and apart from Him nothing came into being that has
come into being" (John 1:3). This includes everything from
cheetahs to the ingredients in Cheetos. If it exists in its natural state, Christ created it. And if you ever wondered if God
has a sense of humor, check out some of His critters! (Avoid

mirrors.) There is no such thing as a natural phenomenon. If it exists in its natural state, Christ created it.

This includes the time dimension. Christ had a need for time, so He created it (Colossians 1:16b). As author C. S. Lovett taught me, *faith cannot exist outside a time dimension.* First, we believe (by faith), then we experience the result. Time is mandatory in this process. This puts anyone who desires a relationship with God in the position of *having* to believe He is a God of impeccable integrity, even though our time-bound five senses don't always render that conclusion.

Trust is the foundation of any lasting relationship, and trust can either increase or decrease as we come to know the object of our trust. Satan's plan is to sow seeds of distrust in our mind. He's constantly accusing God (in our mind) of being unjust, unfair, mean-spirited, capricious, indifferent, etc. God has more than proven these things false by giving His only Son in order that you, too, might become His child, which belies all of that trash talk. God allows us to live in such an environment in order that He might continue to prove His worthiness to us and give us the opportunity to believe or disbelieve His love for us. So you can see why "without faith [that God is trustworthy], it is impossible to please Him" (Hebrews 11:6). Again, my Sunday-school teacher says that *faith is acting like God tells the truth.* Everyone ought to have a Sunday-school teacher like my friend, Carroll Ray, Jr.

As Christians, it's helpful to understand how the pieces of God's plan fit together. Old Testament believers, functioning under the limited revelation made known to them, looked forward by faith in God, believing that He would fulfill His promise of eternal life to them (see Isaiah 53:1ff.). New Testament believers, on the other hand, look backward at the cross and, by faith embrace God's promise of eternal life through Christ. Meanwhile, God sees the entire panorama of

His "freeway" on which you travel as "present tense" through the window of the helicopter. The Deceiver's goal as you travel the freeway is to keep you so immersed in the traffic, so preoccupied with the curves and potholes in the road, that you miss the beautiful vistas and the intimate fellowship with Jesus and the Father that are available to you.

god of the Circle

Adam and Eve didn't sin against God by breaking the Ten Commandments, as these didn't appear on the time line until Moses' day. So what was the offense for which they were banished from God's presence? As previously stated, Eve made the suggestion, and then *Adam made the first declaration of personal independence from God.* His action said, in effect, *"I'm* in control here! *I'll* determine good from evil. *I* have my own ideas about such things, and *I* intend to do things *my* way." Alas, most of us are under the deception that independence is a virtue worthy of our pursuit! We seek it for ourselves and teach it to our kids, failing to realize that God hates independence. He designed us to *depend* upon Him.

God's job description is that He runs things. That's what gods do. There is one true God, but about six billion wannabes. As each descendant of Adam shows up on earth, he draws an imaginary circle around himself and declares himself god of that circle (god with a little g). The audacity of it! As if he had a "right" to claim anything as *his*. "The earth is the Lord's, and all it contains, the world, and those who dwell in it" (Psalm 24:1). But "little g's" attitude is: "This is *my* life. I've got *my* rights to run *my* circle. I *must* stay in control!" He establishes his own independent kingdom juxtaposed against God's kingdom. Look at him standing on his hind legs going head-to-head with God! Uh-oh, where have I seen that face? Arrrgh! In my mirror.

69

The Weakest Man in the World

Whereas the world defines *independence* as "virtuous self-sufficiency," God calls it *sin* because it sees *self* as a worthy source of power. If independent self-sufficiency were the benchmark of true strength, then Jesus Christ was the weakest man who ever lived because He never committed a self-empowered, independent act. "The words that I say to you I do not speak on My own initiative, but the Father abiding in Me does His works" (John 14:10b). The power you see in Jesus was *the Father* expressing His life *through* Jesus! "Have I been so long with you, and yet you have not come to know Me, Philip? He who has seen Me has seen *the Father*; how do you say, 'Show us the Father' " (John 14:9).

The world's definition of *personal weakness* is "a lack of individual power or strength—one who must depend on another." By that definition, Jesus of Nazareth was the weakest sound-of-mind-and-body human who ever lived because He totally depended on the Father in Him.

Examine the temptations He endured. Satan tempted Him to go independent to satisfy His personal need of the moment: to turn a stone into bread when He was 40-days hungry; to kick off His ministry with a bang by diving off the top of the Temple and swooping in for a two-point landing; to throw off the bondage of being under submission to the Father and take over the earth—all of which would have been independent acts! Have you ever noticed that Jesus did not say that *He* could call down thousands of angels to rescue Himself from danger? "Do you think that I cannot appeal to My Father, and *He will* at once put at My disposal more than twelve legions of angels?" (Matthew 26:53, emphasis added). Jesus never lifted an independent hand for 33 years!

— Compare that kind of submission to our own independent, self-serving life before salvation. A lord of the ring condescends to let God handle the heavy stuff, like sunrises, etc., but he is determined to control "his" circle. I call him "lord of the ring" (to put a different spin on Tolkien's phrase). The last words in the Book of Judges describe such a person's ways: "Everyone did what was right in his own eyes." Situation ethics—the product of personal independence from God.

The Flesh

/ Your strategies for living, which you developed by employing your lord-of-the-ring approach, are referred to in Scripture as "flesh" (Philippians 3:3-7).[1] Think of these old ways as habit patterns of how you think, how you act, and how you feel (mind, will, and emotions). For most of us, our major goal as we developed these flesh patterns was twofold: to obtain love from others and, if successful, to bestow love (self-respect) upon ourselves. And we strived to stay in control in order to maintain these. Why would getting a steady supply of love be so important to us? The Bible says that God *is* love, so He created man with a giant need to be loved, because if we didn't need to be loved, we wouldn't need God. However, not knowing about God, but being born with an intense need to be loved, lords of the ring immediately sallied forth trying to extract their love supply out of *people and self.* Some are very effective, most are moderately so, while still others grow up in a loveless environment. I've labeled the three flesh-types which result from their experience USDA Choice, Plain Vanilla, and Yucky. The first two groups keep working at building their skills for earning love, while the last group typically develops skills for merely *surviving* in a world without love. These latter folks become better able to handle rejection than love. They *want* love, but when they get it, they're like a dog who chases cars and finally catches one. *(What do I do with this?)* Most of these folks keep others at arm's length—including God and even their spouse and kids! The other two groups, however, go merrily along their own way, employing their fleshly techniques to milk their love supply out of people and the world system. Although Christ solved the problem of being tyrannized by our own flesh, we must know *how* He has done so and *how* to embrace the victory He promises.[2]

How We Got into Our Fix

To see how we all got caught in this flesh trap, let's zoom in to get a tight shot of Adam on the time line (see Figure 5A). When Adam sinned, he committed spiritual suicide. God had warned him of sin's consequences, but he rebelled anyway. In the very day you sin "you shall surely die" came true that *very day* (Genesis 2:17). Adam died spiritually, not physically, or you would have never shown up. By dying spiritually, the first couple's progeny were all spiritual stillbirths. The wavy line emanating from Adam (man) represents the spiritual characteristics you inherited from him: dead-to-God spirit, enemy of God, lost, son of Satan (John 8:44), guilty, rejected by God, child of wrath, etc. The straight line represents the *physical* characteristics the first Adam passed along to you: lungs, liver, etc.

We Inherit Physical and Spiritual Characteristics from Adam

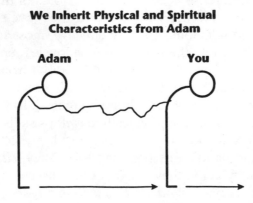

Figure 5A

Man's Identity Problem

Remember the title of this chapter? "God Wishes Christians Knew That Birth, Not Performance, Determines Identity." Because of your spiritual heritage in Adam, you can see that you were in big trouble merely by being born. Every person is born with the same identity crisis. We each showed up in the spiritual lineage of the first human rebel, Adam. This is a very important point to grasp. Here's why: *Birth, not performance, always determines identity.* A toad is not a toad because it croaks and eats bugs. I wouldn't recommend it, but you could eat bugs till you croaked, and it wouldn't turn you into a toad. A toad is a toad because it was *born* a toad.

You're a human by birth. Your mom didn't pause between labor pains and pray, "Oh, God, please let it be a human!" *Birth* determined your human identity. This holds true in the spiritual realm as well. As a spiritual product of Adam, you are a sinner by *birth* (Romans 5:19a). Your performance had nothing whatever to do with your acquiring this identity. *Being born on the wrong side of the spiritual tracks is what condemns sinners to hell,* and God wishes Christians knew this. Then they could inform the lost. Sinner-men go to hell; saints go to heaven. Each of these identities is acquired by birth. Psalm 51:5 says, "I was brought forth in iniquity, and in sin my mother conceived me." That's not talking about sexual intercourse. It means that human parents produce sinner-babies. You and I were sinner-babies by birth. Apparently, the fatal spiritual seed is passed on to the children by the dad. If Jesus had had a human dad, He would have been a sinner-baby by birth. Jesus is the only One in Scripture who is referred to as "seed" of a woman (Genesis 3:15) because no human male produced Him. In light of this, you can see that denying Christ's virgin birth reveals spiritual blindness. God does not want people sitting under such teaching.

73

When witnessing to lost folks, I used to tell them that if they could live a perfect life they would go to heaven, but since they've already blown that one, they need a Savior. Although a person can come under conviction and get saved via this method, my theology was wrong. Even if it were possible for man to keep God's Law perfectly, he would still go to hell because of the spiritual identity he acquired at birth. There will be no sinner-men in heaven. Sinners are not declared to be sinners because they sin, but because they were *born* sinners. All you have to do to spend eternity in hell is show up on earth! Man's ticket to hell is a birth certificate. Folks, spiritual identity is *huge!* And this problem can't be fixed by simply cleaning up your act. You've got to die in Christ as who you are and then be reborn as a new spirit critter. Refusing God's provision to change one's sinner identity to a saintly one through faith in Christ determines one's eternal home—hell. Man's *performance,* on the other hand, determines either his level of punishment in hell or his rewards in heaven, which we'll discuss later.

God has a great deal to say about hell being a literal place of unimaginable punishment that was created for Satan and the angels who participated in the hostile heavenly takeover attempt described in Revelation 12:9: "The great dragon was thrown down, the serpent of old who is called the devil and Satan, who deceives the whole world; he was thrown down to the earth, and his angels were thrown down with him." Simply to live forever in the total absence of love and beauty sounds horrible, to say nothing of the agony of the physical and psychological pain the Bible describes. Jesus said hell was never created for humans, but "for the devil and his angels" (Matthew 25:41). Humans are not *sent* to hell; they *choose* to go there rather than submit to the altruistic action of Jesus Christ on the cross. They have to walk over the crucified body of God's Son to get through hell's gate. What a colossal waste.

74

Small Children Are Not Lost

"The first man, Adam, became a living soul. The last Adam became a life-giving spirit" (1 Corinthians 15:45). Because of your heritage in "the first man," you began to sin (Romans 5:12). Your performance began to reveal that you were yet another lord of the ring by birth. God makes it clear, however, that small children are exempt from this condition. In Matthew 18:10, Jesus said about them, "See that you do not despise one of these little ones, for I say to you, that *their angels in heaven* continually behold the face of My Father who is in heaven." Lost folks don't have personal angels! Jesus also pointed out in this discourse that these children can be led into sin: "Whoever causes one of these little ones who believe in me to stumble, it is better for him that a heavy millstone be hung around his neck, and that he be drowned in the depth of the sea" (Matthew 18:6). (That's a sobering truth for self-styled social engineers.) So the child apparently matures enough to become accountable and then becomes "lost." To be *lost* means "I used to own it, but now I don't." Then Jesus relates the parable of the lost sheep—a picture of the Holy Spirit lovingly searching for the person who became lost, who can then get "saved" by faith in Jesus.

David and Bathsheba had an illegitimate child whom God said He was going to take. David cried, fasted, and prayed for days, asking God to change His mind, but the child died. David's servants were afraid to tell him, for fear he would harm himself, but he overheard them whispering and asked for a report on the child's condition. When they told him the child was gone, he showered, dressed, and asked for food. They were amazed and told him of their fears. He explained: "While the child was still alive, I fasted and wept; for I said, 'Who knows, the Lord may be gracious to me, that the child may live.' But now he has died; why should I fast? Can I bring him back again? *I shall go to him,* but he will not return to me" (2 Samuel 12:22-23). Where did

75

David go? To heaven. Where is the child? Where David went. Little kids are considered innocents by God.

Knowing this is precious to Anabel and me as our son, Mason, was profoundly retarded and went to Jesus at age 12. He's 38 at this writing. We can hardly wait to see him and get acquainted with the real Mason. The problem, you see, was not with Mason, but with his faulty earthsuit. Its brain could not process information. Mason spent his years in virtual solitary confinement inside an earthsuit through which he could not communicate. Now that he has ejected, he's fine (2 Corinthians 5:1-4)!

God Becomes Man

Figure 5B depicts Eternal Life (Christ) dipping down to earth to inhabit a tiny newborn earthsuit. Christ is without beginning or end, thus His life extends forever into both the past and the future (John 1:1-4; Hebrews 7:3).

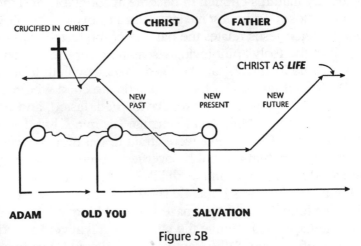

Figure 5B

Look at your innate spiritual identity in Adam when you were still burdened under the weight of your sins. You traveled the time line until you reached the point where you recognized your spiritual condition (sinner) and repented. You asked Jesus Christ by faith to forgive you, to come into you and change you. I've depicted salvation by the erect figure. The line which pierces this figure's breast represents Christ's lifeline, which goes forever into both future and past.

At salvation, several dramatic changes took place in you. Your crucifixion, death, and burial in Christ (Romans 6:6,4,8), your rebirth as a new creation in His resurrection (2 Corinthians 5:17), and your ascension in Him to the right hand of the Father (Ephesians 2:6), all came "on line." You were instantly changed into a brand-new spirit critter! Look at you in Figure 5B, standing tall in Christ! You have left your old spiritual heritage in the dust of earth. You now have a new spiritual *present*. Christ is now your life (Colossians 3:1-4; Galatians 2:20; John 11:25). You also have a new *future*, depicted by the arrows flowing forward in Christ's life. Now notice the arrows flowing backward to the cross. When Christ was crucified, you were *in Christ*, crucified and then buried in Him. When He was resurrected, you were re-created in Him (Ephesians 2:10). Because you are now a spiritual descendant of Christ and your old spiritual past was crucified in Christ ("Old things [have] passed away"—2 Corinthians 5:17), *you have been given a brand-new (holy) spiritual past! God changed your identity from sinner to saint* (2 Corinthians 5:17)! The sinner, along with his spiritual heritage in Adam, was crucified in Christ (Galatians 2:20), and the saint, along with his spiritual heritage in Christ, was born anew of Christ's resurrection! This is not so much to be understood as it is to be believed. It's difficult enough for us humans to believe it, let alone understand it. Don't let anyone talk you out of this fantastic truth, especially those of you with a painful past. You've always wished you could have a new beginning as someone new? Well, congratulations! You've just won the spiritual lottery! "Blessed be the God and Father of our Lord Jesus Christ, who *has blessed* us with *every* spiritual blessing

77

in the heavenly places in Christ" (Ephesians 1:3). Remember, God gets to make the rules. You get to begin life with a clean sheet of paper. You are no longer a sinner-man by your first birth, but a saint (holy one) by your *new birth!* Your spiritual heritage is no longer rooted in the *first* Adam; you're done with him! Your spiritual heritage is rooted in the *last* Adam— Jesus Christ. The word *Adam* means "man." "For since by a man came death, by a man also came the resurrection of the dead.... So also it is written, 'The first man, Adam, became a living soul.' The last Adam became a life-giving spirit" (1 Corinthians 15:21,45). You came out of the *last* Adam's Spirit loins. Just as the first Adam's spirit-history dictated your old, dead spirit-characteristics, the last Adam's spirit-history dictates your *present*, new spirit-characteristics! *Christ's* spirit-history is now your spirit-history, because from the helicopter view you have now been *in Him from before the foundation of the world.* Look at this: "Just as He chose us in Him before the foundation of the world, that we should be holy and blameless before Him" (Ephesians 1:4)! All who are in Christ are "now holy and blameless before [God]." "Now take a deep breath and ask the Holy Spirit to let you feast on all of this amazing truth which is yours because of Jesus. Praise Him!

I find that diagrams are helpful, so I'm printing Figure 5C, depicting your death and burial as the spiritual sinner-man you were, your rebirth and ascension as the new saint you now are in Christ, and Christ as life replacing your old Adamic, self-serving, lord-of-the-ring life on earth. This must be acquired on earth by faith and will then continue forever after your earthsuit dies. Eternal life is not an extension of the Adamic life you inherited from your parents. Eternal Life is *Christ*—the Person (1 John 1:1-2). Don't worry if you can't figure it out. Just take God's Word for it, and then begin to act like it's true, by faith.

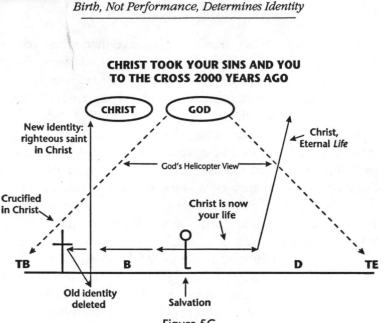

Figure 5C

Believe God, Not Man

⌣ This is so astounding that it's difficult to believe, especially in light of the fact that very few Bible teachers in our day teach it. But it hasn't always been this way. Obviously, Paul taught these truths to the early church. Perhaps you say, "But, Bill, I simply can't buy the idea that I'm a saint. Saints don't commit sins, do they? I still give in and sin. I wish I could stop it, but I can't. I know myself and you don't. I'm a sinner through and through. That's just not true. My pastor warned us against listening to men like you."

It may surprise you that I agree with your pastor. You shouldn't believe the things you read or hear about Christianity *unless they square with the Bible.* I don't delight in proving pastors wrong, but I trust you'll agree that if the Bible documents teaching which a pastor denies, you must follow the truth. No one has *all* truth. Let me ask you a question. If you're born again, why do you believe that your sins are forgiven? What proof do you have that, when you die, God won't be waiting for you with a list of your millions of sins and banish you to hell? Is it because you believe certain humans or believe certain doctrines you may have been reared under? Hopefully you would answer, "Bill, the Bible says that Jesus took the penalty for my sins and that if I come to Him in faith I'll be saved—forgiven of all my sins— and I'll be welcomed into heaven. God said so!" That's right! Good for you! You answered like a wise Christian. Did you notice that your only *tangible* proof of your forgiveness is the Bible? Rows of black print on white paper which you believe, by faith, state categorically that Jesus has the power to forgive sins for all who place their faith in Him. You did that. At this point it's not a feeling which persuades you that you're forgiven, it's your faith in His Word. You believe that you're forgiven and will be accepted into heaven because God said so. Good for you! That's great!

/ Now those same rows of black print on white paper state categorically that you were crucified in Christ and then born again as a new creation. A third-grader can understand that the Bible teaches this. Why do Christians not believe that our old identity died before being reborn, when the Bible says so? I believe it's because it's not taught by most seminary professors; consequently, the trickle-down effect manifests itself in most pastors not teaching it to their people. And then the people propagate the error by passing it along to their kids and others. All of these precious people continue to believe Satan's same old arguments that our crucifixion in Christ is a figment of God's imagination, when it's just as real as Jesus Christ's crucifixion! God said so. It's been my observation that most Christians never mature beyond the level of their pastor. Thus, they remain in the dark about the reality of their true identity. We are literally saints who are literally empowered by Christ's life. The same God whom you believe for forgiveness says that He changed you from a sinner to a saint by first executing you in Christ and then rebirthing you in Him. Are you going to believe Him—or some man-generated, neutering explanation by well-meaning theologians?

Since our basic identity is spirit—not physical, and we now have this miraculous new spirit identity (past, present, and future), can you see the healing that's possible for the Christian whose earthly past is fraught with rejection, trauma, gross sinfulness, etc.? The cry of his/her heart has been, *If only I were someone else—someone I could respect.* Well, congratulations are in order. God has *literally* answered that passionate prayer through Christ! God is not merely "playing like" this is true when, in fact, it's not. God gets to make the rules. It's His universe. If He says you're new, you're new. Embrace it! *Act* like it! Rain on how you *feel.* Rain on what some poor, well-meaning soul teaches to the contrary. He's out of order.

The Bible records that God allowed you to die in Christ so you could start all over as a new person, a holy one. And because He ascended, you, too, are now in the heavenly places *in Christ*: "Even when we *were* dead in our transgressions, [God] *made* us alive together with Christ ... and *raised* us up with Him, and *seated* us with Him in the heavenly places, in Christ Jesus" (Ephesians 2:5-6). Isn't that awesome? You are now not only *permitted* into heaven, you're already *at home* in heaven. *Look at those verb tenses.* You have found your place in life! You fit in. You don't have to strive for acceptance from others or earn it from yourself anymore! As a saint, a son/daughter of God, you are as accepted as elder Brother Jesus is. You are accepted by the One who counts the most! So stop expending so much energy seeking acceptance from people and self. You've got it. Go ahead and shout (unless you're on a plane)!

Two Sides of the Salvation Coin

— Folks, I reiterate: *Identity* change is a critical factor in salvation. Sixty times after Christ's sacrifice on the cross,

Christians are called "saints" (holy)—not because of their performance, but because of their new *birth* in Christ. You can see that even a lifetime of performing religious rituals or traditions can never change a person's identity one iota. Jesus said, "You must be born again" (John 3:7). This may or may not be accompanied by a zippy feeling; feelings are not the issue. It's fine if God gives you a feeling of euphoria at salvation, but it typically comes with about a 30-day warranty. We Christians live by faith, not by feel.

Salvation is similar to a coin in that it has two sides: "Christ in you" (heads), and you "in Christ" (tails). Every Christian knows the heads side (Jesus is in me), but to many believers the tails side (I am in Christ) remains a mystery, mere rows of black print on white paper. When some brothers from Grace Fellowship International showed me what it means to be "in Christ" in 1975, it launched me on a fresh, new walk with the Lord. I ultimately counted all of the "tails side" verses (in Christ, in Him, in Jesus Christ, in Christ Jesus, in whom, etc.) in the New Testament, which I then compared with the Christ-in-you-verses (heads). For every Christ-in-you verse, there are *ten* you-in-Christ verses! That's right. A ten-to-one ratio of you *in Christ* over Christ *in you*. If this realization impacts you like it did me, and you've embraced only the "heads" side of the coin, you're already asking God to show you what you're missing. *God wishes all Christians understood and walked in the truth of being "in Christ."* That's how we became saints!

Your True Identity in Christ

I lovingly challenge you to consider the following *facts* about your identity as declared by God's Word, then juxtapose them with your feelings and the world-system programming of your flesh. How you feel and act are not the indicators of your true identity—God's Word is. As you consistently choose to walk in the truth and in the power of the Holy Spirit, God will begin to make real in your experience what is true of your identity—who you are in Christ.

WHAT I THINK OR FEEL ABOUT MYSELF	WHAT GOD SAYS ABOUT ME
I'm too weak to resist sin.	Christ freed me from sin's controlling power (Romans 6:7).
I feel like God has given up on me.	I am neither condemned now nor in the future (Romans 8:1).
I feel like no one loves me.	I'm fully accepted in Christ (Romans 15:7).
I'm not a saint, you know.	All who are in Christ are saints (1 Corinthians 1:2).
I feel so inferior.	I am part of Christ's body and equal to all (1 Corinthians 12:14-16).
I'm such a failure; I'm hopeless.	I'm *always* in *His* triumph, despite appearances (2 Corinthians 2:14).
I can't understand the Bible.	My hardened mind has been removed (2 Corinthians 3:14).
I'll never change.	I've already been changed. I'm a new creation; The old things "passed away" (2 Corinthians 5:17).
I know that no one is righteous.	I am the righteousness of God in Christ (2 Corinthians 5:21).
I have no parents.	I am a child of God and His heir (Galatians 4:7).
I'm inadequate and lacking.	I am complete in Christ (Colossians 2:10).
Each person must live his own life.	Christ will express His life through me (Colossians 3:3-4).

WHAT I THINK OR FEEL ABOUT MYSELF	WHAT GOD SAYS ABOUT ME
I would have it made if I won the lottery.	I've been blessed with *every* spiritual blessing (Ephesians 1:3).
I'm always the last one chosen.	I *am* chosen by the One who makes the rules (Ephesians 1:4).
I feel guilty all the time.	The One who makes the rules says I'm forgiven (Ephesians 1:7).
I worry about the future.	My glorious future is set in spiritual concrete (Ephesians 1:10-11).
I feel so insecure and anxious.	I've been sealed with the Spirit; I'm safe (Ephesians 1:13).
I hope to go to heaven when I die.	I'm *already* in heaven (Ephesians 2:6).
I can't find direction for my life.	I was re-created for *good* activity; the Holy Spirit will lead me as I trust Him (Ephesians 2:10).
God always seems so far away.	I've been brought near to God (Ephesians 2:13).
My problems are too trivial for God.	I have boldness and confident access to God (Ephesians 3:12).
My mind is crammed so full.	His peace guards my heart and mind (Philippians 4:7).
What if I fail or lose my job?	All of my needs (not greeds) are supplied (Philippians 4:19).

Focusing on What You Know

The above is a partial description of your true identity—who you are now. Peace with God is attainable for you (Romans 5:1). Merely giving a nodding approval to what God says about you, however, will not produce the peace of mind you seek. If God has touched your heart with the truths in the right-hand column, you must passionately, tenaciously claim them as your own with your teeth gritted, then get off your knees and step out in their reality. *Act like the thing is true which God says is true!* This is living by faith. You must know:

- what a hypocrite—a phony—is. Jesus branded the Pharisees "hypocrites" because they pretended to be something which they were not—God's holy "in group" (Matthew 23:13ff.). *A hypocrite is someone who pretends to be something he is not.* Now, wouldn't you know that the Deceiver has faked out the world by his definition of a hypocrite, which is 180 degrees different than God's? He's got the world believing that a hypocrite is anyone who acts contrary to the way he *feels.* He wants to keep us believing that our *feeler* is our main criterion of truth. That's a lie. God's Word is our *only* criterion of truth.

- who God says you are in order to experience God's rest—you must know your identity in Christ. Why is this imperative? Because you will "life out" whatever you believe about yourself to avoid feeling like a phony, a hypocrite. Believe that you're a lousy, no-good sinner, and you'll live life accordingly. *Knowing* that you are not this at all, *knowing* your true identity in Christ, will change what you believe about yourself and empower you to change the way you live.

- that Christ is your life and that His will is to express Himself through you, and that giving this a good effort will give you a supernatural inner peace of mind.

Consider Jesus.... Knowing what His Father said about *His* identity, plus *knowing* what His role was, plus *knowing* the definition of a hypocrite dramatically affected the way that He lived His life: "Jesus, *knowing* [not 'feeling'] ... that

He had come forth from God, and was going back to God, rose from supper, and laid aside His garments; and taking a towel, He girded Himself about. Then He poured water into the basin, and began to wash the disciples' feet" (John 13:3-5).

Jesus *knew* His true identity. He knew that He was the Son of God; that he was God's Savior-Lamb; that He was not first and foremost a carpenter (2 Corinthians 5:16). Because He knew this, He was free from having to play social power games to enhance His self-esteem. He didn't have to drive the hottest wheels or sport the latest fashions or flash his gold card or own the house in the suburbs or be a name-dropper to *feel* better about His image. He rested and was secure in His identity. And this was based upon what He *knew*, not upon how His *emotions* happened to be reacting.

And because He knew the true definition of a hypocrite, Jesus knew that as He "lifed out" His true identity, He was *acting like who He was*, not "pretending to be something He was not." All of this is what gave Him the inner security to wash the feet of the very creatures He had created in order to demonstrate His love for them and show us that we, too, are free to so humble ourselves. Why are we liberated from these things? Because of our *unshakable identity*. It doesn't have to be continually pumped up.

You are armed with these same truths. You know that you are an "[heir] of God and fellow [heir] with Christ" (Romans 8:17), and you know that acting like Christ is expressing His life through you (even though you may not *feel* like He is doing so) does not make you a hypocrite. It makes you obedient. Christ is your life. When you live like this, you are acting like who you are (John 15:5).

Your emotions, your behavior, and certain thoughts from the devil may be declaring you a member of the "great un-washed." If you *act* on those lies, then you will be pretend-ing to be something you are not. *This would make you a hypocrite!* However, by applying only a mustard seed of

86

faith, your mind can agree with God's view of your identity.
You must frequently act like who you are *despite what your
emotions and the Deceiver may say.* This is the only way any
of us can avoid the label "hypocrite."

/ The Holy Spirit within us arouses us to the point of
being overwhelmed by the pure, undiluted grace and love
of God toward us; to be in awe of such a gracious, altruistic
God, who did not shrink back even from sacrificing His
dearly beloved, only Son on our behalf (doubtless His
dearest Confidant and Friend), that we, the unworthy objects
of such mercy and affection, wonder of all wonders, might
also become the very sons of God. Not, that is, mere devo-
tees of some false, unworthy-of-the-lofty-name god such as
Allah, or Buddha, but actual sons by birth—genuine, bona
fide, *spiritual sons* of the God of infinity!

What manner of love is this who loves the unlovable
such as I, who extends infinite grace to the undeserving,
who seats us in the place of highest honor at His royal table
to celebrate the most regal banquet of infinity—the marriage
of His dear Son—even seats us in the place reserved for the
beloved bride-elect? And, as if that were not enough, as if
that were not far more than we could ever imagine or even
entertain with our finite mind, what manner of love is it that
would motivate our Bridegroom, Christ, the reigning Ruler of
creation, who is without beginning and without end, to lay
aside His infinitely high and lifted-up position, to devote 33
long, painful years to His favorite charity—"Operation
You"—which would culminate in allowing His own creation
to *torture the very Author of life until He died,* while praying
aloud for God to forgive us?

The Turning

Giving mere intellectual assent to the truths discussed in
this chapter is powerless. We must step beyond merely com-
prehending truth; Truth Himself must be enthusiastically

embraced. When the unregenerate sinner recognizes his hopeless, guilty condition before a holy God, and his need for Jesus Christ, truth Personified, to become his personal Savior and the *Lord of his ring;* when he chooses to turn 180 degrees and trust in Christ to forgive him of his sins, to come into him and change him on the inside, God calls such a turnaround *repentance*, which I see as mandatory to regeneration. This is not mere human opinion. I believe the Bible teaches this. You must *want* to be changed into a new person before God will change you into a new person. The person who loves his life as is has no motivation to change. He likes things as they are. He is in the category which Jesus addressed, "He who loves his life loses it; and he who hates his life in this world shall keep it to life eternal" (John 12:25). The renowned C. I. Scofield said, "Repentance is not an act separate from faith, but saving faith implies that change of mind which is called *repentance*."[3]

- John the Baptist paved the road to Jesus by preaching only one message: "Repent, for the kingdom of heaven is at hand" (Matthew 3:2) Jesus' forerunner taught repentance as the forerunner to salvation, by faith.

- As Jesus launched His earthly ministry, God says, "From that time Jesus began to preach and say, 'Repent, for the kingdom of heaven is at hand' " (Matthew 4:17). You might say that Jesus preached repentance as the "front porch" to salvation by faith (2 Corinthians 7:10).

- Jesus commissioned Peter to be the "apostle to the Jews." Peter subsequently preached, "Repent therefore and return, that your sins may be wiped away" (Acts 3:19). Peter called for the Jews to repent.

- Jesus commissioned Paul to be the "apostle to the Gentiles." Paul subsequently preached, "God is now declaring to men that all everywhere should repent" (Acts 17:30). Paul preached repentance to Gentiles.

• Everyone on earth falls into one of those two categories: Jew or Gentile. Jesus, John, Paul, and Peter— the four great preachers of the New Testament—all preached that man must turn from the direction he's heading (repentance) and come to Christ in faith.

Take Up Your Cross

"Whoever does not carry his own cross and come after Me cannot be My disciple" (Luke 14:27). You can be saved, but you can't be Jesus' *disciple* until you agree to the terms of the cross. You don't crucify yourself. That's the stuff of monasticism—a false understanding of Scripture. You have *already been crucified* in Christ, but it will do you no practical, *earthly* good until you agree with and embrace this truth with all of its ramifications. This is "taking up your cross." It's a moment-by-moment attitude of mind and heart.

How many rights do you have on a cross? A man who has agreed to take up his cross has no rights. His confidence and hope lie in Another. A man who has agreed to the cross is no longer in control; how much control do you have while hanging there? None. His destiny is in the hands of Another. A man who has agreed to the cross can be unjustly humiliated by the world; the cross takes away all of his pride. His comfort and acceptance are in the hands of Another. A man who has agreed to the cross no longer seeks to take care of number one; he trusts in Number One to take care of *him*, however He may choose to. A man who has agreed to the cross has given up all hope of finding meaning in this world system; he has found meaning and purpose through intimate fellowship with Another.

You Don't Need More Faith

The act of appropriating Christ as life is accomplished by using the same faith that you used to claim Him as personal Savior and Lord. You simply apply that faith to embracing the truth of your identity in Christ—same Jesus; same faith in Him. You don't need "more" of it to take *this* step of faith. Jesus said, "Take [*your*] cross and follow after Me" (Matthew 10:38). The cross you are to take up is not arthritis, or an unhappy marriage. The cross is an instrument of death. You agree that you have given up your old life in exchange for Christ *as life*. God wishes all Christians would do this. Jesus said this is the key to life: "Whoever wishes to save his life shall lose it, but whoever loses his life for My sake, he is the one who will save it" (Luke 9:24). The first step into abundant life is to abandon what you have called *your* life and embrace Christ *as* life (Colossians 3:1-4). This is the key to true life, the door to "abundant" life on earth, and I'm not referencing the "name it, claim it" message. Jesus never lived that way, nor did the disciples.

You may feel that you do not have all the answers to experience the "life [that] is hidden with Christ in God" (Colossians 3:3). I can identify because this was the case when I claimed Christ as life, by faith. I had no one to discuss it with. I couldn't have verbalized my need had there been such a person to come alongside me. I was so desperate because of the mess I was in that, when God showed me this truth in the Bible, I simply *chose to believe* that Christ was my life and started *acting like* He was, by faith. Feelings? I *felt* like I was faking it! But I persevered, *believing* I was "faithing" it. It was my only hope. And it began to work! It was still not a feeling. It's still not a feeling after 28 years! Although I feel fine and circumstances don't put me on the ropes feeling-wise, I do not set my mind on how I feel, but on what I *know* about Christ and my relationship with Him and Dad.

Our loving Father is so tenderhearted toward you. If your desire is to walk in your true identity, bow your head and confide in Him, won't you? He'll fill in the blanks in due time. Don't insist on a *feeling* as proof that God has heard you and that you have begun a whole new way of living. God is not dodging back and forth behind trees, playing hard-to-get. Remembering the great price He paid to win your hand is proof enough of that. Whisper the prayer of your heart, and trust Him to make the wonder of your identity in Christ an experiential reality to you in His own time and in His own way. If you wish to bring this walk on-line, by faith, just tell Jesus and then start *acting like* it's the reality that it is. When you see who you really are and the unique circumstances that it took to reveal it to you, you're going to love being who you are.

6 THAT WE ARE NOT FIGHTING AN INNER CIVIL WAR

Mary! You're never goin' to believe what I just seen
wi' me own two eyes! You know them army tanks
that they've stored in the pasture down the lane? Well,
our old bull busted through our fence, and blamed if
'e didn't get in wi' them tanks! 'E just backed off and
rammed into one of 'em. The blighter poked a hole
right through its side! And, Mary, that tank just let out
a whoosh through that 'ole that Buster 'ad poked in
'er! Them tanks is nothin' but big balloons.[1]

THAT IS REPORTEDLY A TRUE story of an English farmer's
experience in World War II. The "tank" was part of a ploy to
deceive the Germans as to where the Allies would attempt
to invade the European continent. Had you flown over
Britain at 30,000 feet in those days, your mind and emotions
would have told you that the Allies were preparing for a
tremendous military operation to be launched across the
channel from Pas de Calais when the true invasion was to
occur at Normandy. In the southeast, a gigantic fake army
was assembled. Acres of army tents were erected in military
precision, all of them empty. Mess tents were raised, from
which smoke poured three times per day cooking imaginary
meals to feed thousands of phantom soldiers. Army vehicles
churned about kicking up lots of dust to be seen from
30,000 feet above the fake ammo dumps, maintenance de-
pots, etc.

"Fleets" of canvas troop barges floated on barrels in the
Thames. They even constructed a phony oil storage field of

painted canvas. When the Germans shelled it, men lit magnesium fires to simulate a burning oil tank farm.

Wind machines created dust appearing as frenzied preparation for the invasion. The Royal Air Force maintained a fighter cap over these sites to force Nazi reconnaissance to stay above 30,000 feet so their cameras could not reveal the sham. This apparently paid off because the German Panzers did not arrive in time to repel the Normandy invasion.

In this chapter you're going to discover that you've been deceived many times each day because Satan has "kept you above 30,000 feet," where you would be unable to penetrate his subterfuge. The Bible calls Satan a "deceiver" (2 John 1:7). He *camouflages* his method for influencing our choices. But God wishes Christians understood that *He* unmasked the Deceiver's strategy in His Word way back in Genesis.

As we drive on God's freeway, we'll soon see an ugly, desolate area. There it is, up there on the left. That's a rest stop, although you would never guess it, because its entry is cleverly camouflaged in hopes that unwary travelers will pass it by. That's part of the enemy's strategy of keeping us "above 30,000 feet." But if you look closely, you'll see the words "Exit for Deception Alley." It has no landscaping or attractive parking area; Satan has seen to that. He wants all travelers who are speeding toward heaven to *bypass this exit*. It's working, too, because although all Christians believe that Satan is somehow involved when they sin, most would be hard-pressed to explain exactly *how* he influences us to "not [practice] what [we] would like to do, but [do] the very thing [we] hate" (Romans 7:15). All right, Tiger, push the stick of your fighter plane forward, dive through the enemy fighter cover till you're "below 30,000 feet," and then level out, land, and we'll get briefed on the revelation that this rest stop contains.

Look, we're the only ones here. It's OK to get out. The Holy Spirit will take care of any enemies that hang out here

who intend to deceive us. Your job is to remember that
Jesus said, *"One* is your Teacher" (Matthew 23:8). That "One"
is the Holy Spirit who indwells you. Although He may *use* a
teacher, He alone can give us understanding. Visiting this
rest stop will yield one of the most powerful, liberating
truths that the Holy Spirit has ever revealed to you.

Looking Beneath the Camouflage

This is going to sound like strange teaching to many of
you because Satan has managed to keep a lot of Christians
"above 30,000 feet" here, so stay with me on this till I have
time to show you many verses which document it. For
heaven's sake, don't stop reading in the middle of this chapter.
That would make the devil very happy. The Bible teaches
that an evil power called *sin* is at work in man. Gang, I'm
not speaking of *a* sin here, but of a *power* called "sin." I believe this power called "sin" is Satan's secret weapon against
us. God reveals Satan's strategy for deceiving us with this
power early on. The *power of sin* first rears its ugly head in
Genesis, where God is speaking to Cain as he is contemplating murdering Abel: "If you do well, will not your coun-
tenance be lifted up? And if you do not do well, *sin is
crouching at the door; and its desire is for you, but you must
master it"* (Genesis 4:7). Hidden within this verse is the key
to unmasking the devil's means of deceiving us! Follow me
now. The Hebrew of the italicized portion of Genesis 4:7 is
literally translated, *"sin* is crouching at the door; *his* desire is
for you, but you must master *him."* Do you see what God
revealed to us here? *He has unmasked Satan's means of deceiving us! God personified the noun sin in this verse, revealing a fantastic secret to us!* Personify means "to represent as
having personality or the thoughts ... of a living being."

Folks, the word *sin* in this verse is not a verb (action
word); it is a *noun* (person, place, or thing). It's extremely
important to understand that God is not referencing *a sinful*

act here, but a *person, place, or thing* which "crouches," which "desires" Cain (and us), and which *can be* "mastered." (Please read that sentence till you are sure you understand it.) Folks, *God personified sin—the noun.* God is saying that an entity called "sin" somehow had the ability to influence Cain. Without question, God said that a power which He called "sin" was playing a key role as Cain was pondering the killing of his brother.

Folks, I realize that this will be a new teaching to most of you. This is not a figment of my imagination or the result of eating a bad hamburger before bedtime. This is God's revelation from the Bible. Reread this section slowly, trusting the Holy Spirit to unmask this deception for you. Something called sin is waging war against Cain's mind here! I certainly am not teaching that we're all demon-possessed, but you'll have to agree that this verse indicates that we were born with a subversive agent within us that is precisely what God says it is: a power which has the capability to deceive us. And in this chapter we're going to use the New Testament to see how that same power controls *you!* In Genesis 4:7, God portrays sin as having the ability to:

- *persuade* Cain
- *entice* Cain
- *tempt* Cain
- *lead* Cain to take matters into his own hands
- *suggest* that Cain solve his problem by rebelling against God
- *suggest* that Cain murder Abel!

God, not Gillham, either implied or said all of the above, gang. God is penetrating Satan's camouflage for us—and He does so repeatedly in the New Testament. *This persona which God calls "sin" is a noun;* it's not a verb. Using this insight that God has given us through studying how the power of sin influenced Cain to kill his brother, let's step over and study that large information board that God has prepared for us. It contrasts some characteristics of our true Teacher, the Holy Spirit, with those of the power of sin. This will give us a better understanding of exactly how the power of sin will try to influence us to do evil or fail to do God's will.

GOD'S HOLY SPIRIT	THE POWER OF SIN
Teaches truth	Teaches lies
Credits Jesus and the Father for good, blames Satan for the bad	Credits chance, circumstances, luck for good, blames God for the bad
Interprets and validates God's Word	Denies validity of all or part of the Bible
Validates reality of God and Jesus and directs praise and honor to Them	Portrays God as impotent; Jesus as a weak, effeminate, tragic figure
Teaches that following God's Word is best for man	Teaches that following "cultural correctness" is best for man
Convicts us of sin	Dulls our sensitivity to sin
Indwells your *spirit* (1 Corinthians 6:17)	Indwells your *body* (Romans 7:23)
Gives thoughts to your mind	Gives thoughts to your mind
Persuades you	Persuades you
Seeks to lead you in the paths of righteousness	Seeks to lead you in the paths of unrighteousness
Convicts you when you sin	*Condemns* you when you sin
Uses valid guilt feelings	Uses false guilt feelings
Portrays God as a loving Dad (Galatians 4:6)	Portrays God as an Unfair Tyrant
Promotes intimacy with Christ and God	Promotes terror of God

GOD'S HOLY SPIRIT	THE POWER OF SIN
Draws you to God	Alienates you from God
Interprets your circumstances according to the true knowledge of God	Interprets your circumstances *against* the true knowledge of God
Always tells the truth	Always lies or distorts the truth
Guides you with Scripture, using its true context	Guides you with Scripture *apart from* its true context

I believe our failure to recognize sin, the power, is because Satan always seeks to camouflage the English word *sin* to us as a verb rather than as a noun. They both look the same and sound the same in the English language. A Greek-speaking culture, such as that of the churches in the New Testament, would *never* be confused about differentiating between sin, the noun *hamartia* (person, place, or thing), and sin, the verb *hamartano*. Someone has said that if English is a Chevy, Greek is a Cadillac. The English language plays right into the Deceiver's hands here.

A Profound Revelation

In the mid '70s, one of my counselees was a beautiful young woman whom I'll call Mary. Although she had the cheerleader, popular-girl-on-campus pedigree, she was a troubled young woman. I'll never forget the day I received the call that Mary had taken her life.

I agonized over the loss of this Christian. I loved her. Such a waste. I stayed before the Lord for weeks, asking Him to reveal to me how Satan had influenced her to commit this act. And God showed it to me. Once you embrace it, this truth will be a fantastically powerful weapon against Satan. The power of sin "talked" Mary into taking her own life, just as it had deceived Cain in Genesis! This agent of the Deceiver, called "sin," wages war against both sinners and saints. And the seventh chapter of Romans gives us the details of how he goes about it.

Count the actors in Romans 7:15: "For that which *I* am doing, *I* do not understand; for *I* am not practicing what *I* would like to do, but *I* am doing the very thing *I* hate." How many actors do you see in the verse? One: "I." However, verses 17 and 20 both indicate that there are *two* actors in this scenario: "I," plus the power called "sin."

"So now no longer am *I* the one doing it, but *sin* which indwells me" (verse 17). Notice the two actors: "I" and "sin."

"But if *I* am doing the very thing *I* do not wish, *I* am no longer the one doing it, but *sin* which dwells in *me* [is doing it]" (verse 20). There they are again: "I" and "sin."

I am not moving toward teaching "the-devil-made-me-do-it" nonsense. I am pointing out that there are now *two* actors in the scenario: "I" plus "sin." These verses indicate that I am not flying solo when I embrace a sinful thought or commit a sinful act. This power called "sin" is flying copilot. I want to make it very clear that I believe that I am totally accountable when I commit a sinful act or embrace a sinful thought. *I am not teaching the false idea that I can blame my sins on my mythical, nonexistent sinful nature.* That would be a cop-out. The person who takes that unbiblical position projects the blame for his sins on the nonexistent old man who died in Christ (Romans 6:2-8). That is denial. That cannot be documented in the text of Romans chapters 6 through 8. This error promotes the false notion that it's normal for Christians to sin dozens of times a day in our thought-life, plus overtly. That deception is from the father of lies. God says that a *second actor* has entered the scene here who is involved in my sinning: it's the noun called "sin," that same power which God showed us in Genesis.

I'll reprint Romans 7:15 for easy reference, and then I want to make two points: "For that which *I* am doing, *I* do not understand; for *I* am not practicing what *I* would like to do, but *I* am doing the very thing *I* hate."

Point Number 1. When God says something once, we had best pay attention. When He repeats Himself, we had best post it on the door of the fridge! It's mega-important. The second actor in Romans 7:17 and 20 is that noun "sin." I said, "Lord, there is only one actor in verse 15, but there are two in verses 17 and 20. I know that sin was in this man in verse 15 because it came into man at the fall. Sin, however, doesn't surface until verse 17. How did sin go underground in verse 15?" Thoughts came to me which I believe were from the Holy Spirit:

- The power of sin keeps a low profile by injecting thoughts into the mind with first-person-singular pronouns: *I, me, my, myself, mine, etc.*

- In our battle against the power of sin, these "thought-bullets" are triggered into the mind through the old flesh patterns in the brain.

- A Christian who does not understand that the old man was crucified will naïvely receive these thoughts, believing that they originated in his own mind!

There is Satan's secret! God has blown away the smoke and dust camouflaging Satan's "rubber tanks and canvas ships." This is such a powerful revelation from God! Do you see that it is imperative for me to *know* that my old man was literally crucified in Christ (Romans 6:6) and that I am literally a brand-new creation (2 Corinthians 5:17) who *longs* to walk uprightly with God (Hebrews 10:16)? If I do not claim this, I leave myself wide open to the devil's lie that I have *two* spiritual natures: a righteous one and a sinful one who constantly fight against one another! That's the view from 30,000 feet! The old "good dog, bad dog" teaching that we all cut our spiritual teeth on is the devil's smoke-and-mirrors baloney. It's not biblical. The Bible teaches unequivocally that the old man died in Christ and was buried with Him (Romans 6:2-8). Although my counselee Mary had been taught about her crucifixion and rebirth as a new creation, I had not yet received the revelation to teach her about the power of sin and how it operated. Consequently, she was deceived into taking her own life.

Folks, the old you was crucified in Christ before the new you was reborn. Because of this fact, we can believe that:

- A dead man cannot wage war against the new man in Christ.

- A dead man cannot resurrect himself, as we hear some imply: "You've got to keep that old man on the cross." Hey, since when do you have to *keep* a man on the cross?

- If the old man didn't die, then Jesus didn't die because they were both crucified on the same cross, and the Bible states categorically that they died simultaneously (see Romans 6:2-8).

- Satan does not have the power to bring the old man back to life.

- It would be theologically pointless for God to crucify the old man only to bring him back to life again. Why kill him if you're going to bring him back?

- It makes *perfect* theological sense for God to crucify the old man in Christ's death and then re-create the *new man* in Christ's resurrection, which is precisely what the Bible says happened (Romans 7:4).

- The old man is history! Gone!

- I'll use the dreaded *e* word which many theologians rail against—the sin nature is *extinct!* It's a dinosaur for Christians! Write it in the sky in smoke! Shout it from the housetops! Hold a street dance! The "wicked old witch" is dead! *Christians do not have a sinful nature!*

- Christians have only *one* nature—a *holy, righteous new nature.* "He has granted to us His precious and magnificent promises, in order that by them you might become partakers of the *divine* nature" (2 Peter 1:4). That's us! That describes our nature!

Although, based upon our *experience,* our *thought-life,* and our *feelings,* it certainly *seems* illogical to believe that the old man was literally crucified, God's Word teaches that a new creature in Christ has *no sin nature,* due to our having been crucified in Christ (Romans 6:6, et al.). Please don't write to me and quote the New International Version to "prove" me wrong. The *well-meaning* theologians who translated the NIV Bible took unbiblical liberty by translating the Greek word *sarx* as "sinful nature" (see Romans 7:18, et al., NIV). Folks, that's not translation—that's religious tradition; that's human *opinion.* They made an honest mistake. One of them is a good friend of mine. I hasten to credit them for all of the good things about this translation. But I don't recommend that you use it to exegete Romans 6–8 because you'll see the old man portrayed as having the miraculous ability to survive the crucifixion. It's absurd to believe that we must "keep him on the cross." He's deader than a hammer! That old man took one trip to the cross. Then God *buried him!* We regularly celebrate the reality of this truth via believer's baptism—a one-act depiction of our death as the old man, our burial, and as we burst up out of the water, our new birth in Christ's resurrection.

"But, Bill! I still sin, and you wouldn't believe some of the thoughts that I have! I have a constant war going on inside me. How can you claim that I do not have a sinful nature?" Just because a Christian doesn't have a sinful nature doesn't mean that we don't struggle in our war against sin. I agree that we all have a war going on inside us. The Bible documents this: "I see a different law in the members of my body, waging war against the law of my mind, and making me a prisoner of the law of sin which is in my members" (Romans 7:23). But just as you can pick apples without having an apple-picking nature and eat pork without having a hog-eating nature, you can sin without having a sinful nature. *Nature* is defined as "a fundamental characteristic." Sinners *love* sin. Saints *hate* it. Sinners plan ahead for more innovative ways to sin. Saints attend seminars to learn how to overcome it. Our fundamental characteristic is to *avoid* sinning. The Bible does not document that our battle is between the old man and the new man; the Bible describes our battle as *the new man fighting against the power of sin* (Romans 7:23). Gang, you and I are not warring against ourselves; we are not engaged in a *civil* war. Although it may seem like a civil war, we must believe the Bible. We're engaged in a good-guys-against-the-bad-guys war, and *we are the good guys—saints.*

Point Number 2. Although Romans 7:15 is commonly cited to prove that saints have two natures—one good, the other evil—it actually *proves the opposite*—that we are *good.* Is Paul *thrilled* to be practicing evil things? Does he *love* to sin? Is even a tiny part of him *delighted* that he has some mythical excuse for failing to carry out his good intentions (i.e., the old man came back to life)? Does part of him lie awake nights trying to figure out how he can sin and get away with it? Is his attitude, *Oh well, God will forgive me if I sin, so what's the big deal?* No! No! No! A thousand times no to all of these absurdities! *This man is miserable because he can't get victory over his sins!* This man *longs* to do good; he absolutely *hates* it after he has sinned, and he can't figure out why he can't quit it. If, on the other hand, this man had

103

the mythical two natures that the Bible does not document, Romans 7:15 would read like this:

> For I understand very well what I am doing; for I am practicing what I *love* to do. When I feel like sinning, I sin and love every moment of it; when I feel like obeying God, I do that, too. I do the very thing that I feel like at the moment and I am quite happy about it. Isn't it fun to know that we're on our way to heaven?

/ Paul would be similar to a southern California man in March who loves snow skiing and waterskiing equally well. His problem is choosing which he would rather do today. Folks, Paul has a flat spot on his forehead from hitting himself with the palm of his hand crying, "Aye, yi, yi, yi, yi, yi, yi! Why can't I get my act together?" He's miserable because he finds it impossible to carry out his good intentions! This man is holy, through and through. Enough of the devil's nonsense that this verse depicts the mythical "evil you" fighting against the good you—the only you! *It depicts the power of sin fighting against the good you!* Verses 17 and 20 prove this. If you're a new creature in Christ, you have been given a new *godly* nature. "By this, love is perfected with us, that we may have confidence in the day of judgment; because *as He is, so also are we in this world*" (1 John 4:17).

Satan deceives us and influences us to do evil or fail to follow through on our good intentions through the power of sin. *Sin uses the pronouns* I, I'm, me, my, myself, *etc., when interacting with your mind. I believe sin triggers such thoughts through the old patterns for living which are still in your brain.* I believe these are old memory traces. This way you'll be vulnerable to accepting sin's thoughts as if they were your own, especially if you've been taught that you're mostly sinner and a teeny bit saint. Those sinful thoughts will seem as natural as the sunrise! As the power called "sin" bombards your mind with first-person-singular-pronoun thoughts, your resolve may weaken till you end up committing the sinful act. Even if you don't actually commit the sinful act, those thoughts or images will continually assault your mind like a worrisome gnat as the Deceiver seeks to keep you from experiencing the peace of God.

W. E. Vine's *Expository Dictionary of New Testament Words*[2] explains that the Greek word *hamartia* (which translates to the English *sin*) is a noun, while *hamartano* (also translated to the English *sin*) is a verb. In Romans 6:14, where Paul writes, "*Sin* shall not be master over you," *sin* is a noun; while in the very next verse (15), "Shall we *sin* . . . ?" it is a verb, an action word. In Romans chapters 5–8 the word *sin* appears 41 times, only *once* as a verb, *40 times as a noun!* Look at that! Only one time in these critically important chapters dealing with the key to victory over the power called "sin" does the word *sin* mean the *act* of committing a sin! But *if you interpret the word* sin *in Romans 5–8 as a verb, you will never understand these chapters that are so critical for walking in victory.* We have been conditioned to perceive the word *sin* as an action word. Thus, when we read it in the Bible, we think, *Yep, that's when I cheated on my taxes.*

In Romans 5:21; 6:12,14,17; 7:11,14,17,20,23,25; 8:2; 1 Corinthians 15:56; Hebrews 3:13; 11:25; 12:4; James 1:15b, *hamartia* (*sin* as a noun) appears and, as Vine points out, "*This governing principle is personified.*" Sin controls (governs), and it is a persona. As such, *sin presents thoughts to your mind for your consideration and deceives you by making them seem like they're your own thoughts!* Folks, the power of sin is Satan's secret weapon!

A Dialogue, Not a Monologue

Experiencing the thoughts which sin (the persona) feeds up to your mind with first-person-singular pronouns, you'll swear that the old man has been resurrected. You'll think a *monologue* is going on in your mind, when in fact it is a *dialogue* (Romans 7:23). This explains why many Christians teach that the old man is still alive. They believe their *experience* is reality, rather than God's Word. The power of sin is deceiving their minds on the issue of the crucifixion of the old man which, in Romans, is "as plain as the nose on your face."

It's impossible to accurately interpret chapters 5–8 of Romans, verse by verse, and prove the "old man" lives. God states categorically that he died in Romans. Since only God has resurrection power, *the old man has not been resurrected.* The Christian is not at war against the old man, the so-called sinful nature. We must, therefore, search the Word to see what God identifies as our opponent in this inner battle we all experience. Romans 5–8 identifies it as this power called "sin."

"But I see a different law in the members of my *body,* waging war against the law of my mind, and making me a prisoner of the law of sin which is in my members" (Romans 7:23). First, notice that God says our opponent, *the law of, or power of sin,* does not reside in the *mind* where our thoughts are generated, but in the *body.* God says your mind is at war *against* this power from the evil one which entered the world at the fall (Romans 5:12).

Every war must have at least two opposing sides. The power of sin always supports Satan's program. Since Romans 7:23 says your mind fights *against* this power, whose side does your mind *have* to represent: God's or Satan's? *God's side, else there would be no inner war*—you and sin would be on the same team! That was the case when you were lost. Think, Christian. Don't leave these last statements until you understand them. Ask the Holy Spirit to teach this to you. Your mind now fights *against* the power of sin because you have the law of God written *on your mind* (see Hebrews 10:16). You *want* to obey God. Although you are *tempted* to sin, you don't *want* to sin. "We have the mind of Christ" (1 Corinthians 2:16). "I will put My Spirit within you and *cause* you to walk in My statutes, and *you will be careful to observe My ordinances"* (Ezekiel 36:27). Hebrews 10:15-16 indicates this prophecy has already been fulfilled for new creatures in Christ. You have a deep inner longing to obey God.

Gang, I reiterate: You and I are not engaged in a *civil* war. We are fighting in a *bipartisan* war, and we're on God's side. "By this, love is perfected with us, that we may have confidence in the day of judgment; because *as He is, so also are we in this world"* (1 John 4:17). When you recognize that a thought you are experiencing is not your own, the trick is to immediately take it "captive to the obedience of Christ" (2 Corinthians 10:5) simply by refusing to accept it. Think, *No! I'm dead to the power of sin* (Romans 6:7). (You're not dead to sinning; you're dead to the *power of sin.*) Think: *The power of sin has no control over me!* Then instantly generate godly, true thoughts contrary to the thoughts being served up by sin. Let's illustrate with some hypothetical situations in which six Christians experience a dialogue with sin:

CASE NUMBER 1

The Power of Sin: "Boy, *I'd* like to go to bed with that one." (Notice the pronoun.)

Instructed Christian: "No! Thank You, Jesus, that I didn't generate that thought! Thank You that You are living through me, overcoming my flesh. Lord, You really have a problem here. I'm glad *I* don't." And then *act like* Jesus is living through you by diverting your eyes away from the temptation and setting your mind that Christ is overcoming this temptation for you, through you! He will do it!

CASE NUMBER 2

The Power of Sin: "It's no wonder that I have no friends! I'm such a drip! I'm such a worthless loser!" (Note the first-person-singular pronouns.)

Instructed Christian: "No! Thank You, Jesus, that because of You I am a holy, righteous, and blameless saint. Thanks to You, I am the very apple of my Father's eye! I'm not a loser. I am '*more* than a conqueror through You.' I'm not a reject. You have a fruitful day planned for me (Jeremiah 29:11; Ephesians 2:10). Let's the two of us be alert to allow You to *agape* some folks through me today. Thank You that I am such a loved, accepted person. Thank You that I am a *lovable* person, and that out of Your vast love-reservoir within me, I can experience victory over *sin*—the lying power."

CASE NUMBER 3

The Power of Sin: "I can handle this."

Instructed Christian: "No! Jesus, thank You that I am never to 'handle' situations independently. You will handle this through me, for me. Jesus, what liberty to know that You are my Burden-bearer, that it's not only not my job to bear burdens, it's sinful to do so. What a way to live!"

CASE NUMBER 4

Sin, the Deceiver, "speaks" to the mind of a Christian woman with low self-esteem flesh while she watches the Miss America Pageant on TV: "Oh, if only *I* looked more like that, *then* maybe *my* husband would love *me*. (Sigh.) But what's the use.... God made some vessels for common use, and *I'm* just one of them. (Sigh.)"

If she sits there and receives these lies as if they were her own thinking, she not only becomes accountable, but will become depressed by the time the program is over. However, by knowing her true identity in Christ, she can discern that these thoughts are lies. Look at the pronouns sin used, attempting to deceive her: *I, me, my, I'm.* Also notice how sin used the self-depreciating flesh patterns in her brain to slip these thoughts into her mind with first-person-singular pronouns. Although the devil can't *make* her sin, if she embraces these thoughts, she becomes accountable.

⟋ Launching Your Offense

Victory over the power of sin is as close as her will switch. She must throw it toward "setting her mind" on what a lovely, holy, blameless, treasured new creation she is in Christ. If she understands this and has prepared herself for just such situations by rehearsing truths about new creatures in Christ—practicing for future times of testing (Hebrews 5:14)—Christ will overcome the power of sin for her, through her. In this manner she will be *acting like* an instructed Christian. She'll be adding obedience to her faith (James 1:22). That way she will realize that she is being lied to in this situation and will be "loaded for bear."

She cranks up new, true thoughts about her identity in Christ: *Thank You, Jesus, that I know who I really am! I'm not a loser in Christ; I "overwhelmingly conquer through Him"* (Romans 8:37). *I don't win by a field goal as time runs out. I overwhelmingly conquer—I win by 64-0! I am "the righteousness of God in [Christ]"* (2 Corinthians 5:21). *I am the bride of Christ* (2 Corinthians 11:2). *I've been "blessed . . . with every spiritual blessing in the heavenly places in Christ"* (Ephesians 1:3). *I am righteous. I am holy. I am a new creation. My Creator does not look upon my earthsuit to identify me the way humans do* (2 Corinthians 5:16). *He looks upon my new heart that He transplanted into me* (Ezekiel 36:26). *I am "seated . . . in the heavenly places, in Christ"* (Ephesians 2:6). *When I want to look at my spiritual Dad, all I have to do is turn my head to the left, and there You are next to me—smiling at me!*

By supersaturating her mind with such truth from God's Word about all new creatures in Christ, she will ultimately overwhelm the thoughts from the power of sin. Christ will have given her the victory! And this is a *lasting* victory in that she will become strengthened in the inner man over time. There need be no giant letdown from the victory over the devil and the flesh. All she has to do is consistently "set her mind on things above," where she is literally sitting in glory in Christ. "[God] made us alive together with Christ (by grace you have been saved), and *raised* us up with Him, and *seated* us with Him in the heavenly places, *in Christ Jesus*" (Ephesians 2:5-6). Look at those verb tenses. That's not future; that's *past* tense! If we are in Christ and He is seated at the right hand of the Father, where are we right now? We're already relaxing in heaven next to the Father. How's that for acceptance and security!

Don't let sin convince you that this is an ethereal fantasy. Remember that *God's* view is seen from the helicopter, and you are riding shotgun in Christ at His right hand. If this seems too far away to be practical, think of it this way. The Bible says that heaven is up, but it doesn't say how far up, so let's play like heaven is just one inch above the earth. Pretend that heaven "kisses" the surface of the earth, surrounding its entire surface. Viewing it this way, do you see how you are inhabiting your earthsuit, yet "seated in the heavenly places" simultaneously? Sure! Set your mind on this. It will transform you into an indestructible, radiant beauty. God said so (Romans 12:2).

CASE NUMBER 5

A Christian husband's secretary has been sending signals to him that she's interested in beginning a relationship. She's just finished reading his computer monitor while leaning over his shoulder, pressing her body against his back, and is now sauntering toward the door with a seductive walk. She pauses, holds eye contact with him, and flashes a warm smile. Sin "speaks" to his mind. "Wow! *I* can't stand much more of this! But what's the harm, anyway? Half the guys in my adult Sunday-school class have told *me* about the affairs they've had. It's like Harry said, 'God forgives us; He under-stands our weakness.' *I* think *I'll* ask her out to lunch today." Look at those pronouns: *I, me, I'll!* Folks, those are not *his* thoughts; they are coming from the power of sin (Romans 7:20,23). This man is experiencing all-out war.

First, we must understand that this man's sex drive is not evil; it's from God. And his sex drive didn't get crucified in Christ. However, the power of sin is trying to capitalize on his *stimulated sex drive* to tempt him to do evil here. If he does not *instantly* trust Christ to live through him to over-come sin in this perilous situation, he'll be matching wits against someone with an IQ of 20,000. This world is his turf, and if we are foolish enough to match personal strength with him, he will win! Like in the 12-step program, the first step is to agree that *you* can't. But unlike that program, the second step is to agree that "Christ, who is our life," not only *can*, but He *will* defeat the evil one through you!

This man's victory strategy is to move quickly away from the contact she's made with his back, thinking: *Thank You, Jesus, that You are moving me away from this temptation.* (He continues to distance himself from the woman.) *It's wonderful to experience Your power and see You overcoming this situation through me by walking me around to the other side of the desk as if I need to get these papers off the shelf.* Hey, this guy is no robot! He's not on autopilot! *He's the one who's swinging his legs,* but *he's believing by faith that it's Christ through him* who is empowering his movements.

Thank You, Lord, for Your victory over my flesh! You are so faithful! Then he wiggles his lips and lets Christ say, "Oh, Laura, would you please step back to your desk and call my wife? I would like to surprise her by asking her to have lunch with me today. She's such a honey. I wish every man could have a wife who is as wonderful as she is. I never dreamed that marriage could get better and better. God is so good to me." *And the situation is defused. Jesus won the victory over the power of sin!* He may have to help matters along by rinsing his face with cold water, but Jesus won the battle for him!

As you trust Christ as life like this, He will empower you for whatever the situation calls for (Philippians 4:13). If it's wisdom, trust Christ as your Wisdom; if it's compassion, Christ is your Compassion; if it's patience, Christ is your Patience; if it's forgiving others, Christ is your Forgiver; etc. Christ Himself is your Victory over sin. Our source is a Person, not a set of rules or principles or standards by which to live. Our strength is Jesus Christ, our very life.

The Promise Keeper

Incidentally, let me make an *agape* observation to my brothers in the Promise Keepers movement. I think it's marvelous that men of God are getting together to support one another and praise the Lord. I support this movement financially and by attendance. But *Christ is our only trustworthy Promise Keeper.* Making a promise *in the power of your own flesh* is an open door for the devil to demand the right to "sift you like wheat," to knock the props out from under such a promise. You can believe from Peter's and Job's experiences that you're no match for the devil when God gives him permission to test you, which may happen at times. Check the record in Luke 22:31 and Job 1:12; 2:5-6. Those two men bit the dust by trusting in themselves, and modern Christians will as well. Only Christ through us is able to keep our promises, by faith. I believe we must make our promises like this: "Lord, strictly by Your grace, I trust Christ to keep this promise through me." Then *act like* He is doing so.

CASE NUMBER 6

Sin will approach us by using combinations of the devil's three roles (tempter, accuser, deceiver), seeking to defeat us. A single-parent Christian woman is well qualified and has been efficient in her job for seven years. Life would be much simpler if she could get a promotion. Everyone in the office knows that one of her coworkers is a flirt who uses personality and a cute figure to butter up the bosses and board members. Our sister has been with the bank four years longer than the flirt, who doesn't do her work as well as she should because she spends so much time spreading butter. Guess who gets promoted to the supervisor's position? You guessed it.

Sin says to the Christian lady's mind,

> Lord, it's just not fair! That sorry excuse for a human no more deserves that promotion over *me* than the man in the moon! Why did You let that happen? *I've* tried to be faithful to You! *I've* worked so hard and planned so long for that promotion! You *knew* how *I* was counting on that, and You let *me* down! *I'm* just crushed! Why, *oh, why* did You allow that to happen? Sometimes it just doesn't seem worth the effort to serve You!

Look at those pronouns, gang! Of course she's crushed, but those thoughts are not hers, they're sin's (Romans 7:17,20).

The power of sin will even present hateful, critical thoughts to our mind about *God,* and if we're naïve enough to accept them as our own, the power of sin will slamdunk us with accusations for having had "such outrageous thoughts"! And here sin was the one who gave you those hateful thoughts against God in the first place! He's the "accuser of the brethren," gang. He plays dirty pool. He gives you a thought and then accuses you for having it as if *you* had generated it. Of course, if you receive such thoughts, they instantly become yours. The trick is to instantly "capture" them and reject them.

You are especially vulnerable to being inundated by thoughts from sin if you are angry—doubly so if you're *justifiably* angry, like our sister in the example. That's why God cautions us: "*Be* angry, and yet do not sin" (Ephesians 4:26).

113

Anger is a good emotion. Sometimes it's OK to be angry. Jesus expressed anger by taking a whip to those doing business in the Temple, but we must really keep our guard up here because sin is "crouching at [our] door" in such situations. That's what happened to our sister in this example. She grabbed those thoughts about God as her own. In fact, she kept accepting such thoughts from the power of sin for months until she became a bitter, disenchanted, depressed Christian. I've included a discussion in a later chapter on how to handle your emotions during such times. Adverse emotions give sin a leg up on us, and we must be quick to bring Christ-as-life on-line in such circumstances. Each moment's delay will prolong your battle against sin.

Folks, life on this planet is not fair at times. No man has ever been treated as unjustly as our Savior, so it's obvious that it takes a dose or two of unjust treatment thrown into our hopper to move us through the process of being "conformed to [His] image" on the assembly line (Romans 8:29). The instant our sister heard about the promotion, she should have set her mind on thoughts such as these:

> Lord, this is crushing to me! You know that I had my heart set on that promotion! I thought the raise would make a big difference for my kids and me. But hard as it is to say it, You know best! You're in control. If You wanted me to have that promotion and raise, Satan himself couldn't have stopped it from happening.

> Even though I may feel like my world has come to an end, in my mind I know it hasn't. It's going to be agony to submit to her as my new supervisor; she's so incompetent. But I know that you will handle that through me, Jesus. You're the expert at humbling Yourself. Bad as I hate to say it, I give You permission to humble Yourself again, this time *through me* as *we submit to her* leadership together. Thank You, that You're going to do it *through* me. And by the way,

Lord, my kids and I sure would appreciate the next promotion.

Folks, *that's* the way to let Christ handle such disappointment. If she places her trust in Him to act this way in such trials, not only will she *not* become bitter and depressed in the ensuing months, God will so pour out His grace on her that later on she'll actually testify that this was one of the best experiences with Christ she's ever had.

A Subtle Trap

After reading these examples of how sin implants thoughts into our minds, perhaps the idea just came to you, "Now I know how to catch the power of sin in the act of deceiving me. I'm going to really stay on the lookout for those lies." No. That, too, is from the Deceiver. Striving to catch sin's lies is setting your mind on death. "For the mind set on the flesh is death, but the mind set on the Spirit is life and peace" (Romans 8:6). When you set your mind on the former, you're on Satan's turf again, where it will be relatively easy for sin to outfox you. On the other hand, when you set your mind on relaxing in Christ in heaven, one inch above the earth, praising Him for being the marvelous Savior, Lord, Companion, Friend, Spiritual Husband, etc., that He is, while trusting that He is meeting life through you, sin is faced with the daunting task of penetrating such thoughts to deliver his junk mail. You readily see that *such thoughts from sin will often stick out like a sore thumb*, enabling you to take "every [such] thought captive to the obedience of Christ" (2 Corinthians 10:5).

We've examined six different Christians, each with unique fleshly temptations, but all of whom are warring against sin—the power—by embracing Christ's work for them to give them victory. You must refuse such thoughts *at the threshold* of your mind, the instant you become aware of them. When those thoughts are presented to your mind by the power of sin, just act like no one's at home. Ignore the doorbell. Say, "Rain on you, hot shot! Peddle your lies somewhere else!"[3]

The Big "Cop-out" on Accountability

Do you understand now what a cop-out it is to embrace the lie that we still have a sinful nature? *It excuses our sin!* Though we can never reach sinless perfection, our normal experience is to overcome sin. Embracing the truth about the death of the old man, along with understanding how the power of sin accesses your mind via first-person-singular pronouns, will reduce your sinning to a trickle.

Romans 6:11-14 gives you God's formula for victory:

> Even so consider yourselves to be dead to sin [the persona], but alive to God in Christ Jesus. Therefore do not let sin [the persona] reign in your mortal body that you should obey its lusts, and do not go on presenting the members of your body to sin [the persona] as instruments of unrighteousness; but present yourselves to God as those alive from the dead, and your members as instruments of righteousness to God. For sin [the persona] shall not be master over you, for you are not under law, but under grace.

God wishes Christians knew that the word "sin" in Scripture:

- is often a persona, not a sinful action.

- has intelligence.

- obeys its master, Satan.

- can introduce thoughts into your mind with first-person-singular pronouns (*I, me, my*, etc.).

- seeks to control you.

But by Christ's life through you, you do not have to give in to sin's urgings or believe sin's accusations against your identity. It is only in following the imperative of these truths that you can realize consistent victory over sinning (the verb). Sound doctrine will set you free, brothers and sisters.

OK, let's hop in the car and blow this place. It's depressing. I'd rather study about Jesus than the devil, wouldn't you?

7   WHAT IT MEANS TO BE FREE FROM THE LAW

NEARLY EVERY SMALL TOWN HAS its "rich man." Our town had "Mr. Stone." He had a garage with an electric door opener. That's no big deal today, but believe me, that's hot stuff when you've got a remote garage with no door!

Hidden behind Mr. Stone's magic door rested two sparkling-new dream cars: a black four-door Packard with whitewalls (the kind the bad guys drove in the gangster era); and a Lincoln Zephyr coupe, the prototype of the Lincoln Town Car.

They were both 12-cylinder cars, and those babies could lay their ears back and fly. There were no banked curves on highways then because when the speed of your old clunker is 35 MPH, flat turns are no problem. There were no speed limits. If we had driven our old Chevy wide open, it might have reached a sustained speed of 40 MPH for a few miles, and then it would have sounded like the pistons were swapping holes. Not so with Mr. Stone. He could blow by us doing 70!

Was Mr. Stone a speeder? No, because there was no speed law by which to differentiate between Mr. Stone and the rest of us oil-stained wretches. Soon, however, the state legislature recognized the need for a safety measure and established a new law: speed limit 50 MPH. Now when Mr. Stone aired out his wheels at 70 MPH was he a speeder? Yes. Why? Because of *the law.* "What shall we say then? Is the speed law sin? May it never be! On the contrary, Mr. Stone would not have come to know sin except through the law; for he would not have known about speeding if the law had not said, 'You shall not speed' " (Romans 7:7, with minor changes).

The Purpose of the Law

/ Some congregations recite the Ten Commandments in every worship service. It would seem like reciting them weekly would be a deterrent against sinning. But for the uninstructed Christian, this practice could produce the opposite results. What if you were to begin each day with repeating "Keep off the grass" ten times? This would tempt you to walk on grass that you had hardly noticed before. Hammering away with oughts and ought nots is not God's plan for stimulating Christians to good works. *Grace* is to accomplish this desirable goal (Romans 6:14). People are motivated to live up to (or down to) the image they have of themselves. If you comprehend that you are the holy, pure, righteous, virgin bride of Christ, you'll want to live like it. Grace produces this.

Have you ever seen a bird dog that tucks its tail and cowers at your approach? Law likely produced that. Its master crushed its "spirit" by intimidating or perhaps beating it into submission. This animal has no joy. Its purpose for experiencing its created role (hunting) has been quenched by a hard taskmaster's abusive law.

— Consider on the other hand a bird dog which is owned by an *agape* master who has its best interest at heart. It was first taught the master's will for him through law (rules), reward, and discipline, then trained how to best experience the role for which it was created (hunting). It "lives in vital union with its master" as they work and play together. The dog's greatest delight is to simply please its master. Its master has been careful not to crush its "spirit," but to bring its will into line with his own for the dog's best good as well as for his own pleasure.

This dog manifests a zest for living. He has a sparkle in his eye as he ranges out in a grid-like pattern, according to his master's will. He is not restrained by a leash (law), but by the law of love for his master. *He yearns to submit to his master's will. He delights in it. Obedience has become the joy of his life.* This demonstrates "the law of love." This animal does not perceive himself as being controlled by a burdensome taskmaster, but as cooperating with his *life-companion, the love of his life.* Sure, at times he needs correction, and because it's administered to him properly, he is the better for it. He delights to please his master.

Is the evil one beating you down with law, deceiving you into believing that *God* is doing this, or are you constrained by the invisible leash of Christ's boundless grace and love for you? "For *the love of Christ controls us*" (2 Corinthians 5:14). Understanding this will be a fresh breeze to your spirit. Sound exciting? Let's examine it in God's Word.

The "Ministers"—Death and Condemnation

"[God] made us adequate as servants of a *new covenant*, not of the letter [the Law], but of the Spirit; for the letter *kills*, but the Spirit gives life" (2 Corinthians 3:6). Kills? Does that say that Law "kills"? Indeed it does. Verse seven says, "But if the ministry of death, in letters engraved on stones, came with glory...." Does this say that the Law is a "ministry of death"? Indeed it does! And just to be sure we get it, God says it a third time in verse nine: "For if the *ministry of condemnation* has glory, much more does the ministry of righteousness abound in glory." How do we explain this? Although those verses are not to be found in any packet of memory verse cards I've ever seen in the bookstore, they ought to be posted on every Christian's refrigerator door. Christians are not under the Law: "For sin shall not be master over you, for *you are not under law*, but under grace" (Romans 6:14).

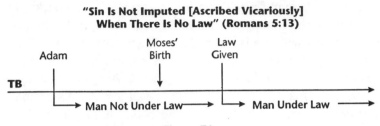

"Sin Is Not Imputed [Ascribed Vicariously] When There Is No Law" (Romans 5:13)

Figure 7A

In Figure 7A, TB stands for *Time Begins*. God's time line then depicts Adam's fall and his propagation of a race of sinners as a result of their *birth*. These folks were unaware of the *consequences* of being born with such a spirit identity (Romans 5:14). Like Mr. Stone's example, there was no benchmark by which they could be measured to identify with being lost sinners. Romans 5:12-13 says, "Through one man [Adam] sin entered into the world, and death through sin, and so death spread to all men, because all sinned—for until the Law sin was *in* the world; *but sin is not [ascribed to man] when there is no law*." In other words, there must be a violation of Law, or sin doesn't register on God's radar screen; if there is no law to be violated, there is no accountability for sin. Mr. Stone wasn't identified as a speeder until the speed law was enacted.

Lot committed some serious violations of God's Law, but it had yet to be handed down when Lot walked the earth. It's puzzling to see him called "righteous Lot" in 2 Peter 2:7; God took into account Lot's naïveté of God's ways (laws). God gets to make the rules; it's part of His job description. Lot was righteous because God *declared* him to be righteous. And that settles that.

An important aspect of Moses' ministry was the giving of the Law: "For the Law was given through Moses; grace and truth were realized through Jesus Christ" (John 1:17; see Figure 7A). Notice, grace and truth were not imparted to man via Law—and it will never be so. Condemnation and death were imparted to man via Law—and it will always be so (Romans 3:20). That's worth rereading, gang, because many well-meaning teachers teach that keeping God's law is our means of attaining or retaining His acceptance. In fact, if you removed Law from their sermon barrel, it might be a big step toward solving our paper shortage. Using Law to motivate Christians to godly behavior is actually counterproductive. "The *power* of sin is the law" (1 Corinthians 15:56). Pouring Law into a Christian actually *fuels* sin's engine, making it stronger! Remember the "Keep off the grass" illustration? I realize that it may be difficult to accept this if it is a new concept to you. This new concept, however, is as old as the New Testament. God wishes that mentors understood that grace is what moves Christians to obedience, not Law. God designed it this way. Have you not noticed that the preacher who rails the loudest against sexual sin is often the one who runs off with another woman?

— Now, I am not teaching what theologians call *antinomianism*—that since we are "not under law" (Romans 6:14), we can violate God's Law while He smiles at our antics like an indulgent Grandpa and says, "Boys will be boys." Absolutely not! Christians are governed by a higher law, "the law of love (*agape*)," which is written on our heart (Hebrews 10:16). Christians *long* to do the will of God. They *wish* they could overcome their sin (Romans 7:15). That's a ten! Paul verbalizes it for us: "For I joyfully concur with the law of God in the inner man" (Romans 7:22). Does that sound like we crave sin? Ridiculous! The reason that God can trust us by taking us out from under the Law is because He has written the desire to obey Him on our heart and mind (Hebrews 10:16). We're on a love tether.

Just as the speed law identified Mr. Stone as a speeder, God's Law identifies all unregenerate people as sinners. But here the similarity ends. Mr. Stone could cease to be a

123

speeder by obeying the speed law. Man's law holds that *performance* determines a person's identity—speeder or law-abider. Man says that you are what you *do*—a performance-based identity. But you'll recall that in God's economy, *birth*, not performance, determines identity. A sinner is born a sinner, and he can never become a saint by performing up to the standards of God's Law.

Performance-Based Acceptance

I looked upon the Law as God's standards to which I must measure up. However, my *emotions* carried it further than that. Having been conditioned by living on earth, my feeler "told" me that God's *acceptance* of me fluctuated according to my ability to keep His Law. This is called *performance-based acceptance*, the norm in human relationships. If you perform in ways that please folks, they will accept you; if you don't, they'll reject you. This holds true whether you're in the pub or, unfortunately, many churches.

But God's rules state that *all men are sinners by birth; performance has nothing whatever to do with acquiring this spirit identity nor with getting rid of it.* That's as impossible as changing your ethnicity from Caucasian to Asian by frequenting a tanning salon.

The Myth of Sinless Perfection

The only way a human can change his spirit identity from "sinner" to "saint" (who sometimes sins) is by dying and then being reborn as a holy spirit critter. Am I saying then that we Christians can attain a sinless state? Of course not; both the Bible and our experience disprove the notion of attaining such "sinless perfection" (1 John 1:8). Jesus made certain that all men understood this by intensifying the Law from the committing of overt sins to the committing of covert sins—sins of the thought-life. No man can gain perfect control of his thoughts.

"But, Bill, if we're not under the Law, what's to keep Christians from going off the deep end into sins?" God's Word answers this question: "Shall we sin because we are not under law but under grace? May it never be! ... Thanks be to God that though you *were* slaves of sin, you became obedient *from the heart* [and] ... became slaves of righteousness" (Romans 6:15,17-18). Did you see where the dynamic for your obedience is located? It came "from the heart." This new "law of love" (for God) which He "has written on our hearts" (Hebrews 10:16) is God's plan to be our motivation to godly behavior. This is not a set of rules God has typed across our mind and heart, but is the Spirit of Christ Himself—the Holy Spirit. *He* is the law of love; *He* is our life; *He* is *agape.* Will *Christ* living through us desire to life out God's *agape* law? Of course! We're now on a love leash, and it's a gentle bridle.

Reopened Under New Management

God describes the miracle by which He has implanted supernatural love in our control center (heart): "The love of God has been poured out within our hearts through the Holy Spirit who was given to us" (Romans 5:5). Here are a few more references to the change of heart that we now have through Christ: Romans 2:29; 6:17; 2 Corinthians 3:3; 5:14a; 6:12; Hebrews 10:16.

I believe the heart is the deepest dynamic that motivates a person. The lost person's heart is described as "desperately sick" (Jeremiah 17:9). He refuses to bend his will to that of Jesus Christ as his Lord. He seeks to stay in control of *his* environment and get his needs satisfied *his* way. The Christian, on the other hand, has undergone a *change* in his heart. He now loves God and longs to please Him; those are tens.

The physical and psychological appetites we have, such as our need for rest, food, sexual satisfaction, self-esteem, etc., were part of God's blueprint for us *before* Adam fell. Jesus had these identical human needs (Hebrews 4:15). These are *good* needs and are to be met according to God's will. Satan's game plan is to tempt us to go independent, rebel against God, and spend our lives seeking to satisfy our human needs. You and I no longer want this. Done that. Turned away from that (repented). Our desire is to seek Christ first and rest in His righteousness, while trusting *Him* to supply all our needs (Matthew 6:33; Philippians 4:19). Admittedly, although no Christian aces this, God planted the *desire* to do so in our new heart (Hebrews 8:10). That's why God has said He will give you the desire of your heart: Your new heart is godly (Hebrews 10:16).

A new creature in Christ no longer *desires*, no longer *craves* to live a sinful life. That's why Christians find such a life deeply unrewarding. Granted, it feels good to get your needs met, but when you sin to accomplish this, you feel rotten. The reason *for* this is that God has given us the heart transplant which He prophesied in Ezekiel 36:26-27 and fulfilled in us through our death and re-creation in Christ. This isn't bypass surgery, gang; He *removed* that old, lost, rebellious, desperately sick heart and replaced it with a heart of love for Him. We must consistently remind ourselves and one another of this fact instead of talking about how "desperately wicked" our heart is. That is the Old Testament description of the unregenerated heart in Jeremiah 17:9.

Back when they had one-room schools, the teacher would often assign a fifth-grader to sit next to a third-grader to help him with his "guzindas," as Jethro on the Beverly Hillbillies called it: two guzinda four two times, three guzinda six, etc. If we try to motivate the third-grader by assigning the fifth-grader to whack him when he makes a mistake, he'll likely become intimidated or rebel and drop out of school. Although Christian "fifth-graders" who attempt to motivate "third-graders" by whacking their knuckles with

126

the Law may mean well, this is not God's plan for yielding godly obedience. Christians resist snuggling up to a God that they believe is temperamental or angry. Hey, who will cuddle up to a lighted stick of dynamite? But, gang, God took out all of His righteous anger on Jesus! He's not mad at Christians!

God says, "The love of Christ controls us" (2 Corinthians 5:14). This explains why new creatures in Christ are not *externally* controlled by the Law, as was the case for Old Testament believers. This is not to say that you and I will never need correction by the Lord, a spouse, or friends. Neither do I believe it means that our fallible love for Christ empowers us to obedience, but rather that *His* infallible love *within* us does so—when, that is, we understand how to allow Him to live through us. The more we set our minds on how great His love is for us the stronger we'll become. But it doesn't all happen by Saturday night. We're on a pilgrimage, gang—a lifelong adventure with Christ.

God describes Christ as our *internal* control center in Romans 8:2: "For the law of the Spirit of life in Christ Jesus has set you free from the law of sin and of death." You can identify His law of love within you—it's *an inner urging, a longing, a strong sensing, a desire* to live in a manner that is pleasing to God. That's the Spirit of Christ in you, and it beats the daylights out of living under a hard taskmaster who continually badgers you with "you *ought* to, you *must*, you *should*, you *have* to," etc. Law has no *life* in it. It "ministers" condemnation (2 Corinthians 3:6,9).

Man's Attempt to Please God

The Old Testament Jewish leaders, seeking to be Law-abiding, taught that the road to becoming acceptable to God lay in keeping the Law. This view prevailed for centuries, and indeed continues to be embraced today by many who purport to carefully follow the Bible. They, however, are

127

failing to discern the Word of truth. Left to his own devices, man (with help from the Deceiver) comes up with some bizarre attempts at meriting God's acceptance. From the jungles of South America to the canyons of Wall Street, men do strange things seeking God's favor.

— During the 400-year period between the Old and New Testaments, God was relatively silent; He raised up no prophets, no spokesmen on His behalf. It's no wonder that people developed an outlandish interpretation of God's Law when you consider how the liberal Supreme Court has distorted the U.S. Constitution in just a few short years. This was the period in which the Pharisees sprang up. They developed an elaborate set of hoops that men must jump through to merit both earthly blessing and eternal life. The Pharisees had hundreds of dos and don'ts to be strictly observed. They felt they had the market cornered on pleasing God, and got their kicks by comparing their performance with that of the poor ol' guys on the back pew who couldn't get the hang of it.

✓ Finally, in God's wisdom, it was time for Jesus Christ to hang His crown and regal robes on heaven's hall tree (Galatians 4:4-5), shrink His majesty into a microscopic human package (Philippians 2:6-8), and be implanted by His Father's Spirit inside the womb of a teenage virgin named Mary (Luke 1:35-38). Amazing! God was donning a tiny earthsuit! (Praise God that Mary was pro-life.) No more prophets would speak for God. Jesus Christ, the Son, would finally *reveal* God to man: "God, after He spoke long ago to the fathers in the prophets ... in these last days has spoken to us *in* His son" (Hebrews 1:1-2). Notice that it does not say *through* His Son, but *in* His Son. I'll ring the bell again: Jesus Christ put a "face" on God for us. "God was *in* Christ, reconciling the world to Himself" (2 Corinthians 5:19). "He who has seen Me has *seen* the Father" (John 14:9). You've always wanted to know what God is *really* like? Check out Jesus! As C. S. Lovett says, Jesus was God in an earthsuit.

Jesus' purpose was to convict "speeders," call them to repentance and to faith in Him, fix their speeding tickets, change their interior, trash the old motor, and install a new one in them that's designed to run best by obeying the speed limit. They were thus equipped to begin a marvelous, warm, intimate love relationship with God. To understand how He accomplished this, it's important that we clearly understand two facts about the Law:

- Jesus' entire ministry occurred *under the Law*, not under grace. *The era of grace was ushered in at Pentecost after His death, resurrection, and ascension* (see Figure 7B). As such, we see only a foretaste of God's "grace plan" for man in the four Gospels—it is revealed in its entirety *after* Christ's ascension, primarily through Paul's teaching.

Jesus' Earthly Ministry Was Under the Law

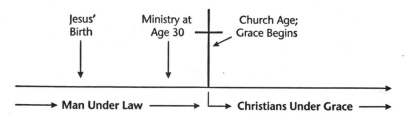

Figure 7B

- As we saw earlier, the Law is a minister of death and condemnation (2 Corinthians 3:6-9), designed to convict the unsaved that they are sinners and guilty before a holy God. This is God's whetting-the-appetite technique at work; a man must be convinced that he's hopelessly separated from God before he's "hungry" enough to want his problem fixed. The Law serves this purpose. It "pours salt in man's wounds."

Now let's see how Jesus used the Law to produce in sinners a "hunger" to repent, and to motivate them to claim Him as their personal Savior and Lord.

The Sermon on the Mount: Intensifying the Law

Perhaps the following illustration will clarify Jesus' motive as He began His ministry. He had just returned from His 40 days in the wilderness when He approached the masses who were striving to gain God's acceptance by adhering to the Law. He asked, "How're you guys doing in your quest for eternal life?"

> Not too well. We try to keep the Mosaic Law, but we just keep slipping off the chinning bar. About the time we get one phase working, the priests and their "in group" explain another one that we're flunking. To tell You the truth, it's looking pretty grim.

> Now, if you want to talk to some guys that really have their act together, you need to check out the Pharisees. They are so zealous for God that they discuss the Law all day. They don't even hold down day jobs!

So, Jesus strolls down the street to visit the Pharisees and says, "Hey there, how are you guys doing in your quest for God's acceptance?"

> Just great! We never slip off God's chinning bar. Of course, with one of our main attributes being humility we don't like to brag; but since You asked, the truth is, we're perfect. We can't deny reality.

> Now, Jesus, we don't mean to tell You how to run Your business; but after all, You being an uneducated carpenter from the wrong hometown and we being

130

God's favorites, knowing the Scriptures by heart. . . .
Don't waste Your time preaching to us. You need to
work on those folks across the tracks. *There's* Your
mission field! You talk about sinners! We thank God
that we're not like them. They don't have a prayer of
making heaven.

And Jesus said, "Sit down, boys—I think I feel a Sermon
on the Mount coming on." And He began to preach.

Jesus lays down some heavy Law (alongside some grace)
in that sermon. He tells them, "Not only are you guilty if you
commit murder, but you're hopelessly guilty if you are angry
with your brother." "Not only are you guilty if you commit
adultery, you're condemned if you've ever daydreamed
about it." And He was just warming to His subject!

After He intensifies commandments five and six, He goes
on to say "tear out" your wandering eye if you've got one,
and "cut off" your thieving hand (Matthew 5:29-30). Wow!
Do you see what He is doing? Talk about laying the Law on
people! Jesus makes things tougher than ever in this sermon.
He takes the Law beyond the realm of overt behavior and
moves it into the thought-life. He shows them that not only
are they speeders if they've driven 70 MPH; they are speeders
if they've ever seen Mr. Stone whiz by and *thought*, "Wow, I
wish I could do that." And, in closing, just before He strolls
down the hill, He says, "Oh, and by the way, be as perfect
as God is" (see Matthew 5:48). Try that one on for size,
gang! If that won't convince you that you need a miracle
from God—a Savior—to obtain eternal life, nothing will! Had
you been among the multitudes at the Sermon on the
Mount, your response would have been the same as theirs
most likely was; "Oh, no! We'll *never* make it to God now!
Please don't help us anymore, Jesus!"

Since they believed that God had men on a performance-
based acceptance, they concluded that Jesus had just delivered their death sentence. They were wrong on the first

count, but correct on the second. This is why Paul said, "The letter [Law] kills" (2 Corinthians 3:6). He clarified that by saying, "I would not have come to know sin except through the Law; for I would not have known about coveting if the Law had not said, 'You shall not covet.' ... For sin, taking opportunity through the commandment, deceived me, and through it killed me.... I was once alive *apart from* the Law; but when the commandment came, sin became alive, and I *died*" (Romans 7:7,11,9).

The Law convinced him that he was spiritually dead as a lost man. It convicted him of his need for God's mercy—of His need for a supernatural Savior. This is what happens to all of us who experience the purpose of the Law. Some of Jesus' listeners understood that they were doomed, hopeless insofar as their being able to solve their own dilemma. *By producing such hopelessness, Jesus had set them up to need a Savior.* But the attitude of the Pharisees? "Kill the bum! Who does this country yokel think He is, God Almighty?"

And, of course, they finally had their way with Him. In their blindness they killed their Savior, got rid of the body before the Sabbath, and doubtless repaired the veil covering the Holy of Holies so everything would be shipshape for worship the following day.

Law and the Rich Young Ruler

Tracking Jesus' ministry through the four Gospels, you'll see that He uses this same technique again and again in order to produce hopelessness in people insofar as their being able to perform well enough to merit eternal life. Jesus was using the "ministry of death and condemnation" to accomplish His *agape* purpose: to lead people to their Savior. The realization of a *need* to be changed must always precede a *desire* to be changed. Why would anyone want to fix something that he believes ain't broke?

Consider Jesus' encounter with the rich young ruler
(Luke 18:18ff). The man asks Jesus what he can do to inherit
eternal life. Jesus laid five of God's laws on him, to which he
replied, "Aced those." He passed! If he had simply walked
away, he would have had Jesus' affirmation, right? But Jesus,
knowing all things, knew that the ruler's second question
would be, "What else must I do?" He knew the man was
uncertain in his heart as to whether or not he was "doing"
enough to merit eternal life. Jesus was setting him up to realize his need for a Savior. So when the rich man asked,
"What else?" Jesus said, "Oh, just one more thing: Give away
all your money and come follow Me." Look at that. He told
him to birdie every hole in the Jerusalem Open! The rich
man now had a problem that he couldn't solve. He had
bitten the lure and was hooked deep. He couldn't throw
that hook! When he approached Jesus, he felt that his performance was well above average, yet wondered if it was
good enough. When he walked away, he *knew* he was a
doomed, helpless sinner who needed a Savior. Jesus had
accomplished His goal.

Skeptical? If you were witnessing to a wealthy person,
would you tell him that his first move toward eternal life
must be to give away all his money? No? Jesus did, so why
don't you follow His example? It's because you *know* that
you live under the grace umbrella of faith in Jesus Christ.
You realize through *revelation* that giving your money has
nothing whatever to do with obtaining eternal life. Jesus,
however, did not minister under grace, but ministered *under
the Law*, and what He said to the rich man was the perfect
response to set him up to need a Savior. First the Bible says,
"Sin, taking opportunity through [Law], deceived me, and
through it killed me" (Romans 7:11). Then it says, "The Law
has become our tutor *to lead us to Christ*, that we may be
justified *by faith*" (Galatians 3:24). Do you see that Jesus
combined these two truths to convict the rich young ruler of

his need for a Savior? Jesus knew that the ruler thought he was doing well—performing his way to heaven. So, first the man needed an intensified dose of Law to "kill" him—lead him to think that his chances for eternal life were hopeless. He got that when Jesus told him to give away all of his wealth. Then the next step in Jesus' plan was for this painful condition to act as "tutor to lead [the rich man] to Christ [salvation by grace, through faith]." And by the way, the verse following Galatians 3:24 says, "But now that faith has come, we are no longer under a tutor." This verse says that when we were convicted of our own sinful condition by measuring ourselves against the law and it led us to Christ, the law had served its purpose for us, and we're no longer under the law, gang (Romans 6:14). We don't need a tutor to lead us to salvation by faith anymore. Been there; done that.

— Although I used to surmise that the rich ruler went to hell because he loved money more than Jesus, understanding the function of the Law for the lost has led me to a new opinion. I hope to meet that rich man in heaven one day. It wouldn't surprise me to hear him testify that he sprinted down the aisle when the Holy Spirit kicked in and opened his eyes at Pentecost to realize that God didn't want money; God wanted *him*—wanted a warm, intimate relationship with him. My guess is that heaven will reveal that the rich man's period of reflection over his seemingly hopeless condition was the "tutor that led him to Christ."

The Greatest Mistake

Deuteronomy 21:21 says that a rebellious son is to be stoned to death. Having reared four sons, I've thought about trying to reinstate that one a time or two! This verse, among many others from the Mosaic Law laid down in the Old Testament, might be cited as "proof" that God has us on a performance-based acceptance. Not so. With Christ's death on the cross, God put all people, both the lost and the saved, on a *Jesus-based acceptance.*

Of course, Jesus' sacrificial death was according to God's plan. Even so, murdering God's Messiah was not the biggest mistake for those who were responsible for His crucifixion. No, their greatest error was refusing to be open-minded enough to examine Jesus' claims about Himself and failing to accept the *risen* Christ as their personal Savior and Lord.

Each person faces this same choice during his or her earthwalk. Where do you land on this very personal watershed issue, dear friend? Jesus threw Himself in front of a train for you. He let the wheels grind Him up because of His great love for you, that you might enjoy an eternal love relationship with your Creator, beginning right now. Have you repented of who you are by birth—Adam's offspring—and of how you've treated your Creator? Have you cast yourself upon Jesus Christ to claim His mercy and forgiveness, trusting Him to change you? Or are you merely "religious"? The latter is flesh, not truth, dear friend. Why not settle this issue right now before reading further? You'll never be sorry. Ask Jesus Christ to include you in the marvelous sacrifice He made for sinners.

Pray, "Jesus, I'm sorry for the way I've treated You. Forgive me. You've opened my eyes. I want to turn away from what I am. Come into me and change me. Forgive me and make me into a new creation." He will do it.

8 WHERE THE NEW COVENANT (TESTAMENT) BEGINS

I WANT TO GO ON RECORD as stating unequivocally that I believe the Bible is totally God-inspired and infallible. It is God's revelation to man and is absolutely true.

Here are some basics about the Bible that I embrace:

• The Bible was inspired by God's Holy Spirit.

• It was penned in Hebrew, Greek, and some Aramaic.

• Alexander the Great conquered the Middle East in 330 B.C. His philosophy was to impose *Koine* Greek upon those he conquered. Consequently, it was spoken throughout the Græco-Roman world when the New Testament was penned. Greek was later banned by Roman decree and eventually became a *dead* language. So, *Koine* Greek became "frozen" in the cultural time-zone spanning roughly 330 B.C. to A.D. 200. Thus, *Koine* Greek will *never become corrupted*. This phenomenon assures us that the Word of God will never change.

• The time gap between the originals and our oldest manuscripts of Plato's and Aristotle's writings is 1200 and 1400 years, respectively. We have seven such copies of Plato's and five of Aristotle's. The gap between the actual events and our oldest Greek manuscripts of the New Testament is only 150 to 300 years and we have some 25,000 copies! Go figure.

- Although the Word of God *never* changes, *language* changes. For example, when I was a teenager the word *cool* indicated temperature, whereas today's culture attaches multiple meanings to this word. We must always consider the *original* meaning of a word when interpreting the Bible.[1]

- This necessitates ongoing, new, *accurate* translations of the Bible into the multiplicity of earth's languages.

- Religious tradition says the New Covenant (Testament) begins with Matthew chapter 1, but *Jesus* seems to disagree (Luke 22:20). Knowing the truth on this critical issue will give you a wonderful tool for interpreting the Bible more accurately.

Remember that only the Holy Spirit can guide us into all truth. Our emotions can't. They can't even think! For many years when I read the Gospels, I would often be confused because I was attempting to filter all of Jesus' teaching through the "grace glasses" we enjoy as new creatures in Christ. My mind-set was that all of those teachings targeted *me*, and I found that Jesus frequently raised standards which were impossible for me to attain. For example, "Therefore you are to be perfect, as your heavenly Father is perfect" (Matthew 5:48). "Goodness, Lord, how can *anyone* except You accomplish that?" But praise God, He solved my problem by revealing to me that the words I was reading were spoken to man *before* God's grace plan was brought on-line in Acts chapter 2! These words were directed at *unregenerate people* who were *under* the Law. They could not have been born again because Jesus had not gone to the cross.

Please stay with me now and give me a chance to explain why I believe that the New Covenant (Testament) begins in Acts chapter 2 rather than Matthew chapter 1. This is a dynamite truth which I believe you will find to be a powerful tool in better understanding the Bible you love. It's going to answer a lot of questions that may have troubled you for years. Here we go. A minute ago I said I believe the Bible is God-inspired. But that is not necessarily true of certain things such as chapter divisions, verse divisions, the numbering system, the topical headings added by translators or editors, and also the words *The New Testament* on the clean, white page preceding Matthew 1:1. How can I be so presumptuous as to include those hallowed, precious words—*The New Testament?* Please let me explain. The Greek word *diatheko* translates to our words *covenant* or *testament*. This means that the terms *new covenant* and *new testament* are synonyms, *either of which* could be used in Matthew 26:28; Mark 14:24; Luke 22:20; 1 Corinthians 11:25; 2 Corinthians 3:6; Hebrews 8:8,13; 12:24—all passages of Scripture which speak of God's new "grace plan" for man through Christ. Elementary spiritual discernment reveals that the New Covenant *could not begin* until Jesus ascended and made the Holy Spirit available to take up residence in new creatures in Christ. I urge you to ask the Holy Spirit if this is correct rather than checking with your emotions—they can't even *think!* The New Covenant (New Testament) has to begin *following* the four Gospels, *not at their inception.*

Now, I realize this is a radical departure from theological tradition, but as you read, place your trust in the Holy Spirit and the Bible to test this teaching. This truth opened my eyes to an understanding of certain verses/passages in the Gospels that had puzzled me for years. Let's pull into this rest stop of "Crucifixion Week" on God's freeway, discuss the Last Supper, and examine Jesus' statement pinpointing the beginning of the New Covenant (Testament).

Where the "Rest" Begins

Jesus taught His disciples many truths during their last supper together, including the watershed between God's old covenant and new covenant, *which was about to be put in*

139

place through Jesus' crucifixion, resurrection, and ascension.
He said, "This cup which is poured out for you is *the new covenant [diatheke] in My blood*" (Luke 22:20). Jesus is identifying the point where the New Covenant, or *New Testament*, would become available to man. Up until the glorious event of the atonement, the radical change which occurred through the advent of the New Testament was not anticipated by any of these folks because its mystery had yet to be fully revealed to them by the Holy Spirit. All spiritual truth comes by revelation, not by human intelligence: "No one knows the thoughts of God except the Spirit of God" (1 Corinthians 2:11, text rearranged for clarification).

Jesus' statement indicates that the New Covenant (Testament) *begins* at the death, burial, resurrection, and ascension of Jesus Christ and the coming of the Holy Spirit. Let me rephrase this to emphasize the powerful truth it contains. Jesus' statement means that *the New Testament does not begin with Matthew chapter 1*, but with His death, burial, resurrection, and ascension, along with the coming of the Holy Spirit—*Acts chapter 2!* This not only makes spiritual sense, but logical sense in that Jesus' entire ministry was carried out *under* the Law. *Matthew 1:1 falls 33 years short of the beginning of the New Covenant in His blood.* Although it's obvious that the New Testament couldn't have had a beginning unless Jesus had been born, there was no Covenant (Testament) resulting from Jesus' birth at Bethlehem!

Jesus' goal was to use the Law to reveal man's shortcomings and his need for a Savior (God's grace). We *must* differentiate between Jesus' Law teachings and His grace teachings in order to avoid theological quicksand. Many, *though certainly not all*, Scriptures in the four Gospels become perfect fits only when viewed as the Law teaching they are. Law reigned during Jesus' entire earthly ministry (Galatians 4:4-5), but grace now reigns from His *heavenly* ministry. The "crossover" occurred at His death on the cross,

His burial, resurrection, ascension, and the coming of the Holy Spirit (see Figure 8A).

Where the New Covenant (Testament) Begins

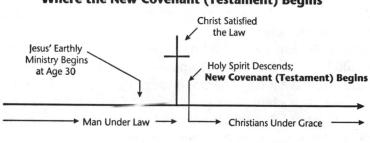

Figure 8A

By way of comparison, the Abrahamic Covenant didn't begin when Abraham was a baby, nor were the tablets of the Law handed down to Moses as he lay in his basket in the Nile River. They would have sunk his little ship, just like they'll sink the ship of any adult who seeks to find life through striving to keep the Law. The Abrahamic Covenant began through *adult* Abraham. The Law was handed down through *adult* Moses. Similarly, the New Covenant (Testament) did not begin with *Baby* Jesus in a manger in Bethlehem— tender and special as that blessed event is to us. The New Testament began 33 years later with the events surrounding *adult* Jesus' crucifixion, burial, resurrection, ascension, and the coming of the Holy Spirit.

"But, Bill, Jesus said, 'The Law and the Prophets were proclaimed until John; since then the gospel of the kingdom of God is preached.' " Yes, Jesus announced His *arrival*— that the "kingdom of God is *at hand*"—but, gang, it was impossible to get into the kingdom of God *via regeneration* during Jesus' *earthly* ministry. God's new grace plan via faith in Christ did not become available until Pentecost, following Jesus' ascension. The gospel Jesus preached was *yet to be*. Those folks had to look *forward* in faith that God would

141

grant them eternal life, whereas, we look *backward* by faith in Christ that He already has granted eternal life.

— Solid assurance of salvation was a hidden mystery at that time which was all according to God's plan. We are so blessed that we live today and not in Jesus' day. Don't ever entertain the notion that following Jesus around the Holy Land 2000 years ago would have been more exciting. We would have been Delbert Dumb—just like His followers were. We have it far better than they. The masses were puzzled about much of what Jesus taught. Jesus said, "I speak to them in parables; because while seeing they do not see, and while hearing they do not hear, nor do they understand" (Matthew 13:13). Gang, God was not being unfair here. He was using the techniques of piquing their curiosity while laying on the conviction in order to prepare them for the consummation of the gospel at Pentecost.

The Law of God Is Good, Not Evil

"[God's] Law is holy, and the commandment is holy and righteous and good" (Romans 7:12). Even though man can never be saved through the Law, we must be careful to not fall into Satan's trap of considering the Law of God to be the bad guy, our problem. Scripture makes this clear: "Is the Law sin? May it never be! On the contrary, I would not have come to know sin except through the Law" (Romans 7:7). It's the same for us. God's Law nailed our sorry hides to the wall. It convicted us that we were sinners headed for hell and motivated us to come to Christ. We might say that the Law is somewhat like the sidewalk leading to salvation's door. It reveals the holy character of God and how woefully short we fall of His standard for acceptance. After realizing this, understanding the purpose of Jesus' sacrifice, and claiming Him for our salvation, "do we then nullify the Law through [our] faith? May it never be! On the contrary, we *establish* the Law" (Romans 3:31). The Law served a great and glorious purpose for us. The Law is what "crowded" us toward coming to Christ for salvation (Galatians 3:24).

The Watershed in God's Word

God's Word contains a confluence of law and grace in each of the two testaments. These respective doctrines are often best identified as they are juxtaposed, and *they must be discerned correctly if the reader is to optimally understand the Bible.* When Christians read portions of the Bible which appear in the section labeled "The New Testament," their perceptual mind-set is that they are reading grace teaching intended for Christians. But just as the solution to the "four-dot" illustration in the introduction cannot be understood by a seeker with a "box-solution" mind-set, truth cannot be understood by filtering the four Gospels through the mind-set that *all* of Jesus' teaching is intended for Christians. *Much of it is Law.*

For example, He said, "If you forgive others for their transgressions, your heavenly Father will also forgive you. But if you do not forgive others, then your Father will not forgive your transgressions" (Matthew 6:14-15). These verses are easily misconstrued if we fail to remember where the New Covenant (Testament) begins. This is a Law teaching which is *not* directed to Christians. It can't be, gang, because the Bible says *after the cross,* "And when you were dead in your transgressions and the uncircumcision of your flesh, He made you alive together with Him, *having forgiven us all our transgressions,* having canceled out the certificate of debt consisting of decrees against us and which was hostile to us; and *He has taken it out of the way,* having nailed it to the cross" (Colossians 2:13-14).

However, since Jesus' words are recorded in the section labeled "The New Testament," I would venture to say that most Christians do not discern that this teaching is intended for those yet unsaved to convict them. Apparently, many fail

143

to see that this actually teaches that we must *earn* God's forgiveness. Of course, Jesus did not teach a falsehood! He was merely using this difficult-to-attain, lofty standard to *intensify* the listeners' need for a Savior. He taught truth according to the revelation given to man in that day. My friend Frank Friedmann says, "Jesus taught perfect truth under an Old Testament economy. He taught perfect truth for a new covenant (testament) which was going to be established." Jesus is teaching that we must forgive the person who wronged us before God will say, "Now I'll forgive you." If you'll trust the Holy Spirit, I believe He'll show you that I'm simply passing along His truth. Matthew 6:14-15 would seem to teach performance-based, merited forgiveness and, to make it more irrefutable, the words came from the lips of our Savior Himself! But we Christians know that no man can merit God's forgiveness via performance. Forgiveness comes by grace through faith in Christ's work *alone*. How can this seeming contradiction be explained?

✓ Let's say it's approaching midnight and you're driving alone on a dark, lonely road. Your car's gas gauge is approaching empty; you've passed two darkened gas stations. Your interest in discovering *any* lighted sign along the roadside signaling an open station increases dramatically. Educators call this the "discovery" method of learning. You and I experience an increased interest in seeking closure to a problem in direct proportion to the intensity of our need.

Jesus was a great teacher who often used this method in His ministry. Step 1: Identify the listener's need; Step 2: Create a situation in which the listener will identify his need; Step 3: Cause the need to intensify in the listener by describing his dilemma; Step 4: Give clues (guidance) to the listener for "discovering" the yet *future* Solution to his need (Christ), usually allowing ample time for the listener to wrestle with the "improbability" of there being such a solution, so as to further intensify both his need and his search.

— By teaching Law, Jesus dropped His listeners into a deep cistern with slick walls. As they thrashed about, He would deliver yet another Law pronouncement which, in effect, added more slime to the walls. Hold it now. I'm not portraying our beloved Savior as a sadist who delights in causing misery! He loves us enough to die for us. Gang, *need-deprivation always produces hunger! Indeed, there is no other way to produce hunger!* Jesus' *agape* goal was to produce a hunger for eternal life through His teaching. As the listeners heard more and more unreachable standards (Law) being taught, their burden of hopelessness, condemnation, and guilt got heavier, yet they kept returning to hear more because they sensed that He held the key to eternal life (John 6:68).

Our eyes have been opened via regeneration, which gives us the ability to understand Jesus' altruistic motive. Gang, God changed a lot of the rules after the cross. Let me remind you of the episode with the Canaanite woman who asked Jesus to heal her demon-possessed daughter in Matthew 15. "He ... said, 'It is not good to take the children's bread and throw it to the dogs' " (Matthew 15:26). Great day! Would any Christian believe we should teach this simply because Jesus said it? Absurd! Then why did Jesus say this? When you're God, you get to make the rules, and the rules *at that time* said, "Salvation for Jews Only—Everyone Else to the Back of the Bus." But praise God, He changed the rules! Jesus' finished work on the cross enabled God to fling open the gates of heaven and shout, "Whosoever will may come (via faith in Jesus)!"

God Wishes Christians Understood the Role of the Law

When reading a teaching such as Matthew 6:14-15 (on forgiveness, cited earlier) we must remember that the material was taught *before the cross.* Therefore, it may include both grace and Law. Next we must discern if the passage is a Law teaching or a grace teaching. Upon discovering that it teaches *merited reward*, not undeserved favor (grace), we discern it to be Law. Then we must ask the Holy Spirit to show us why Jesus taught it. I believe that perhaps He knew there were some individuals in His audience who could not identify with His condemnation of such sins as adultery, or hatred, etc., but who simply could not forgive: "Forgive that back-stabber? No way!" Jesus' Law-teaching on forgiveness swept him to the edge of a snake-filled swamp and commanded, "If you swim across at midnight, God will forgive you." He withheld the fact that God would eventually "drain the swamp" by providing a Savior because *it was not yet time.* He skewered everybody on that mountain with conviction, guilt, condemnation, and the certainty of everlasting death. And a good portion of those same slings and arrows of Law continue to accomplish their intended purpose with lost people today. This is good; this is one of Law's purposes (Romans 7:7-9).

First Timothy 1:8 says, "We know that the Law is good, if one uses it lawfully." But the implication is that the Law can be used *unlawfully*, and if so, it is *not* a good practice. We must realize that the next verse explains, "Law is not made for a righteous [person]," coupled with the fact that all new creations in Christ are *righteous people* (1 Corinthians 5:21). Gang, Law arrows were never intended to be fired at new creatures in Christ, "for you are not under law, but under grace" (Romans 6:14). Let me hasten to avoid a misunderstanding here. The verse following says, "Shall we sin because we are not under law but under grace? May it never be!" The reason God is able to trust new creations in Christ is because He has lavished such incredible grace and love upon us, not the least of which is our open-heart surgery. He "put [His] laws upon [our] heart, and ... mind" (Hebrews 10:16). If you're born again, you now *desire* to obey Christ.

You *yearn* to obey, to please Jesus. Of course, you don't always accomplish this, but you *wish* that you could. New creatures don't have to be cajoled into obeying Jesus; we long to do so. The "law of love in Christ" has elevated us to soar with Jesus like the law of aerodynamics enables a plane to be free from the law of gravity.

I am not teaching that we Christians should disregard such Holy Spirit-inspired teaching as the Sermon on the Mount. I'm teaching that we must trust the Holy Spirit to differentiate between Law and grace, especially in the Gospels. Some portions of the Sermon on the Mount are right on target for the saved: "You are the light of the world. A city set on a hill cannot be hidden" (Matthew 5:14); "but you, when you pray, go into your inner room, and when you have shut your door, pray to your Father who is in se-cret, and your Father who sees in secret will repay you." (Matthew 6:6). But those who do not differentiate between Law and grace in the gospels often "push *Christians* into that snaky swamp at midnight" by quoting verses to them on forgiveness, like Matthew 6:14-15. Many well-meaning Chris-tians attempt to mix Law and grace into a stew and force-feed it to Christians as a deterrent against sinning. Good motive, bad method—because it's unbiblical. It piles false guilt upon false guilt, false condemnation upon false con-demnation, and produces defeated, intimidated Christians or dropouts. Folks, the Bible teaches that we Christians are *already* forgiven. We do not have to forgive someone to merit our own forgiveness. That is a Law stipulation, and we are free from the Law (Romans 6:14).

The Model Prayer

⌐ Another example which calls for a clear understanding of where the New Covenant (Testament) begins is Jesus' model prayer. Many people are unaware that the Lord's prayer reminds God that He should forgive us because we

deserve it: "And forgive us our debts, as we also have forgiven our debtors" (Matthew 6:12). The petitioner is asking
for *merited* forgiveness. If you disagree with that, look at
verses 14-15: "For if you forgive men for their transgressions,
your heavenly Father will also forgive you. But if you do not
forgive men, then your Father will not forgive your transgressions." It seems pretty clear that Jesus was teaching *conditional* forgiveness—we must forgive others before God
will forgive us. But how can this be? We know that we're
forgiven by grace alone through faith in Christ. Has God
solved this dilemma in your theology?" Here's the answer:
There were *no new creatures in Christ* when Jesus taught
believers to pray the model prayer. Some of this prayer is
Law teaching, which was intended to depress sinner-men as
a part of "tutoring" them to Christ (see Galatians 3:24-25).
This was the case for the entire population of the world
when the Master modeled it to the disciples. (Remember, the
disciples as well could not be regenerated until Pentecost.)

As you will often find in Jesus' teachings, the model
prayer contains both Law and grace. "*Our* Father . . ." This is
fantastic grace. What did we do to rate such a lofty status
with the living God? Nothing! We simply believed on the
Lord Jesus as our personal Savior and Lord, and God instantly
became our Father. "Forgive us our trespasses, even as we
forgive others their trespasses against us" (from Matthew
6:12). As stated previously, this is Law. By making this statement, we're saying, in effect, that due to the fact that *we*
have done the noble thing, that *we* have taken the high
road, we're asking Him to do likewise—forgive us. Folks, I
choke on that; I simply cannot pray that statement to God.

Of course I believe it's God's will that we forgive those
who sin against us, but we're motivated to do so by grace,
not by Law. How can I be sure? Look at what God's Word
says in the actual New Covenant (Testament): "And be kind
to one another, tender-hearted, *forgiving* each other, *just as*

148

God in Christ also has forgiven you" (Ephesians 4:32). Here
we see that we Christians are *already forgiven* of all our
sins, and that knowing this is to motivate us to forgive any
who have sinned against us. We're motivated by grace, not
by Law. *This is the exact opposite of Jesus' teaching in the
Sermon on the Mount.* Is that a fresh breeze or what? Whew!

Location, Location, Location

The solution to the Law/grace dilemma in the Gospels is
not, "Oh well, Paul had his ideas and Jesus has His. I'm
going to side with what Jesus said. It can't be wrong if Jesus
said it." No! No! No! Jesus wasn't wrong. It's like they say
about assessing the value of real estate: location, location,
location. On which side of the cross is the teaching located?
Jesus was teaching unregenerate people, which included His
disciples. And Ephesians 4:32 is not Paul's viewpoint, it's the
Holy Spirit's. The same Holy Spirit inspired both Matthew
and Ephesians, but each presents a different side of the
Law/grace watershed. Dear people, we must differentiate
between Law and grace in order to realize our awesome
liberty and forgiveness in Christ. And absolutely critical to
this realization is understanding where the New Covenant
(Testament) begins. Without understanding this, we will
propagate the error of a false view of God—an angry God
withholding His forgiveness until such time as we merit it by
first forgiving others *via our own power*, to say nothing of
the many other blind alleys that will be encountered if we
attempt to mix Law and grace!

Not by Rules, But by Our New Heart

Why do Christians *not* need a set of rules to follow? He
installed a Holy Guidance System in our new spirit: the Holy
Spirit of Christ.

"For the law of the *Spirit of life in Christ* has set you free from the law of sin and of death" (Romans 8:2). God contrasts embracing Christ as life versus the law. Again, "for indeed what *had* glory [law], in this case has no glory on account of the glory that *surpasses it*" (2 Corinthians 3:10). It's like finding the light switch with a match. The "glory" of the room's light overwhelms the flame.

It's like a sparrow and a convict in the prison exercise yard. The wall is not intended for the bird. It is *created* free from the law of gravity, whereas the convict is bound by this law. Similarly, a superior law, the law of the Spirit of life in Christ Jesus, has negated the necessity of our being constantly reminded of our failure to measure up. *Christ* measured up for us. *Christ* is our "Measurer Upper," by faith! We *have* measured up in Him. What incredible grace is the New Testament of God!

The Scriptures say that God has written His laws on our hearts and minds (Hebrews 10:16). Let's clarify that. Romans 13:8-10 says that agape love summarizes the whole law. Jesus was asked what the greatest commandment was. He gave two imperatives that summed up *the whole law* of God: "...'You shall love the Lord your God with all your heart, and with all your soul, and with all your mind.' This is the great and foremost commandment. The second is like it, 'You shall love your neighbor as yourself.' *On these two commandments depend the whole Law and the Prophets*" (Matthew 22:37-40). That summary of the whole law is "written on your heart and mind." Let me prove it. You love God, and that's a ten! You don't always act like it, but you love Him at level ten. Now for the second part: You love people. You may not like them, but you love them—even the world's current despot. You wish he could get saved. You hate what he does, but you wish he could know Jesus, and that's a ten! You realize that under other circumstances you could have been just as weird as that guy is. Right? The fact that you have these two loves proves that you've had the heart transplant spoken of in Ezekiel 36:26-27.[2]

The Beatitudes Revisited

The Bible indicates that Christians have *already attained* many of the goals that Jesus' Law teachings either teach or imply that we must strive for. You be the judge as to whether these verses taken from the Gospels on the Law side of the watershed are intended for saints.

Matthew 5:6—"Blessed are those who hunger and thirst for righteousness, for they shall be satisfied."

Remember that *righteousness* means to be *all right* with God—accepted by Him. Although some of these folks may have "thirsted for righteousness," it seemed unattainable because identifying such hunger and thirst via introspection would be a subjective judgment; you could never be certain that your hunger or thirst was intense enough to qualify. And in the case of those who had no such thirst, how could they ever generate it? Jesus presented a lose-lose situation.

Now we'll "cross" over into grace. "He made Him who knew no sin to be sin on our behalf, that we might become *the righteousness of God* in Him" (2 Corinthians 5:21). New creations are *already righteous* in Christ! We have already been accepted by God. Our righteousness is not man-generated, but Christ-generated.

Matthew 5:7—"Blessed are the merciful, for they shall receive mercy."

That's a promised mercy based upon *man's* performance, and the payoff is once again a subjective call. When am I being merciful enough to merit God's mercy? God's mercy was but a shaky, future hope for those who try hard enough. There was no way of attaining any security. It was based upon some hazy, future measuring stick wielded by a God who was viewed as having unattainable standards.

Let's put on our grace glasses: "Blessed be the God and Father of our Lord Jesus Christ, who according to His *great mercy* has *caused* us to be born again to a *living* hope through the resurrection of Jesus Christ" (1 Peter 1:3). We are already recipients of God's mercy! No man can merit this. And it's not a future hope, but a present, "living" hope—we *have* this hope because we have Christ.

Before we consider the next verses let me remind you of our definition of "heart" from the last chapter: *the strongest dynamic that motivates a person.* The unregenerate heart is set on living *his* life *his* way. Hebrews 10:15-16 describes our heart: "The Holy Spirit also bears witness to *us*. . . . I will put my laws upon their heart. . . ." Because of this, we *yearn* to obey God. We *wish* we could perform perfectly. This is *proof* of our new heart.

Matthew 5:8—"Blessed are the pure in heart, for they shall see God."

Ouch, how would that one have landed? This was seen as performance-based, thought-life-based purity, which was absolutely impossible to attain. Who in Jesus' audience would dare to believe he qualified to see God by this standard? I believe most Christians believe we still have the heart spoken of in Jeremiah 17:9: "The heart is more deceitful than all else and is desperately sick . . ." But, folks, that verse describes the unregenerate man before the cross.

And as for "seeing God," look at 1 John 3:2: "We know that, when He appears, we shall be like Him, because *we shall see Him* just as He is." We're going to see God forever and ever![3]

Matthew 5:9—"Blessed are the peacemakers, for they shall be called sons of God."

If this is how to become God's child, all of us have flunked.

Let's see what God has to say to those who are under grace: "For you are all *sons of God* through faith in Christ

Jesus" (Galatians 3:26). That's the *only* way we can become God's child. Speaking of attaining peace, "For [Christ] Himself is our peace...." (Ephesians 2:14). We have the privilege of speaking to others about peace with God. We are "peacemakers."

Matthew 5:20—"For I say to you, that unless your righteousness surpasses that of the scribes and Pharisees, you shall not enter the kingdom of heaven."

These guys, mistakenly viewed as God's favorites, wouldn't even carry a needle in their lapel on the Sabbath. Jesus said that even *that* didn't impress God. Jesus offered His listeners little or no hope.

But our righteousness far exceeds that: "But by *His doing* you are in Christ Jesus, who *became to us ... righteousness* and sanctification, and redemption" (1 Corinthians 1:30). Our righteousness is not a phenomenon, but a Person.

Matthew 5:22—"But I say to you that everyone who is angry with his brother shall be guilty ..."

Not that we Christians are looking for a loophole to get angry with the brethren, but look at Romans 8:1: "There is therefore *now* no condemnation for those who are in Christ Jesus."

— That's *now*, gang; there's zero condemnation *now, at this very moment, as well as in the future,* for those who are in Christ! How different this is from the insecurity produced by Matthew 5:22! The Holy Spirit will condemn what you *do* when you sin, but He will never, never condemn *you.* The Holy Spirit will "say," *That was wrong.* The Deceiver will communicate: *I'm a sorry Christian; I'm no good,* etc.

Matthew 5:25-26—"Make friends quickly with your opponent at law while you are with him on the way, in order that your opponent may not deliver you to the judge, and the judge to the officer, and you be thrown into prison. Truly I say to you, you shall not come out of there, until you have paid up the last cent."

Jesus is not teaching His listeners how to avoid litigation. The "opponent at law" is God's Law; "while you are with him on the way" refers to your earthwalk; the judge is God; the prison is hell; and the inescapable penalty is eternal damnation. This is laden with threat and Law. One slipup, and you're outta here.

Do you see what Jesus' goal is in all of these verses we're examining? He is piling on the condemnation and insecurity in order to crumble the foundation of people's mistaken notion that they can attain eternal life via good performance. By creating this feeling of hopelessness, He is increasing the likelihood of their repenting and rushing to Him as their Savior and Lord at Pentecost (Acts 2).

Gang, those verses don't apply to Christians. Look at Ephesians 2:12-13,19: "You were at that time separate from Christ . . . having no hope and without God in the world. But now in Christ Jesus you who formerly were far off have been brought near by the blood of Christ. . . . So then you are no longer strangers and aliens, but you are . . . of God's household." We're actually members of His household (Galatians 4:6)! We are born of His Spirit's gene pool (2 Peter 1:4).

Matthew 5:30—"And if your right hand makes you stumble, cut it off . . . for it is better for you that one of the parts of your body perish, than for . . . [you] to go into hell."

But look at a *grace* verse about Someone else's hand in John 10:28: "I *give* eternal life to them, and they shall *never* perish, and *no one shall snatch them out of My hand.* Here we see grace teaching from the *Gospels* intended to comfort new creations in Christ. This was presented to Jesus' listeners as a future hope for all who would come to Him. The key here is to trust the Holy Spirit for discernment (and we get to keep our hands).

Matthew 5:48—"Therefore you are to be perfect, as your heavenly Father is perfect." (The Greek word translated *perfect* means "complete" or "finished.")

How's that for an unreachable standard condemning all to utter hopelessness? That's Law, troops. Those words are a minister of condemnation (2 Corinthians 3:9). But look at this! "And we proclaim Him, admonishing every man and teaching every man with all wisdom, that we may present every man *complete in Christ"* (Colossians 1:28).

The Greek word translated *complete* here is the same word Jesus used to describe His Father, which the translators have rendered *perfect.* What astounding grace! We're *not perfect performers,* but we're *perfectly made* in Christ. This is an identity issue, gang, not a performance issue.

Acts chapter 2 is the knife-edge which separates those under Law from those under grace. We are free from the condemnation of the Law. But someone asks, "What's to keep Christians from going wild?" "The *love of Christ* controls us" (2 Corinthians 5:14). Sure, we love Christ, but the higher truth in this verse is that it is *Christ's* love—*Christ, the Lover— within us* which is our control center. Born-again people are righteous, and righteous folks long to *live* righteously. This explains why, as we saw earlier, God said, "Law is *not made* for a *righteous* man, but for those who are lawless and rebellious, for the ungodly . . ." (1 Timothy 1:9). We're now righteous ("all right" with God) through Christ (1 Corinthians 1:30; Philippians 3:9). Got it?

As I was teaching this material to our staff, Joyce Ray brought out that these teachings in Matthew all center on *man's* responsibility to measure up, whereas the post-cross verses focus on *Christ* and the *Father*—we have already measured up in Christ, by grace, through faith.

A Preview

I was visiting with a friend some time ago and he mentioned that, God willing, we will see the year 2000 roll around. Two thousand years! What a milestone!

There was once a celebration of such a watershed event on God's time line, only it focused on a *spiritual* bench mark, not a chronological milestone. This wasn't a mere once-in-a-lifetime event; it was a once-in-eternity event: "Now where there is forgiveness of these things, there is no longer any offering for sin" (Hebrews 10:18). No more sin offerings! Jesus was the perfect offering for sin. Man, there was dancing in the street when spiritually hungry, hurting people who had labored under the Law all of their lives realized what God had done through Jesus Christ on the day of *His* atonement! They had felt under condemnation for so long. Now God, through His Son, had made a new covenant with man. He revealed the reality that had been prophesied. They came to understand that "Christ is the *end of the Law for righteousness* to everyone who believes" (Romans 10:4). Romans 10:4—now there's the ultimate "10-4" that radio buffs quote to signal that their "work" is finished. Christ *finished* His work! It's not half-finished or almost finished, it's finished. "Righteousness to everyone who believes." W. E. Vine defines *righteousness* in this instance as "the gracious gift of God to men whereby all who believe on the Lord Jesus Christ are brought into right relationship with God."[4] That means we're OK with God.

God explains the process by which the watershed transition from Law to grace took place in Galatians 3. "Before faith came, we were kept in custody *under the law*, being shut up to the faith which was later to be revealed" (verse 23). This describes the condition of the Old Testament believers and today's sinner-man. "Therefore the Law has become our tutor to lead us to Christ, that we may be justified by faith" (verse 24). The Holy Spirit uses the valid guilt that the Law produces to make the unregenerate man's heart sensitive to his need to be rescued. This produces an openness to the gospel. Law has "tutored" him to place his faith in Christ. "But now that faith has come, we are no longer under a tutor" (verse 25). Once this step of faith in Christ is taken, a person becomes born again and no longer needs the Law to "tutor" him to Christ. "For you are all sons of God through faith in Christ Jesus" (verse 26).

However, we must understand that there are *two dimensions* to God's righteousness equation in the New Covenant:

- The first is the *state* or *condition* of righteousness. This righteous *identity* is acquired by our new spiritual *birth*. Christians are righteous via our birth in Christ.

- The second involves righteous *performance.* Although we are now righteous by birth, *acting* righteously is a moment-by-moment choice. Only when we let Christ express His life through us, by faith, do we produce righteous (acceptable) behavior. Although a Christian can produce *righteous-looking* behavior independently, such action is rejected by God as unrighteous (see Habukkuk 1:11; Jeremiah 17:5). Folks, no man works for God. He doesn't need our help. It is our privilege to offer ourselves to God as a living and holy sacrifice (Romans 12:1), allowing Christ to do the will and work of God through us, by faith (Romans 15:18). This alone produces righteous (approved) work.

These two dimensions of righteousness (identity and performance) must always be considered as separate entities. The first is by faith alone; the latter is by faith combined with your obedience (works). Blurring the line which delineates these will lead you into theological quicksand.

Receiving the Holy Spirit

I believe we should look at one more example of failing to discern Law and grace in the Gospels before we move back onto God's freeway, because Christians can easily get confused on this issue.

Jesus said in Luke 11:13, "If you then, being evil, know how to give good gifts to your children, how much more shall your heavenly Father give the Holy Spirit to those who ask Him?" On the basis of what we've discussed about the dividing line between the Old and New Testaments, who is Jesus addressing? Unregenerated people! It is a grievous error to present this teaching to Christians. By being armed with the knowledge that the New Testament does not begin until Acts chapter 2, Christians can discern:

- that Jesus was addressing unregenerate (evil) sinners, not regenerated (holy) saints.

- that *none* of Jesus' listeners could obtain the Holy Spirit because the Holy Spirit would not be available to people until Pentecost in Acts chapter 2.

- that God says, "If anyone does not have the Spirit of Christ (Holy Spirit), he does not belong to Him" (Romans 8:9). You can't get reborn without getting the Holy Spirit.

Please understand that I am not discarding the precious words of the Gospels from the Bible any more than I am discarding the Psalms, the Pentateuch, the Prophets, etc. There is much, much grace teaching in all of these!

Attempting to explain the liberating truth of where the New Testament begins to your pastor as you shake his hand after the Sunday service would be most inappropriate. First, *earn the right* to recommend this book by your gentleness and love toward him and his family. He must see Christ through you to become open to your counsel. The same applies to your Christian friends. Be wise. I pray this truth will bring you into a deeper relationship of intimacy and obedience to our Lord.

9 THAT THE ASCENDED CHRIST DISCIPLED ONLY ONE APOSTLE

HERE'S A BRAINTEASER. Name a Bible character who occupied one of the most important positions in the New Testament. He was a member of the most elite group of powerful insiders in the history of the world, yet his name is mentioned in only one episode in the Bible. He never did anything of renown, never spoke a line; we know nothing about him or his family tree. Although he was doubtless highly respected as a man of great integrity, I daresay you don't know anyone who was named after him as with Peter, Paul, and Mary. His big moment in the sun occurred when he won the Jerusalem lottery, but then he quickly faded to black. Can you name this man? It's Matthias, the apostle who was chosen by *lot* to replace Judas.

Who chose Jesus' 12 disciples? Jesus. Who taught and discipled them? Jesus. When Judas turned out to be a bad apple, it was no shock to Jesus. He knew that Judas had a terminal blemish and chose him specifically because of it (John 13:18). It's not that God *made* Judas betray Jesus; He simply knew from the helicopter view that he would ultimately do so. He even knew what Judas would eat for breakfast that day. He's omniscient.

I wonder if Peter didn't jump the gun in Acts 1:15,22-26 by suggesting that the group choose Judas' replacement. It would be in character for him before he was regenerated in Acts 2. You'll recall episodes such as his pledge to protect Jesus from harm (Matthew 16:21-23) and his boasting that he would die with Jesus (Mark 14:29-31). He was impulsive; he had to *do something* in situations that called for action. I can really identify with that dear brother, whose feet took turns occupying his mouth. Had I been present, I probably would have seconded his motion. "Let's get this disciple-selection show on the road. We've sat around here long enough. We're going to need all the help we can get." But in retrospect, I suspect Peter's suggestion was man's plan, not God's. Would the risen Christ entrust this important matter to others? I don't think so. Since Jesus chose and discipled the 12, I believe He would not have delegated the selection of Judas's replacement to a committee of men who were yet to be regenerated and filled with the Holy Spirit. I believe *Jesus'* choice occurred in Acts chapter 9 when He chose Paul. Look what He said: "[Paul] is a *chosen* instrument of Mine; to bear My name before the Gentiles and kings and the sons of Israel" (Acts 9:15). That's quite an endorsement.

Whereas Matthias is never mentioned again, the Bible states 17 times that Paul was an apostle. It also states that he was chosen by God, not by a committee (1 Corinthians 1:1; 2 Corinthians 1:1; Galatians 1:1), and also that he "[considered himself] not in the least inferior to the most eminent apostles" (2 Corinthians 11:5). However, in terms of his worthiness to be chosen, he believed he was the least qualified because he had persecuted the early church (1 Corinthians 15:9). I believe the selection of Matthias was the well-meaning disciples' effort to "help God out." Through no fault of his own, Matthias's selection was similar to Ishmael's birth, when Abraham and Sarah grew weary of waiting on God to fulfill His promise of a son and sought to "help God." Sarah talked Abraham into impregnating Hagar, and when she delivered Ishmael, they all celebrated the arrival of "God's gift." Yeah, right. I don't intend to demean Matthias, but I believe his selection was of man. God never honors the works of the flesh (Isaiah 64:6). I believe this is why Matthias was never heard from after he won the Jerusalem lottery.

Paul Goes to Seminary

The natural thing for Paul to have done after he got hit with Jesus' heavenly stun gun on the road to Damascus would have been to crawl back to Jerusalem to ask the disciples to forgive him, beg to eat crow-supper at their feet, and be taught everything they knew about Jesus. But in Galatians 1:12, Paul tells us: "I neither received [the gospel I teach] from man, nor was I *taught* it, but I received it through *a revelation of* Jesus Christ." Paul says that no human communicated the gospel to him. In fact, he says, "I wasn't *taught* it [period]; I *received* it as a *revelation of Jesus*." Notice, he doesn't say "a revelation *from* Jesus," but *of* Jesus. Apparently, Jesus didn't even verbalize *some* information to Paul, but downloaded understanding into Paul's spirit; *it came in a revelation of Christ Himself, not necessarily in what Christ taught*. Paul had no human mentor; coming to *know* Jesus Christ gave this dear brother everything he needed for life and ministry.

Paul says,

> I did not immediately consult with [man], nor did I go up to Jerusalem to those who were apostles before me; but I went away to Arabia. . . . Three years later I went up to Jerusalem to become acquainted with Cephas [Peter for] fifteen days. But I did not see any other of the apostles except James (Galatians 1:16-19).

What a Difference a Veil Makes

The Bible, speaking of the unregenerated, says, "Their minds were hardened; for . . . the veil remains unlifted, because it is removed *in Christ*. . . . Whenever a man turns to the Lord, the veil is taken away" (2 Corinthians 3:14,16).

Only one disciple had the veil removed from his "hardened mind" *before* he was tutored by Christ. Only one man had been regenerated prior to receiving the revelation that Christ gave him. Only one man was discipled by the *ascended Christ*. Only one man was discipled by Christ with *New Testament* revelation under grace. That passage says that "the veil [which precludes man's ability to understand spiritual things] remains unlifted [until regeneration]." First Corinthians 2:10,12-14 says, "For to us God revealed [the 'hidden wisdom'] through the Spirit .... Now we have received ... the Spirit who is from God, that we might know the things freely given to us by God, which things we also speak, not in words taught by human wisdom, but in those taught by the Spirit.... But a natural man ... cannot understand them, because they are spiritually appraised." Folks, how is a person changed from a "natural man" to a "new man" in Christ? By regeneration which was not available to mankind until the miraculous events recorded in Acts 2.

For three years, 12 men, 11 of whom awaited the lifting of their veil until Pentecost, were discipled by Jesus *during the period of Law*. Paul, on the other hand, *was* regenerated; his veil was removed in Christ *prior to being tutored by Jesus*. This would have equipped him to understand spiritual truth before he spent his three years matriculating in the University of Desert with the ascended Christ. Afterward he went to visit Peter for a couple of weeks, and also had at least one encounter with James. The *ascended* Christ tutored this man one-on-one in Arabia, preparing him for his ministry as apostle to the Gentiles (1 Timothy 2:7). Then, 14 years later (17 years post-salvation), the Holy Spirit gave Paul a revelation that he was to visit the earlier apostles and explain the gospel that the *ascended* Christ had shared with him (Galatians 2:1-2). He said, "Those who were of reputation *contributed nothing to me*" (Galatians 2:6). There was probably little spiritual understanding that those 11 men possessed that Paul did not already understand because their experiences with Jesus had been filtered through veiled minds. I do not believe Paul's claims about his knowledge were arrogance. The teachings Paul presents are not *his* opinion, they're God's, or they wouldn't be in the canon! The man was simply stating facts. He was similar to the great St. Louis Cardinal right-hander Dizzy Dean, who said, "When you've got the best arm in the world and claim you're the best pitcher in baseball, you ain't braggin', you're tellin' the truth."

A Visit to Heaven

Most of us are fascinated by the stories in the Bible about people who have been resurrected from the grave—for example Lazarus, and, of course, that of our Savior's being the epitome. I believe that when Jesus brought Lazarus back from the grave the man wasn't jumping for joy. Talk about culture shock! Have you ever wished you could ask him about his round-trip? I have. But I believe there is one resurrection from the dead that's recorded in the Bible which some may not have recognized. This man recorded much of what he saw and heard after he touched down following his round-trip to heaven. It was Paul.

Years ago, I was studying 2 Corinthians 12, where Paul is discussing the revelations he was given by the ascended Christ: "I know a man in Christ who fourteen years ago ... was caught up to the third heaven ... and heard inexpressible words, which a man is not permitted to speak." I was in the home of a friend at the time in 1975, studying from his Bible, which had dates printed at the top of each page, recording the year that scholars believe the events on the page had occurred. As I came across the "fourteen years ago" phrase, I thought, *I'll subtract fourteen years from the date at the top of this page and see if there is any reference to Paul on the pages bearing that date.* Guess what happened

14 years prior to Paul's penning those words—his stoning at Lystra! "They stoned Paul and dragged him out of the city, supposing him to be dead" (Acts 14:19).

My interest was stimulated, to say the least! Paul was the legalistic Jews' worst nightmare come true. Having watched Saul-cum-Paul's rising star ever since he was a rookie Pharisee, and the way he could make mincemeat of their religious opponents such as the Sadducees in public debate, he had become the Pharisees' champion. In reminiscing about his past, Paul called himself "a Hebrew of Hebrews." Today we would say "a Hebrew's Hebrew." He was an incomparable asset to their team and must have been *the* religious role model of zealous Hebrew males, young and old. This guy was as popular as the Most Valuable Player of the Super Bowl. He was Captain Israel! He could leap tall legalistic buildings in a single bound! You can see why his conversion to Christ was probably more scandalous to them than it would be for political conservatives to hear that Rush Limbaugh had re-registered as a liberal Democrat. Their love and admiration immediately turned into passionate hatred. They chased him all over the map, seeking to "kill him for God."

When they finally cornered him at Lystra, they weren't throwing whiffle balls, gang. It says they dragged him out of town, "supposing him to be dead" (Acts 14:19). It's easy to imagine that at least one of them administered the *coup de grace* with a big rock to the head. These "hit men" wanted to proudly report back to the high priest that God had one less problem.

Apparently, they weren't the only ones who believed him dead. Acts 14:20 says that after the killers left, Paul's disciples were standing around him, staring at his body. They weren't even dialing 911. There must have been no pulse. Then, "he rose and entered the city. And the next day he went away with Barnabas to Derbe" (Acts 23:20). Such simple words, but I believe miracles are revealed here:

- *First miracle*: After this severe bludgeoning, Paul got up *unassisted.*

- *Second miracle*: After becoming a pulverized horizontal target pounded by a crazed mob of religious zealots hurling rocks the size of a baseball, Paul walked *unassisted* back into town, following the grooves that his heels had made in the dust.

- *Third miracle*: Pro football running backs at the peak of their health with muscle definition like Adonis due to genetics, proper diet, and a lifetime of pumping iron and toughened by weekly pummeling from equally physically endowed specimens, most of whom are 20 percent to 25 percent larger than they are, and although protected by high-tech pads and ten huge blockers to ward off the blows, are so bruised after a game that they often have to be helped from a bed the next morning. This 37-year-old little man got up off the ground *unassisted* and walked back into Lystra *unassisted* perhaps only an hour or so following the "rock festival." In addition, not only did he need no assistance getting out of bed the "morning after the game," he stepped out on a *30-mile march to Derbe!* How many running backs could do that?

Paul's Ride in God's Helicopter

I realize that some people will disagree with me, and that's OK, but in my opinion it makes spiritual sense that Paul was raised from the dead. I believe that God was at work here. I certainly don't claim to have the absolute truth, but it seems to me that Paul was murdered; that he ejected from his dead earthsuit; that *he*, not the anonymous man of

2 Corinthians 12:2, was taken up into heaven; that upon his arrival he was given profound revelations by Jesus Christ (2 Corinthians 12:7a). Assuming this was the case, Paul was the one who "heard inexpressible words, which a man is not permitted to speak" (2 Corinthians 12:4).[1]

As we have seen, God gives revelation to man according to His own timetable. Could it be that God, for reasons known only to Himself, was not yet ready for certain of the revelations given to Paul to be revealed to the world? Could it be that God gave such revelations to Paul along with other revelations which were to be shared immediately? This seems plausible to me. And is it possible that He may have lifted His ban by the time Paul penned Ephesians (A.D. 60–62) and Colossians (A.D. 62)? Paul was martyred in A.D. 68. Of course, God knew this before the world was created. Could it be that God commanded Paul to share the secret revelation to the churches before his martyrdom? I'm speculating that this may be the case because Ephesians, Colossians, and Philippians have much to say about the glorious truths of our identity in Christ. The first four chapters of Ephesians, as well as many verses in Galatians, Philippians, and Colossians, address this. On the other hand, this topic is treated much more lightly, if at all, in Paul's earlier writings (1 and 2 Thessalonians, 1 and 2 Corinthians, and Romans).

The fact that no other New Testament scribes record the truths of our new identity in Christ *this extensively* makes me suspect that they were revealed more completely to Paul. Not that I labor under the delusion that I have the market cornered on truth, but I don't see any *major* life-changing, liberating truth in the New Testament other than that of our identity in Christ that man was not permitted to hear for a season. If this is not the secret revelation that was given to Paul, then it seems to me that he must have died with his lips sealed. In addition, if Paul is not the man who was caught up to heaven, I ask myself why God gave such secret, powerful revelation to only one anonymous man and left the rest of the body of Christ in the dark.

Perhaps you question whether it was Paul or one of his acquaintances who was caught up to heaven. In the 2 Corinthians 12 passage Paul writes, "And because of the surpassing greatness of the revelations ... there was given me a thorn in the flesh ... to keep me from exalting myself" (verse 7). "To keep *me* from exalting myself"? In verses 2-5, it seems as though Paul is speaking of an acquaintance who took the trip in God's helicopter, but if so, I ask the Holy Spirit why he didn't become an important teacher in the early church?

Besides this, it's unlikely that Paul would be given a "thorn" to guard him against pride just because he happened to *know* such a man. You and I know an important person or two, but we don't need a special thorn to keep us from going on a lifelong pride trip over it. I believe the apostle is speaking of his own experiences, and that humility prompted him to recount it in the third-person format. Paul speaks of "my" gospel, and hints that he was given unique revelations (see Romans 2:16; 16:25; Galatians 1:11-12; 2:2; Ephesians 3:3ff.; 2 Timothy 2:8). Why would he refer to the gospel as "*my* gospel" if it was a carbon copy of what the apostles preached in the early days? Why not call it *the* gospel?

Sometimes it can get lonely at the top. This is especially true when you feel like you're the only one who is saying or doing something a particular way and you are encountering opposition from those who are ostensibly reading from the same page as you. Did Paul begin to have some doubts about whether his message needed some tweaking? Perhaps so. Human reinforcement is encouraging. God designed the body of Christ this way. The Scriptures say, "Then after an interval of fourteen years I [Paul] went up again to Jerusalem ... And it was because of a revelation that I went up; and I submitted to them the gospel which I preach among the Gentiles, but I did so *in private to those who were of reputation, for fear that I might be running, or had run, in vain"* (Galatians 2:1-2, emphasis added). Paul hadn't visited Jerusalem in 14 years, and during the interim he was constantly hassled by "men from James." But apparently the apostles agreed with what he was teaching. Although it's not recorded in Scripture, perhaps God had been downloading revelation into their spirits as well (see Ephesians 3:3-5). Of the disciples, only Matthew, Peter, and John recorded part of the canon. I believe the Holy Spirit led Paul back to the apostles in order that he might be reinforced to press on with *his* gospel, that the revelation he had received during his helicopter ride did indeed explain *the* gospel of Jesus Christ which God wishes every Christian understood.

Thousands of folks, most of them Jewish, were converted through the good news of the gospel as preached by the apostles and their converts long before Paul's conversion. Is it possible that Paul received revelation about our identity in Christ from the ascended Christ which earlier converts did not receive at their salvation? I believe this is the case. *But it certainly does not mean they were anything less than born-again.* That would be as impossible as being only partially born in the physical realm. How much of God's truth did the Ethiopian eunuch know when he got born again—25 percent? How much did *I* understand about God's truth to get saved—20 percent? Hey, *everyone* understands but a small part of God's truth at salvation! Physical birth is a one-time experience, while physical, mental, and emotional *development* is a process. Spiritual birth is a one-time phenomenon; spiritual *development*, on the other hand, is a process. After salvation the Holy Spirit sets out to reveal more and more truth to us in our pilgrimage with Christ. It's likely that no human comprehends more than the proverbial tip of the iceberg of the gospel.

Becoming spiritually born-again is simply the wonderful *beginning* of something great. Being born physically is also a beginning, but if there were faulty development either in or out of the womb, we call that person *handicapped*. The same thing can happen *after* a spiritual birth. Many Christians are spiritually underdeveloped—handicapped through acquiring a limited view of what Jesus accomplished (Galatians 1:6-7). You can become an American simply by being born in the United States of America, but most "street" people are uninformed as to how to optimally benefit from their citizenship. I believe this may be analogous to the experience of the early Christians, who were saved prior to understanding the revelations of our identity in Christ, which were given to Paul. Doubtless many, if not all, of these folks heard his teachings at a later date, however.[2]

We would agree that although a former big league ball player and his ten-year-old daughter may attend a baseball game together, the dad will enjoy it more because of his greater understanding of the game. Hebrews 5:12-14 teaches that Christians can have a similar experience in the game of life: "For though by this time you ought to be teachers, you have need again for someone to teach you the elementary principles of the [teachings] of God, and you have come to need milk and not solid food. For everyone who partakes only of milk is not accustomed to the word of [his own] righteousness [in Christ], for he is a babe. But solid food is for the mature, who because of *practice* have their senses *trained* to discern good and evil." Some of these Christians were like the little girl. Although they are enjoying being at the "game" with our Dad, they would enjoy it much more if they would press on in the faith. Like the ball player, life is more enjoyable when you are *experiencing* God.

I believe God gave Paul a greater understanding of God's truth than He originally gave to the 11. As evidence of this, note the volume of New Testament Scripture that he either dictated or penned—13 of the 23 *post-cross* books (14 if he wrote Hebrews), not to mention that three-fifths of the

Book of Acts deals with his ministry as penned by Luke. The other New Testament penmen don't dedicate the amount of space in their writings to proclaim our identity in Christ that Paul does. Ephesians 1:3 through 2:10 alone (A.D. 60-62) contains 40 verses proclaiming our true identity! But the 3000 people who came to Christ at Pentecost were not taught this truth in Peter's sermon. I think the earliest converts must have understood only the "elementary oracles of God" because the revelations which Paul received about our identity in Christ were apparently not revealed until later in his ministry.

By being made the custodian of the magnificent truth which puts so many pieces of life's puzzle together for us, it's no small wonder that the man taught and lived with such boldness. Some naively mistake this for arrogance. I disagree. All of us would love to have the walk with Jesus Christ that Paul had, but I'm not sure we would line up to receive the suffering that wrung the world out of him in order that God might accomplish what He did in and through this dear brother.

The Lifting of the Veil

Hopefully, we've settled the issue that *a person does not have to understand all of God's truth to get saved.* Hey, which of us understands it even after we've been saved for decades? As we have seen, the *pre-cross* apostles understood grace through veiled eyes. They received some Law teaching, as well as some grace teaching. God's truth as revealed to Paul, on the other hand, consists *entirely* of grace. I do not demean these 11 beloved brothers in Christ who were regenerated in Acts 2, but am commenting on the facts as I believe the Bible portrays them.

As evidence of this, consider Peter's trying to block Jesus from being crucified, as recorded in John 18:10. At this point in his pilgrimage, he simply did not comprehend the role of the Savior's sacrificial death, resurrection, and ascension for believers. All of this changed, however, when the Holy Spirit entered Peter at his regeneration, as Jesus had prophesied: "But the Helper, the Holy Spirit . . . will teach you all things, and *bring to your remembrance* all that I said to you" (John 14:26). There is no way Peter could have preached his magnificent sermon in Acts 2:14-40 two months earlier. He couldn't have interpreted the teaching he had received from Jesus. Does this mean that Jesus didn't teach *elements* of God's truth to the pre-cross seekers? Of course not. Does this mean that Jesus' teaching was not sufficient to bring man to eternal life? Of course not, but He could hardly teach the *fullness of God's truth* before all of the elements of that truth had been put into place. Which of those folks would have dared to dream that God's Holy Spirit would rip the curtain of the Holy of Holies and vacate the premises to take up residence in *them* as new holy ones (saints)? That mind-boggling phenomenon had been God's secret since before the beginning of time (Ephesians 1:4).

Spiritual blindness is standard equipment for the unregenerate (Matthew 13:13ff.; 1 Corinthians 1:18-24). God says of Israel, "Their minds were hardened; for until this very day at the reading of the old covenant the same veil remains unlifted because *it is removed in Christ*" (2 Corinthians 3:14). The veil is lifted off a man's mind at salvation. This means that *Paul was the only apostle who had this veil "removed in Christ" prior to being given the gospel of grace by Christ.* It was a different ball game for both Christ and Paul when Christ discipled Paul. Christ was ascended, and Paul was regenerated. Think about that, folks. Think about the wonderful difference this would make: Christ could explain what it meant to be born again, and Paul could understand. He could explain that the ripping of the Temple veil was symbolic of God vacating the "temple made with hands" that He might dwell in Paul. And Paul could absorb this miracle! And

171

the beat goes on. Paul was the *only* apostle who was spiritually equipped via regeneration to understand the revelations
he was given by the ascended, glorified Jesus Christ. The
unregenerate apostles who sat under Jesus' teaching, on the
other hand, often stared at Him like a deer in headlights.
They simply couldn't understand many of His teachings.
One of their frequent requests was for Jesus to repeat Himself or explain His teaching to them. And often they *still*
didn't get it any better than you or I did before *we* were regenerated. A person with a dead spirit simply cannot comprehend spiritual truth.

— I believe we can account for the fact that Paul speaks
with such passion and authority for the gospel of grace because he was saturated with grace while matriculating at
Desert University and during his ride in the helicopter. Yet,
the man was not arrogant; he was awed and greatly humbled that he would be chosen to be the purveyor of such
marvelous truth (2 Corinthians 12:5,7; Romans 15:18). He felt
mega-unworthy. He said, "For I . . . am not fit to be called an
apostle, because I persecuted the church of God" (1 Corinthians 15:9). It would seem that his "thorn" served him well
by protecting him from pridefulness (2 Corinthians 12:7).

 James, Peter, and John acknowledged Paul's special
anointing and role after hearing him present the gospel he
was teaching to the Gentiles (Galatians 2:9). Peter also
wrote, "In all [Paul's] letters, speaking in them of these
things, in which are *some things hard to understand*, which
the untaught and unstable distort, as they do also *the rest* of
the Scriptures . . ." (2 Peter 3:16). He acknowledges Paul's
writings as "Scripture" and says that he himself, like many of
us, struggled to comprehend the marvelous revelations
which were given to Paul. You'll also note that he spoke a
sobering caution to Christians who reject what God teaches
through Paul, calling them "untaught and unstable" and
saying that they distort the *rest* of God's Word, too. Wow!

This encompasses truths about the elimination of our old identity (Romans 6:6), our new identity in Christ (Ephesians 1:3–3:21), and Christ as life through us (Colossians 3:3-4), which are foundational in Paul's gospel—which, of course, is really the gospel of Jesus Christ! I want to be careful to not be misunderstood here. I am certainly not teaching that Paul's teaching is more authoritative than that of Jesus Christ. I am saying that Paul's teaching *is the teaching of Jesus Christ after the cross.*

Grace Defended

When teachers came from out of town or arose from within the churches to distort *the* gospel by introducing legalism, Paul blistered them. He recounts in Galatians 2:11-14 how he publicly castigated "men from James," and even Peter, when Peter reverted back to living under the Law. When someone introduced legalism to Paul's flock, he skinned them alive (see Galatians 1:7-9). "Would that those who are troubling you would even mutilate themselves" (Galatians 5:12). Folks, I'll try to say this tactfully. Considering the righteous steam that seems to be coming out of Paul's collar, many believe the Greek word which the New American Standard version scholars tactfully translate *mutilate* probably means he wishes that the legalistic circumcision teachers would let the knife slip on themselves. Paul took no prisoners when it came to fighting against legalism because it is an adulteration of *the* gospel. I believe Paul's round-trip to heaven accounts for this boldness. He understood that God allows zero tolerance for mixing Law with grace. Why would God be so uptight about this? It's because *He refuses to share the glory of (honor of, credit for) the salvation phenomenon with any of His creatures.* God recognizes *His* work alone. He acknowledges no works of the flesh (Romans 15:18; Acts 15:12). Salvation and the overcoming Christian life is all of God, none of man. That's what

173

grace is all about. Jesus, the only Son, paid the supreme price as our Father suffered the agony of having to stand by and watch Him accomplish it. Man's effort has nothing to do with our glorious, merciful salvation by grace, lest he be justified in boasting about what *he* did to accomplish it (Ephesians 2:8-9).

- Legalism is not an alternate view of the gospel.

- Legalism attempts to add man's effort to the gospel.

- Paul's attitude toward legalism is not his own bias; it's in the canon.

- Paul's passion against legalism is *God's* passion against legalism.

The Bible labels Law a "ministry of death" and a "ministry of condemnation" (2 Corinthians 3:7,9). Even though the Law is *good* (Romans 7:12), insisting that Christians keep it perfectly as a means of pleasing God without teaching them how to let Christ "life out" God's ways *for* them, *through* them, produces frustration and "dead works" (human effort to please God). Henry Drummond likened it to standing on the deck and pushing the mast to make the boat go. "The sting of death is sin, and the *power* of sin is the law" (1 Corinthians 15:56). Legalism is the gasoline which fuels sin's engine. The more you teach Law to Christians, the more you empower sin.

Why Be So Concerned over Paul's Role?

"Bill, why did you dedicate a whole chapter to proving that Paul is the only apostle who received the complete gospel of Jesus Christ? Aren't you introducing one more potentially divisive issue that doesn't make that much difference?" Great day, no! Stay with me now.... Who is the major teacher in the four Gospels? Jesus, of course. And when

174

Jesus takes a position on an issue in the Gospels, it's a no-brainer that it must be our position, isn't it? Or is it? Is it possible that new creations in Christ must interpret *certain* of Jesus' teachings in a different light *for us* than was the case for His unregenerated hearers before the cross? Jesus taught as a Man under the Law (Galatians 4:4). Jesus taught other people who were under the Law. Jesus taught *truth* according to the revelation of God to man at that point in time in God's grand scheme of things. Jesus was preparing *man who was under Law* for the opportunity to become *man under grace.* One of His key tools for accomplishing this gracious, merciful goal was to *intensify* the Law, which would cause man to see himself as incapable of attaining eternal life via keeping the Law. Jesus would usher in this marvelous opportunity for all who would place their faith in Him by His death, resurrection, and ascension. The entire ball game would change for the beliver. Christ would take on a new meaning. The Father would take on new meaning. The Scriptures would take on new meaning. Life would take on new meaning.

When comparing the teaching of Jesus with that of Paul, it is imperative we remember that they were *addressing different audiences under two different dispensations,* so we should not be surprised if the teaching *appears* to differ on an issue. It's not that one teaching is in conflict with the other, but that one is appropriate under Law, while the other is appropriate under grace. Proper interpretation must not focus on which of the two is correct, but rather on discerning whether the teaching is appropriate for those under Law or those under grace. Stop and think before the Lord. Ask Him if the fact that Jesus' teaching falls on the Law side of the cross while Paul's falls on the grace side of the cross holds the key to a correct interpretation. This frequently makes a profound difference. If Jesus had been employing His technique of intensifying the Law, your ability to discern that

His teaching was intended for the *unregenerate* and not for Christians could make the difference between bondage and freedom for you.

The teacher who refuses to study this issue out before the Lord, but continues to teach Scriptures such as Matthew 6:14-15 to Christians is in error and places his disciples in bondage. My brothers and sisters in Christ, it matters not if your pastor or study-materials author is world-renowned. If they teach Matthew 6:14-15 to Christians, you must weigh this by the Word and the Holy Spirit (not by your emotions) to discern the truth. Don't believe me; believe only the Word and the Holy Spirit; test everyone else.

God made Paul a steward of mind-blowing truth, and I suggest that this is the reason he refused to remove the thorn from Paul's flesh, because the thorn somehow deterred his tripping out on pride over being the custodian of such treasure (2 Corinthians 12:7). Whatever the thorn was, Paul *needed* that particular thorn, that "messenger from Satan," as a constant reminder to give no "opportunity [to prideful] flesh" (Galatians 5:13). He could have prayed for it to be removed 300 times instead of three times, and he would have gotten God's voice mail.[3]

"Apparent" Contradiction

Let's examine how *apparent* contradictions between pre-cross teaching and post-cross teaching in Scripture may arise by using an illustration from marriage. "Jason" had promised his wife that he would help her rake and bag leaves from the yard and from under the shrubbery this Saturday, and she was anticipating their working together to pretty up the house. It was going to be a "workday," which she loved. On Friday night, Jason's golfing buddy called to ask him if he would like to drive over to a nearby city to play golf Saturday of *next week,* and Jason said he would love to. Mary overheard Jason excitedly planning the details of the "Saturday" golf trip, and jumped to the conclusion that he was welching on his promise. She was crushed! Her feeler shot up to a ten as she rushed into the bedroom, choking back the tears. It took a lot of time explaining and reinterpreting the conversation and forgiving and apologizing to get the mess straightened out because of misinterpreting the facts. *Timing* was the critical issue here. Mary assumed Jason was discussing *this* Saturday instead of next Saturday.

Folks, timing is *essential* in resolving a "supposed" conflict between Scriptures occurring before the cross and those occurring after the cross. By remembering that man was under Law until Acts 2 when we encounter such a conflict, we can *"hear both sides of the conversation."* When a *seeming* contradiction arises between teaching in the Gospels versus that in the Epistles, knowing that God's grace position is far more likely to occur *following* Acts 2 gives us a leg up on resolving the apparent conflict. The Epistles will give us the final (grace) word.

The same Holy Spirit is speaking pure, unvarnished truth in both the Gospels and the Epistles. Timing is everything here! The reason there may be a "supposed" conflict is because the two teachings occur on opposite sides of the cross. Great day, aren't we grateful for the differences? Surely we agree that there are significant differences between many pre-cross and post-cross teachings. The pre-cross Gospel listeners heard truth under Law and *some* grace, while Paul's post-cross listeners heard grace, period.

"A Promise Remains of Entering God's Rest"

⁓ Perhaps this illustration might help. Let's say that an older mechanical engineer had graduated from MIT when manual slide rules were state-of-the-art technology, but had long since switched to an electronic digital calculator. However, he kept trying to integrate *all* of the teaching from the old slide-rule manual with that in the new calculator's

177

manual. Both manuals are true when used properly. It's simply that the new manual contains truth which overrides some of that in the old. His practice of refusing to use the truth found in his new calculator manual to override truth for the era of the old slide rule manual would keep him in a state of confusion. Such a man could never "enter into rest" in his chosen profession.

We Christians can fall into a similar trap. I believe a large percentage of Christians not only attempt to apply all of the teaching in the Gospels to our grace walk, but see the Gospels as *their major source for truth*. Where the Gospels and the Epistles may *appear* to conflict, these folks hold to the teaching of Jesus and reject that of Paul's Epistles. Gang, there is certain Scripture in the Gospels that simply does not apply to saints of God any more than those old slide-rule instructions apply to operating an electric calculator. Christians are "electric" people who operate under a different power system! The Law verses found in the Gospels were never intended to apply to new creations in Christ, but to the unregenerate. Law is intended as a "cattle prod" to crowd the lost toward faith in Jesus Christ. And praise God, it worked for those of us who know Christ. "The Law has become our tutor to lead us to Christ, *that we may be justified by faith*. But now that faith has come, we are *no longer under a tutor*" (Galatians 3:24-25). We are not under Law.

I spoke of the engineer "entering into rest." In Christianity, "there [is] a Sabbath rest for the people of God. For the one who has entered His rest has himself also rested from his works, as God did from His" (Hebrews 4:9-10). In this chapter we've seen an example of the Bible being the best commentary on the Bible. The post-cross Scriptures give us the key to unlock the mystery of much of Jesus' pre-cross Law teaching. By understanding this, we are better able to enter the "rest for the people of God."

I realize that this chapter contains some challenging teaching, but I believe the effort you expend to study it out before the Lord will greatly enhance your walk with Christ. Understanding how to resolve the issue of "apparent" contradictions between certain teaching in the Gospels and that of Paul's letters has helped me experience the "rest" which is ours in Christ.

10   THAT THEY ARE SANCTIFIED

ALUMNAE OF OKLAHOMA STATE UNIVERSITY and Texas A
& M are known as Aggies, and we Aggies wear the label
proudly. But someone in the course of time began making
up "Aggie jokes." (Undoubtedly, it was the devil. Nah, I get
as big a kick out of them as the non-Aggies do.)

> An Aggie alum was driving through rural Texas when
> he spotted a strapping young 18-year-old boy trying
> to row a boat through a plowed field. He was bent to
> the oars, sweat pouring from his face. The Aggie
> stopped his car and strode over to the fence where he
> hollered, "Hey! What are you doing out there?" To
> which the kid replied with a grin as big as Dallas, "I'm
> on my way down to Texas A & M to enroll." "You
> idiot!" the Aggie screamed, arms windmilling. "Here
> some of us are trying our best to create a better image
> for A & M, and it's idiots like you who give us a bad
> name! If I could swim I'd come over there and give
> you a whuppin'!"

I believe Satan has millions of Christians chained to the
oars of such a boat. Its bow is headed in the right direction
and, although the people are pulling with a will, the boat
never moves. Its name is the "Who-Am-I?" The evil one has
been hard at work blurring the differences between the gen-
ders in order to produce generations of males and females
who are confused about their gender-identity roles. Their
numbers are legion and increasing. I rowed with them for
years, but by God's grace, I've shipped my oars.

The Making of an Identity Crisis

I am a male. I didn't *perform* to obtain this identity; I was *born* a male. Remember: Birth, not performance, always determines identity. The doctor simply checks the plumbing and announces your gender identity: "It's a boy!" I, however, didn't look at it that objectively and, due to my formative years, I had an identity struggle. I didn't *feel* that I was "male enough" to merit the title. Even though I passed the physical, my world "told" me that I couldn't hack it as a male. I didn't *feel* like I thought a *real* male ought to *feel*. But, crazy as that may seem, that's the way Satan recruits more oarsmen for his gender-confusion boat.

— My mom and dad were both lords of the ring, as we all have been. They're with the Lord now, and my intention is not to bash them. I love them, but they blew some things, just as I have with my four sons. Since Mom had strong, assertive, outspoken flesh, while Pop's was passive and accommodating, when they married they ignored God's plan for the husband and wife and changed it to accommodate their flesh. Mom "lifed out" the role of husband in that she was the sole authority figure in our home, while Pop totally submitted to his wife's authority over him. Gang, that's like jumping off a cliff to demonstrate how God's law of gravity operates. Some things in their union were destined to spatter when they hit the ground. One of them was me!

When I showed up, programmed at the male factory to ultimately marry a female, treasure her, tenderly lead her, provide for her, protect her from the cold winds of life, and otherwise serve her as Jesus does His bride (Ephesians 5:25), I was confused by trying to match that innate programming with the roles modeled at home. I was ignorant of what a *real* male was by God's definition, so I steered my ship toward one of the world's alternatives: I tried to be a John Wayne clone. *When I get married, things are going to be different! No woman will boss me! A real man is going to run my house!* But I had spent my life programming my flesh by navigating through a gender-confusing home environment, which provided no charts for my build-a-macho-man enterprise. Twenty years and four sons later, I was steering my ship and crew toward a wreck on the reefs without a clue, even though I was a deeply committed Christian and had a doctorate in counseling from Oklahoma State University.

Although I put on the big macho façade, inside I felt weak, insecure, inadequate, and threatened in my masculinity. So I married the only kind of security I had ever known: a female who was a talented self-starter. Let me hasten to say that my precious Anabel is a lovely, feminine saint of God, but she had programmed her flesh to take charge and make things happen. She is mega-organized, creative, and full of stamina. As the smoke cleared from our honeymoon, she began to take charge of the home, and when she did, I unleashed 23 years of pent-up hostility on her with my hateful, punitive sarcasm, invective, ridicule, etc. Anabel and I had a stormy relationship till God began to show us the truths you see in this book. We now could wish that every married couple had a marriage like ours, but I sure dealt her misery for many years, most of them as a committed Christian. To Christ be the glory for the change!

Christ—God's Solution to Our Identity Crisis

I don't have to prove my masculinity now. Anabel no longer lives under the tyranny of a frustrated macho-male wanna-be. She doesn't have to be the perfect wife or be in control now. We each know who we are in Christ, and that settles it. As for being a *real* male, I know my true identity in Christ and pass the male physical, so that settles *that* issue. And rain on what my *feeler's* verdict is! Neither Anabel nor I got any more of the Lord's resources than we had received at salvation in order to turn our lives and our marriage around. It's just that God showed us how to benefit more fully from the Great Resource we had *already* received: the Holy Spirit within each of us, and our identity in Christ. Although we were both sanctified in Christ at salvation, we didn't know it. It stands to reason that since we didn't *know* we were righteous, we certainly didn't know that we had also been given the power to *act* in a sanctified manner toward one another. We rededicated our lives till our rededicators wore out. We made many promises to do better, but they were always broken because they were based upon the power of our own flesh rather than on trusting Christ to carry them out through us. Had we known how to bring Christ on-line to do so, God would have viewed these efforts as *sanctified*. "For I will not presume to speak of anything except what Christ has accomplished *through* me (Romans 15:18).

— *Sanctified* means "holified," "to cause to become holy"; it's like being submerged in bleach. It's more than just forgiveness, wonderful as that is. It's the *purifying of our personhood—our identity*. You and I were stains on God's landscape whom He purified in Christ by crucifying us and spiritually rebirthing us. God initiated a spiritual purge through Christ. Listen to the Holy Spirit as He reiterates these words that He spoke to the penmen of His Love Letter:

- "And for their sakes I sanctify Myself, that they themselves also may be sanctified in truth"—Jesus (John 17:19).

- "I commend you to God and to the word of His grace, which is able to build you up and to give you the inheritance among *all those who are sanctified*" (Acts 20:32).

- "... in order that they may receive forgiveness of sins and an inheritance among *those who have been sanctified by faith in Me*"—Jesus (Acts 26:18).

- "... to those who *have been sanctified in Christ Jesus,* saints by calling, with all who in every place call upon the name of our Lord Jesus Christ, their Lord and ours" (1 Corinthians 1:2).

- "And such were some of you; but you were washed, but *you were sanctified,* but you were justified" (1 Corinthians 6:11).

Two Types of Sanctification

Those last two verses were spoken to the most licentious performers of the first-century churches: the church at Corinth. These guys invented the phrase, "Character doesn't matter." Even though these born-again Corinthians were "lacking in no spiritual gift," much of their *behavior* was reprehensible according to the biblical record. However, incredible as it is to the human mentality, they were sanctified (holy) as far as their *identity* was concerned. God said so! Their behavior obviously didn't match their holy identity. In addition to our *sanctified personhood—identity,* there is a second type of sanctification which the Corinthians lacked: *sanctified performance.*

It's common for Christians to fail to differentiate between these two types of sanctification. They do not simply lump sanctified identity and sanctified performance together into the same ball of wax, however. They're harder on themselves than that. They believe that a sanctified identity (holiness) can only be attained via performance, which makes it seem like climbing Mount Everest in high heels! (Guess who dreamed up this idea.) The result is that many Christians believe they will never become sanctified (purified) on this earth. That's why some folks only bestow the title of *saint* by committee vote on certain high-profile, super-performers. I don't intend to be ugly by saying this. Folks, we just read a few of the multitude of verses showing unequivocally that

185

each person who is in Christ Jesus *is already holy*. The Bible is not speaking of performance here, but of *identity*—who we are, not what we've done. Sanctification is somewhat like being born in Texas. Although this guarantees that you are a Texan, we must wait to see if you buy your boots, big hat, big belt buckle, and brag about Texas to determine whether you act like one.

In addition to this new, sanctified *identity*, sanctified *performance* is also attainable through Christ. This is not achieved by trying harder, but by letting Christ express His life through us. *His* work alone is acceptable (sanctified) to the Father. This is demonstrated by what Jesus says in John 15:5: "I am the vine, you are the branches; he who abides in Me, and I in him, he bears much fruit; for *apart from Me you can do nothing.*" Clearly, the *fruit* produced by Vine-life is acceptable to God, but anything produced by an independent branch is "nothing" (i.e., an imitation, worthless, *not sanctified*, fit only for God's trash heap). And remember, God gets to make the rules. He loves relationship. He loves community. Those are tens with Him. God rejects all independent human effort. He insists on a joint effort; Jesus and the believer or believers. "They will be held guilty, they whose strength is their god" (Habakkuk 1:11). "Thus says the Lord, 'Cursed is the man who trusts in mankind and makes flesh his strength' " (Jeremiah 17:5). This encompasses all independent human effort, ranging from gardening to preaching, plucking eyebrows to teaching Sunday school, mowing the lawn to soul-winning, *ad infinitum*. However, these identical tasks could have become sanctified by Christ performing them *through* the Christian, by faith. Yes, even eyebrow plucking (except for you guys). Such a mundane task can become a sanctified (holy) act when the Christian performs it by trusting Christ as life. Hey, unloading the dishwasher should be done in the Spirit! Let Christ do it.

So, as regards our identity, the New Testament teaches time and again that all who are born again *have* (drumroll) *been* (drumroll) *sanctified in Christ.* End of argument. We're holy and righteous before God. I fear, however, that should a person present himself for membership in most evangelical churches claiming to be holy and righteous, the members would be scandalized. They hold to the power of sin's lie that Christians are sinners saved by grace. Folks, this breaks God's heart. Our *sanctified identity* comes with the salvation package by faith in Christ, never by human performance. God explains why: so no one can brag about his own achievement (Ephesians 2:8-9). Such a beneficent gift speaks volumes about the love, grace, and mercy of the Giver.

While obtaining your sanctified identity in Christ requires faith alone, producing sanctified *behavior* requires faith *plus obedience.* Just as Christ is the focal point of providing our sanctified identity, He is also the focal point of providing our sanctified performance. Behavior acceptable to God *must* be produced by Christ expressing His life through the believer via faith and obedience. There is no other way (2 Corinthians 4:10-11). You are a war zone in which the Deceiver seeks to use every trick in his book to keep you from winning battles, even though he knows that he's lost the war. Let me illustrate how we can become more victorious against the world, the flesh, and the devil.

Spontaneous Recovery

Anabel and I had not planned well, and as a result, we were making a mad dash to a church in our city where we were due to speak. (OK, OK, for my friends who know Anabel, *I* had not planned well; Anabel always plans well.) We were zipping along on Loop 820, my mind on the seminar, when we came to the Airport Freeway Exit. We were *supposed* to go straight, but *I* veered toward the airport! Arrrgh!

187

What a dumb trick! Now we would *really* be hard-pressed to make it to the church on time.

How could I have done such a thing? Simple. I've made the trip to Dallas/Fort Worth Airport a gazillion times. I have well-developed habit patterns for driving this route burned into my memory banks. When my mind became preoccupied, I headed for the airport as was my custom, instead of traveling the new, less-familiar route to the church. In psychological circles that's called "spontaneous recovery." In Poteau, Oklahoma, where Anabel and I grew up, it's called "stupidity." I like the psychological term better. Somehow it sounds more palatable, perhaps even a bit intelligent.

This has a parallel in the Christian life. Your old patterns for living (flesh) which you burned into your memory banks are well-established. By agreeing that God tells the truth, you claimed that you were crucified with Christ (Romans 6:6, *et al)*, and thus you "crucified the flesh with its passions" (Galatians 5:24). This means that victory over its dominance is not only possible, but normal for us through Christ. But how many years did you work at building those flesh patterns? Twenty-five years? Fifty years? Hey, it's no wonder why your car turns toward the airport as you drive on God's freeway by setting your mind on cruise control. However, as a born-again person, you have a desire to "walk by the Spirit" and, as a result, "not carry out the desire of the flesh" (Galatians 5:16). You wish to build new, sanctified patterns for living, patterns of depending upon Christ to express His life through you. You also desire to build new patterns for believing that God tells the truth about your identity, that you are holy, righteous, totally forgiven, and not only as accepted as Christ is, but *acceptable* as a new creation in Him. I believe we're on safe biblical ground by saying that your *desire* to walk in obedience to Christ is a ten (Hebrews 10:16), but the new patterns you're building for doing so are much lower on the scale (Galatians 5:17). Let's pull over into this rest stop labeled

"Building Sanctified Patterns for Living" to plan our strategy for producing sanctified behavior. Good. Now kill the engine and lock up while we get out and stretch our legs. Let's stroll down that shady pathway while we chat.

/ Let's say your car has an automatic transmission. You've logged many years and mega-miles of driving an automatic transmission automobile. Tell me, when you slide under the wheel each morning, do you have to ponder to remember where the ignition keyhole is? Of course not; you can even find it in the dark due to a habit pattern. You don't look for it on the floorboard! As you move away from the driveway, do you have to remind yourself to pull the shift lever down till the indicator points to the letter *D* (for Drive)? Absurd; a habit pattern takes care of this detail. Or do you have to deliberate when making sudden stops? Of course not. Your brain is trained like a bird dog to drive an automatic transmission car from years of building habit patterns.

Let's say that you want to downsize for the sake of economy, and you are thinking about buying a cream puff you've found: a restored VW Bug with a stick shift. You're also attracted by the VW-size parking places in your city which your present car can't squeeze into. Although you've heard folks sing the praises of the reliability of the VW, you've had little experience with them. In fact, you've yet to drive your first stick-shift car. You can't get that spotless, candy-apple-red Bug out of your mind. Oh, how you would love to have it in your garage. As the Bug continues to burrow its way into your heart, you succumb to its siren call and become its proud owner.

Tell me, would you arrange to meet the seller on Friday at 5:20 P.M. at a service station near the entry ramp to the freeway to pick up your new VW? Would you climb into the driver's seat and zoom down the ramp to merge with the rush-hour traffic? Hey, those semis and commuters are ready to play street hockey with you strapped into the puck!

No way. You would ask the seller to meet you Saturday morning at the vacant parking lot of your neighborhood middle school, where you would have plenty of room for making miscues as you became familiar with the new experience of driving a stick-shift Bug. But, meantime, you would ask him to give you the manufacturer's handbook so you could study up on just how a VW operates. You would pore over that book, marking special portions that bore remembering. You would discover that some of your old "automatic-transmission" habit patterns will generalize to the VW. For example, each has a steering wheel, although the VW does not have power steering like your old car does. That means steering it will have a different *feel*.

Oh, oh—here's something that will take some getting used to.... The VW gearshift is down on the floor, whereas you're used to it being mounted on the side of the steering column. And the diagram of the shifting scheme in the manufacturer's handbook looks like a capital *H* with a tail on the left side (see Figure 10A).

Figure 10A

— Oh, look. This car has an extra pedal on the floor. It's called the "clutch," and it must be depressed before you can move the shift lever. This means your left foot will never be available for braking. You'll also have to practice gently raising your left foot off the clutch while slowly depressing

the accelerator. The same technique will also have to be
mastered in order to change gears while underway. That's
going to take a lot of practice.

Whoa! Here's a tricky one—how to shift into reverse.
With the clutch pedal depressed by your left foot, move the
shift lever to the crossbar of the H pattern, which is called
"neutral" (see Figure 10A). With the palm of your right hand
firmly atop the knob on the end of the shifter rod, depress
the rod downward toward the floor. Move it smartly to the
left (toward your knee), then pull it back toward you. That's
really going to take a lot of practice.

Hmmm, the starter is engaged by turning the ignition
key clockwise, just like in your old car. But here's a clever
idea: If the engine fails to start or if it should die, the starter
cannot be reengaged by turning the key clockwise. You
must first turn the key counterclockwise back to the "off"
position before attempting to restart.

Finally, the big day arrives when you're going to get
hands-on experience with the new Bug. You've studied the
book, which somewhat reduces your mild anxiety. As you
are dropped at the middle school by a friend on Saturday
morning, you are pleased to see that the seller is already
there. The sparkling VW is even more beautiful than you
had remembered it. After the final arrangements have been
concluded, the other people have driven off, and you're
alone in your new car. You tentatively start the engine, shift
into first gear, and slowly let out the clutch while depressing
the accelerator. Ouch—a jerky start—and you even kill the
engine! Double drat. You try to turn the key to restart, but it
won't budge. Then you remember that you must turn the
key counterclockwise to the "off" position before you can
initiate the restart procedure. Finally, after sufficient practice,
you feel comfortable enough to drive onto the quiet neighborhood streets leading to your house. You enter your driveway, depress both the clutch and brake and roll to a stop.

Then you practice backing up and pulling forward several times till you begin to feel more comfortable with that tricky procedure. As the weekend passes and your practice has begun to build *new habit patterns* for driving, you become more comfortable driving this delightful little car. What fun it is! It tools around the neighborhood like a toy. You are pleased.

Monday arrives and you psych yourself for the big test: the dreaded freeway. On a 1 to 10 scale, you feel comfortable about your ability to handle the car at about a 6, but you stay in the slow lane all the way to your office, and you allow yourself extra drive time so you won't feel pressured. You make it just fine. As the days pass and you log more freeway time, your comfort zone expands. You really enjoy hitting the gears as you move through the traffic.

Weeks later as you're driving on an artery which passes through the campus of the local university, a traffic light turns amber, and you're going to have to stop. You decelerate and, at the point where your left foot is supposed to lift off the floor to depress the clutch, it doesn't budge. The car begins to jerk violently. You panic, and this triggers an old habit for stamping hard on the brake pedal with both feet. The car has jerked out into the intersection nearly a car length, and the engine has died! Horns blare. Scowls glare. *Restart the car! But the key won't turn! What's wrong with the dumb key! Ob, turn it back to its original position and then restart!* A carload of college kids who've stopped in the next lane is laughing at you. "Hey, Delbert Dumb! You want us to lift your car out of the road for you?" Finally, the engine starts. *Back up! Back up! Where's the reverse? Where's the stupid reverse?* The college kids are howling. Finally, you begin to back up, but by this time your light has turned green, and the drivers behind begin honking at you to move it. This time you move forward without incident and heave a sigh of relief that the nightmare is over.

What happened? Our old friend "spontaneous recovery" interfered with your new habit patterns. Your old habit pattern of depressing the brake with the right foot while resting the left foot on the floor took over without your conscious awareness, and when your car began to jerk, panic hit the "delete" button on your new learning. Escaping from the traumatic intersection has enabled you to recall your new learning, and you bring it back on-line. Your emotions, however, are still elevated a few points on the humiliation scale.

The Application: Walking in the Spirit or After the Flesh?

Let's apply this lengthy example to walking in the Spirit (allowing the Holy Spirit to express Christ's life through you and thinking of yourself according to your identity in Christ). The habit patterns for driving your automatic transmission represent your old ways, or "flesh" as the Bible calls them (see Philippians 3:3-7), which you developed by living independently; your new patterns are those for trusting Christ as life and your identity in Him and are represented by driving the VW. As you trust Christ as life, some of your old patterns may still be effective and will be accessed by the Spirit of Christ as He expresses life through you. For example, good personal hygiene, diligence, ethical behavior, etc. Godly stuff. You have other "flesh patterns," however, that are self-serving, self-debasing, or otherwise un-Christlike. These, of course, will be accessed by the power of sin as it tempts you to take over and live independently again. You will be engaged in a moment-by-moment battle within the mind for the rest of your tenure on earth: "For the flesh sets its desire against the Spirit, and the Spirit against the flesh; for these are in opposition to one another, so that you may not do the things that you [*wish*]" (Galatians 5:17). This is a battle which can be consistently won for you only by the Holy Spirit of Christ. "But I say, walk by the Spirit, and you will not carry out the desire of the flesh" (Galatians 5:16). The trick is to *act like* you are totally dependent upon the Holy Spirit to overcome the flesh for you. It's sort of like playing Lone Ranger and Tonto when you were a kid. You *acted like* Tonto. Well, you are to just *act like* Christ is expressing His life through you, by faith. Don't let the power of sin convince your mind that you're being a phony. Remember the definition of a hypocrite. You're simply *acting like* something is true that *is* true!

Building Sanctified Behavior Patterns

Hebrews 5:14 says, "Solid food is for the mature, who because of *practice* have their senses *trained* to discern good and evil." Once your spiritual eyes have been opened by the Holy Spirit to understand the powerful truth of your identity in Christ, you're going to be surprised to discover that many verses in the Bible (Manufacturer's Handbook) have taken on new meaning for you. Certain verses, and even entire passages, which you've either misinterpreted or passed over without understanding will be interpreted in an exciting new way—a grace-filled way, a liberating way. This is going to require some adjustment; it's going to require building sanctified-behavior habit patterns.

Notice the two words I've emphasized in Hebrews 5:14 above: *practice* and *trained*. In the VW example, through diligent *practice* you had *retrained* your senses to drive the car successfully until the panic episode. Research indicates that it takes about six weeks to develop a habit. You, however, have spent your entire lifetime grooming your flesh— your independent habit patterns for living on earth. Now the Father is giving you the opportunity to allow Christ to overcome your old flesh patterns of thinking, feeling, and acting by expressing His life through you. You are going to learn that "the law of the Spirit of life in Christ Jesus has set you free from the *law of sin*" (Romans 8:2). That's one reason

194

God hasn't beamed you up. Christ did the big part of the job by crucifying you as who you *were* and then rebirthing you as who you *are* in Him. You have been changed from a sinner-man to a godly, righteous saint. Wow—talk about a new beginning! Operating in this truth (practicing) will give you a tremendous leg up on overcoming your flesh.

So, your problem now is, how will you "life out" this new identity? How do you propose to bring it on-line? God poses this same question: "This is the only thing I want to find out from you: did you receive the [Holy] Spirit by the works of the Law [self-effort], or by hearing with faith?"

You respond: "I simply received Him by faith, Lord."

Then He asks, "Are you foolish? Having *begun* by the [Holy] Spirit, are you now being *perfected* by the flesh?" (Galatians 3:2-3). In other words, since you got saved by putting your faith in Christ alone, why would you try to "life out" your new identity by putting your faith in yourself? You were changed from a sinner to a saint at salvation, strictly by faith in Christ's work for you. Don't fall into the trap that the power of sin has laid. Why cast your faith in Christ aside and try to live as an independent-of-God saint, just like you once lived as an independent-of-God sinner? Let me illustrate.

Practicing in the Parking Lot

Sally attends a "Victorious Christian Living" seminar that Anabel and I teach and learns about her true identity in Christ, is deeply touched by the Holy Spirit, and prays to make this a reality in her daily walk. At last, she has discovered the missing ingredient in her powerless life. She claims that Christ is her life. She is unhappily married to George, a difficult Christian man to live with, but she's filled with new hope. *She* no longer has to live with George, but *Christ* will live with George *through* her, *for* her. She can't wait to try this new way of living a sanctified life. George is away on business and will be home in two days. Boy, will he be surprised when he sees the change in her!

For the next two days Sally goes about her daily routine: arising at 6:00 A.M., showering, making up her face, fixing her hair, dressing, making breakfast, getting the kids up and off to school, running the taxi service to Little League and piano lessons, dealing with the plumber, all the while thinking how surprised George will be when she tells him of her newfound secrets of the sanctified Christian life.

Finally, George arrives from the airport to find that seven-year-old Anthony's bike is blocking the garage door. "How many times do I have to tell that sorry excuse for a son that he's *never* to leave his bike in front of the garage door!" George angrily shouts to himself in the car. "As hard as I work for this family, spending time on the road, while Sally and the kids get to live a life of ease at home!" He storms out of the car, *flings* the bike into the yard, gets back into the car, *slams* the door, and pulls into the garage. Sally, having heard the garage door open, rushes out into the garage, ready to let Jesus live through her.

"Hi, Honey!" she coos.

"Don't give me that 'Hi, Honey' stuff! How many times do I have to tell you to teach *your* son that our driveway is not a public parking lot! Where is he? Tell 'im to get into the house right now! I'm gonna teach that kid a lesson he'll not forget! It looks like you could manage the *simple* details of being a housewife while I'm away slaving for the family! Do *I* have to do *everything* around here?"

"You idiot! You blithering *idiot*!" Sally screams. "You fly in from having spent four days in Atlanta staying in a cushy hotel, eating at fine restaurants, all at company expense, while I slave at home taking care of *your* kids, and you have the gall to charge in here yelling at me! Yelling at *me!* You imbecile! Why don't you just back your car out of here and go back to your precious Atlanta! In fact, why don't you just keep on backing clear out of our lives!" And she slams the door dashes through the kitchen into the bedroom, slams the door, and throws herself across the bed sobbing.

"God, why did You let me down?" she screams through her wracking sobs. "Nothing's changed! Jesus, You abandoned me! I trusted You! Why didn't You do *Your* part?"

What in the world went wrong with Sally's new plan? Why didn't Christ come through for her? A better question is, Why didn't Sally *let* Christ handle this situation through her as she had planned? Did George's tirade (or Sally's) scare Christ so badly that He vacated the premises? In light of the learning process with the new VW, do you see why Sally crashed and burned? *She chose the worst possible situation (George's homecoming)—potentially the most stressful episode of her week—to begin trying to let Jesus live through her.* She tried to "drive her new VW" on the freeway during rush hour without a lick of practice or studying the Manufacturer's Handbook (God's statements concerning her identity in Christ and Christ as life through her). Where is the vacant parking lot in Sally's life? I'll tell you where: getting out of bed, taking a shower, making up her face, fixing her hair, deciding what to wear today, fixing breakfast, working on the new blouse she's making for her daughter, etc. Yes! Precisely! Christ is not her life just when George drives up. Christ is her life, *period!* God said so. "For you have died and *your life is hidden with Christ in God.* When Christ, *who is our life*, is revealed, then you also will be revealed with Him in glory" (Colossians 3:3-4). She can't operate on cruise control during the *easy* details of her life, which she has always handled *independently* (sinning), and wait to bring Christ on-line when the tornadoes hit. She is to *practice* the reality of Christ within her as her very life, moment by moment. As she does so, she will build up new patterns of intimacy with God Himself. Here's the way she must develop her new *modus operandi* for facing life:

— Jesus, it's really neat to know that I'm *never* alone, that *You* are washing my face right now—the very face which You tenderly fashioned 35 years ago. Why, without You, I can't even wash my face. You said so in John 15:5: "Apart from Me you can do nothing." Thank You, Sir. It's so wonderful to work together with You like this. I never knew that You wanted to be involved in the menial things in my life, but I should have seen that branches must totally depend upon the life of the vine. A branch withers and dies unless it abides in the vine; it's cut off from its life. You're the Vine, I'm the branch. My goodness, things are really going to be different!

Let's see, what lipstick will we use today? Yes, that's good. We'll use the pale pink. George likes that. He's basically a good man, Jesus. He's just under so much stress in his work, and he often spews it all out on his family. You and I know that he doesn't *want* to act that way, but he doesn't know about letting You live through him. Thank You that You are hard at work on him like You said in Your Love Letter to us: "So then, my beloved ... work out your salvation with fear and trembling; for it is *God* who is at work *in you*, both to will and to work for *His* good pleasure" (Philippians 2:12-13). Ah! I just saw what that "work out your salvation" phrase means! It doesn't mean that I am to work *for* my salvation, but that I must trust in You to complete the work which You began in me (Philippians 1:6) as I live in intimate union with You. You're speaking of *practicing* sanctified behavior here! How wonderful! That was *You* who showed me that, wasn't it? All this time I've been trying to figure that phrase out on my own. Oops, the eyebrow pencil slipped a bit there, Lord. Let's lick a finger and rub it off. There. Now let's redo it. That's better.

Relationship, Not Independence

/ Yes! Absolutely! That's the kind of relationship that the God of the universe longs for with *you*, my sister, my brother (except for the eyebrow pencil, guys). You say, "Bill, get real!" That's exactly what I'm doing. Reality is that God never intended that any person live an *independent* life. Personal independence is the devil's take on life! That's what the original sin was, remember? God re-creates us in Christ to enjoy a vital, intimate relationship with us as individuals, and for the entire church, Christ's body, to live in harmonious, intimate relationship with one another as well. He calls it being "in union" with Him, or "abiding" in Christ. Today we might call it *bonding.* Hudson Taylor points out that when you *abide* with someone, you do such things as eat with them, fellowship with them, discuss the events of the day with them, become well-acquainted with them and their family members, learn their way of life, etc.[1] Independence, separation, self-reliance, self-confidence, self-sufficiency, personal pride—these are abominable sins to the One who created us for intimate, transparent *relationship.* Those characteristics which are so revered by the world represent the very opposite of what and who God is. Such fleshly characteristics cause people to avoid transparent relationships, fearing vulnerability. God sacrificed His only Son in order to build His forever family of loving, obedient, warmhearted, altruistic, gentle, courageous, merciful, generous, dependable, faithful, patient, unselfish, pure-hearted, transparent new creations in Christ who are full of hope for today and the future. And those characteristics are the core, the basic ingredients, of your true identity! Over your pilgrimage on earth, it's possible (indeed, *normal*) for you to develop into a mature version of these by letting Christ manifest them through you. This is building Christian *character!*

Let me illustrate your identity this way: A squirrel buries a pecan, and in time a pecan sprout appears. As this sprout becomes two inches thick, four inches thick, ten inches thick, does it get pecanier and pecanier? Of course not; once a pecan, always a pecan. *It doesn't undergo a change in its identity*—birth determined that. It simply becomes an increasingly more mature pecan tree until the Lord calls it home to pecan-tree heaven. The metaphor holds a truth for you in your sanctified growth process. As you *set your mind* on your true identity in Christ, and as you *act like* Christ is expressing His life through you to accomplish His will on earth, can you become *more* righteous than righteous? *More* forgiven than forgiven? *More* accepted by God than accepted? *Holier* than holy? *Better seated* in the heavenlies than seated in the heavenlies? Absurd. You can't get *more* of any of those awesome characteristics. First John 4:17 says, "As [Christ] is, *so also are we* in this world"; 1 Corinthians 3:17 says, "For the temple of God is holy, and *that is what you are*." Your spiritual nature is Christlike. You are holy! "For *in Him* all the fullness of Deity dwells in bodily form, and *in Him you have been made complete*" (Colossians 2:9-10). You are complete! How can you improve on perfect? That is not to say you are a *perfectly finished* product in Christ, but that you are a *perfectly made* product. As such, you have the wonderful opportunity to cooperate with Christ to let Him express His holy life through you as opposed to offering your "members ... to [the power of] sin as instruments of unrighteousness" (Romans 6:13).

Spiritual Myopia

— The glorious characteristics which, taken together, describe the essence of your identity absolutely *cannot grow* in any Christian who is living *his own* life, striving to *become* the very thing that he already is. Did you comprehend that? There is no such thing as sanctified flesh. Such a person is failing to *practice* living as if God tells the truth about our identity in Christ. For years, all of what I deemed to be "growth" I attained by trusting in my own effort, my own personhood. Although I was sincere, it was mere fleshly effort, which will never be declared a righteous work (a sanctified product) by God (Isaiah 64:6). Insofar as the *power* to live life goes, I operated like the Old Testament Jew. I lived by the strength of my own personality, calling upon God to "help me" when I needed a boost. My experience was a constant struggle rather than the "rest" or "easy yoke" Jesus Christ speaks of, because I never tapped into the powerful Life within my spirit: the Holy Spirit of Christ.

The Christian who penned most of the portions of the New Testament that teach our identity in Christ said, "The things you have learned and received and heard and seen in me, *practice* these things; and the God of peace shall be with you" (Philippians 4:9). Paul is endorsing his sanctified *method* here, gang: Christ as life through him. He's certainly not bragging on himself.

God says in Hebrews 5:13, "For everyone who partakes only of milk *is not accustomed to* the word of [our] righteousness [in Christ], for *he is a babe.*" Christians *are already righteous.* He says that those who deny "the word of [their own] righteousness" remain "a babe"—spiritually immature. Then He reiterates this in verse 14 saying, "But solid food is for the mature, who because of *practice* [at building new, sanctified habit patterns] have their senses *trained* to discern good and evil." Christians who know they are righteous become increasingly skilled at recognizing which of the thoughts they experience are from the power of sin.

He goes ahead to say, "Therefore leaving the *elementary* teaching about the Christ, let us press on to maturity, not laying again [and again, and again, Sunday after Sunday] a foundation of repentance from dead works and of faith toward God" (Hebrews 6:1). God says that Christians must *leave* the elementary truths of the gospel and press on to *plumb the depths of all that our Savior accomplished for us at Calvary if we are to mature in the faith.* Although knowing the "elementary" truth that through faith in Christ we're on our way to heaven is a blessing from God, we must know how to place our same faith in this same Christ for further marvelous benefits that our Father has provided. Don't let the power of sin tell your mind that I am minimizing Jesus Christ's saving work on the cross. I am not guilty of that! I'm saying that the Christian who camps on the *one blessed truth* of our promised heaven to the degree that he never looks beyond it is like a child who is so enamored by the first birthday gift he opens that he never opens the rest of them. He is like a Boy Scout who receives his new Scout knife, but only opens one of the blades. He's like a man with a new car who polishes it daily but doesn't know that its engine will spare him from walking. He's like a man with a chain saw who laboriously saws logs without starting it.

God wishes every Christian *embraced* his identity in Christ, and *lifed it out.* Since the Father has extended His hand of grace much more through Christ than most of us realized at salvation, is it a noble thing to claim that we can "get by without studying out that 'nonsense' about our identity in Christ—just knowing that we're heaven-bound is all we need to know"? God forbid! That's not a noble posture; it's being presumptuous, independent, and disobedient. No instructed Christian would deliberately *choose* to remain in such a position. Such a Christian is deceived—blinded by Satan. Facing life with the wrong view of one's spiritual identity leaves the Christian severely shorthanded to fight the battles of earth. He is self-reliant much of the time, which, in my opinion, explains why we see such devastation among our ranks in the pew, pulpit, parsonage, and seminary. Such a Christian has left himself wide open to Satan's demands that God allow him to "sift him like wheat," which God will permit Satan to do at times (Luke 22:31; Job 1:10-12). Although no believer experiences all of the grace that God has for us on earth, Christians who reject the truth of our identity in Christ are operating with less grace than those who embrace it, and this is so unnecessary. Remember: Faith is simply *acting like* God tells the truth. Rejecting your identity in Christ is unbelief.

11 STOP ASKING HIM
TO FORGIVE THEM

— AFTER READING SUCH A TITLE, some of you may be ready
to run me through the magnetic-imaging heresy scanner! *Let's
have a book-burnin'!* I've got a better idea. Let's compare
our human "religious" view on forgiveness with God's Word.

You've doubtless heard people pray like this: "And Lord,
we ask You to forgive us of all our sins." But hold it. We tell
lost folks—and correctly so—that they can be forgiven of all
their sins through Jesus Christ. This being true, why do
Christians ask for God's forgiveness? Do they not believe
that they are forgiven? Some Christians sporting the bumper
sticker "Christians are not perfect, just forgiven" will ask
thousands of times during their earthwalk for God to do
what their sticker claims He has already done. If they *believe*
they're forgiven, then why do they ask for it repeatedly?

We would consider a man who had 500 dollars in sav-
ings needlessly insecure if he went to the bank daily and
asked to see his money. We would say, "You need to have
faith in your bank, guy. You must be 'persuaded that it is
able to keep that which you have committed unto it against
that day' when you wish to make a withdrawal." Wouldn't
you think that God would have a similar attitude toward the
Christian who keeps asking for something which the Bible
says he already has? Such a Christian is treating God as if He
doles out forgiveness on a piecemeal basis, like humans do.
Mr. A sins against Mr. B; B's offended; A asks B to forgive
him; B grants the forgiveness; then the relationship is OK so

long as Mr. A doesn't keep sinning against Mr. B. If, however, A continues to commit the same sin or new kinds of sins against Mr. B, most humans would write him off. Consequently, our emotions have been conditioned to *feel* like God operates the same way. I've counseled many people who *feel* like God is angry with them and "will not forgive them." But, folks, faith appeals to our *mind* to believe that *God has a different method of forgiving us.*

Let's use the helicopter illustration to help us here.

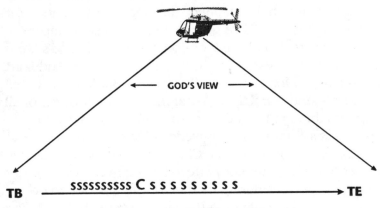

Figure 11A

This represents *my* time line. "TB" is its beginning, and "TE" its ending. The lower case *s* represents sins committed prior to my salvation at *C* (for *Christian*). When I came to Christ in faith, I was shown in the Bible that I was forgiven of all my sins, so all of the *s*'s to the left of *C* were wiped out. It was then explained to me that each time I sinned, I was to ask God to forgive me, and He would according to 1 John 1:9: "If we confess our sins, He is faithful and righteous to forgive us our sins and to cleanse us from all unrighteousness." I adopted this practice. Soon I began to struggle with sins of the thought-life. My asking picked up the pace dramatically. No problem; I kept my ledger balanced.

What If I Forget to Ask for Forgiveness?

But then I began to have episodes that threw a wrench into my forgiveness model. We were running late for church. There was the usual last-minute dash to make sure the kids had their offerings and had visited the bathroom, etc. When we were all in the car, Anabel noticed a run in her hose and had to rush back into the house to change. When she returned to the car, I said, "Honey, it looks like you could check such things *before* you get to the car!"

"Well, if *you'd* help me more with the kids instead of reading the sports page, maybe I'd have more time to check my hose, *Darling!*"

"I wasn't reading the sports page, *Darling*, I was reading my *Sunday school lesson!*" By the time we got to the church, I had committed 15 sins against Anabel and the kids, because they chimed in on her side. Ask God for forgiveness? I was in no mood! I stuffed it, put on my charming smile, and breezed in to tell everyone what a joy it is to be saved! By the time I cooled off enough to forgive Anabel and ask God, her, and the kids to forgive me, I couldn't for the life of me remember all 15 sins. I could recall that one biggie, but some were gone. So I just raked them into a pile and asked Him to forgive me (Figure 11B).

```
                              sssss
                              sssss
                  C           sssss
TB  ─────────────────────────────────────────▶ TE
```

Figure 11B

I asked a mentor how God deals with our sins that we forget to ask forgiveness for. He explained that God only holds us accountable for the sins that we can remember. An alarm went off in my spirit. As I understood the Bible, God is very uptight about our sins; so much so that He had to sacrifice His only Son so we could be forgiven. There was no way He was going to sweep *any* of my gazillion sins under a celestial rug! Much later when I understood that God sees my entire life-line as present tense (the helicopter view), I *really* had questions about my sins which I had forgotten to ask forgiveness for. So I began to study all of the verses I could find on forgiveness, and much to my delight I saw that God forgave us for *all* of our sins at salvation!

I realize that God doesn't have any problems, but in a way He had a problem with you. He loved you, but He couldn't stand to have you near Him! There were two reasons for this: your identity—sinner, and your performance—sins. So, God and Jesus made it possible for you to correct both problems by grace, through faith in the finished work of Christ. Through salvation you were changed from a sinner to a saint, which solved the first problem. And you were forgiven of all your sins, past, present, and future and given Christ as life, which solved the second problem.

When God looks upon you now, He sees nothing but purity, because through your faith in Christ, He has purged away everything about you that would block you from His holy presence. There are no lowercase *s* letters on your lifeline! Jesus' blood has washed them away. They're not "covered"; they're nonexistent! He says, "I am the one who wipes out your transgressions *for My own sake;* and I will not remember your sins" (Isaiah 43:25). See those italics? God has solved His problem with you, both for you and for *Himself!* He has deleted your sins from His hard drive. You are forgiven of *all your sins,* Christian! Praise God for it and marvel at His awesome grace toward us!

God Has Forgiven Us for All of Our Sins

Here are a few verses where God states that we are totally forgiven:

As far as the east is from the west, So far has He removed our transgressions from us (Psalm 103:12).

You have cast *all* my sins behind Your back (Isaiah 38:17).

I have wiped out your transgressions like a thick cloud, and your sins like a heavy mist (Isaiah 44:22).

I will forgive their iniquity, and their sin I will remember no more (Jeremiah 31:34).

He will again have compassion on us; He will tread our iniquities under foot. Yes, You will cast *all* their sins into the depths of the sea (Micah 7:19).

There is therefore *now* no condemnation for those who are in Christ Jesus (Romans 8:1).

Who will bring a charge against God's elect? God is the one who justifies; who is the one who condemns?... Who shall separate us from the love of Christ? Shall tribulation, or distress, or persecution, or famine, or nakedness, or peril, or sword?...For I am convinced that neither death, nor life, nor angels, nor principalities, nor things present, nor things to come, nor powers, nor height, nor depth, nor any other created thing, shall be able to separate us from the love of God, which is in Christ Jesus our Lord (Romans 8:33-35, 38-39).

You were washed . . . sanctified . . . justified (1 Corinthians 6:11).

. . . forgiving each other, just as God in Christ also *has forgiven* you (Ephesians 4:32).

In [Christ] we *have* . . . the forgiveness of sins. . . . He has now reconciled you in His fleshly body through death, in order to present you before Him holy and blameless and beyond reproach (Colossians 1:14,22).

When you were dead in your transgressions and the uncircumcision of your flesh, He made you alive

together with Him, *having forgiven* us all our transgressions, *having canceled out* the certificate of debt
consisting of decrees against us and which was hostile
to us; and He has *taken it out* of the way, having
nailed it to the cross (Colossians 2:13-14).

After saying, "Sacrifices and offerings and whole burnt
offerings and sacrifices for sin You have not desired,
nor have You taken pleasure in them" . . . then [Jesus]
said, "Behold, I have come to do Your will." He takes
away the first in order to establish the second. By this
will we *have been sanctified* through the offering of
the body of Jesus Christ once for all. . . . "And their
sins and their lawless deeds I will *remember no more*"
(Hebrews 10:8-10,14,17).

I am writing to you, little children, because your sins
are forgiven you for His name's sake (1 John 2:12).

Forgiveness Doctrine Must Not Be Based Upon the Gospels

Admittedly, there are a few verses which can foster insecurity about your forgiveness. But the overwhelming majority of such verses are *prior to Jesus solving your problem at
the cross*. And remember, this includes the vast majority of
Matthew, Mark, Luke, and John. Did you get that? Some Christians base their forgiveness doctrine on pre-cross teaching,
often from the Gospels. Don't study the Gospels to glean
verses on forgiveness due to the Law there. For example,
let's look at a story Jesus told Peter when Peter asked Him
how many times he must forgive a person (Matthew 18:21).
The story was about a slave who was forgiven a huge debt
by his master, but who then threw his own debtor into
prison because he could not pay.

> Then summoning him, his lord said to him, "You
> wicked slave, I forgave you all that debt because you
> entreated me. Should you not also have had mercy on

your fellow slave, even as I had mercy on you?" And
his lord, moved with anger, handed him over to the
torturers until he should repay all that was owed him.
"So shall my heavenly Father also do to you, if each
of you does not forgive his brother from your heart"
(Matthew 18:32-35).

Folks, that hard teaching on forgiveness was presented
to all who had yet to be regenerated (including Peter), with
the motive of whetting their appetite for a Savior. All within
earshot must have gone away terrified at the thought of such
a horrible fate! Jesus dealt out some tough teaching with a
mega-tender motive: to bring them to Himself as their Savior.
God forbid that you would misinterpret me as being critical
of His teaching. It was perfect teaching for that time to accomplish a perfect end—salvation, but you will not find
such teaching on the grace side of the cross. Does the grace
of God through Christ throw Christians to "the torturers"
until we forgive our brother from the heart? I refer you to
God's Word for the answer: "Be kind to one another, tender-
hearted, *forgiving each other,* just as God in Christ also *has
forgiven you*" (Ephesians 4:32). We must primarily base our
forgiveness doctrine on what God's Word says about our
forgiveness *after* the cross.

Hebrews 5:12 says, "For though by this time you ought
to be teachers, you have need *again* for someone to teach
you the *elementary principles* of the oracles of God, and you
have come to need milk and not solid food." Paraphrasing
this verse as it applies to God's forgiveness: "You need to
repeat the basic course on forgiveness. It's covered in My
Love Letter to you, but somehow you didn't understand.
Forgiveness is a done deal. Let's settle this issue so we can
move on toward enjoying sweet communion as I conform
you to the image of Christ."

Forgiveness Doctrine Must Not Be Based upon Human Logic

We jump the tracks concerning God's forgiveness if we depend on human logic. Humans, as you know, require that an offender ask to be forgiven for each offense. In addition to this, they do not hold a person guilty until an evil deed is actually committed.

Adopting *God's method* for forgiveness is crucial to experiencing "the peace which passes [human] understanding." How frequently do you hear someone pray, "Thank You that I stand before You a completely forgiven man. Thank You, that I am as spotless as the driven snow"? Such words are rare, but they thrill the heart of God because they demonstrate *faith* that this man believes God, who says we are forgiven in Christ (Colossians 2:13-14). There is no way a Christian who feels like God is increasingly upset with him is going to cozy up to Him. To feel secure in His forgiveness, we *must* believe that He does not hold one single sin against us. It's impossible for a Christian to ask God's forgiveness for a besetting sin the umpteenth time, then snuggle up to Him. He will *feel* like God's patience is being stretched to the limit. (Note: I am not addressing the person here who is mocking God's patience by licentious living, but the true believer who seeks God with a sincere heart.)

Because our heavenly Father is omniscient, He sees all the sins of the lost folks past, present, and future. Therefore, His method of forgiving *has to* differ from that of time-bound humans. In order to obliterate the barrier between us and Himself, He must forgive us of all our sins—past, present, and future. Had He not done so, He would continually see us with egg on our faces!

The Key to God's View of Forgiveness Is in His Helicopter

The thought comes: *Wrong. Can't be right. God can't forgive future sins. I've always heard that.* Well, this agrees with human logic, but let's see if it agrees with biblical revelation. Tell me again, how many of your sins did Jesus bear on the cross 2000 years ago? *All of them.* And how many of your sins had you committed 2000 years ago? *None of them. All of your sins were future sins.* From the helicopter view in Figure 11A, there are no yesterdays or tomorrows. There is only the present. There is no such thing as "future" sins to God. That's how all of our sins were placed on the lovely, innocent Jesus 2000 years ago. *God dealt with your sins while every one of your sins were future sins! You are forgiven of all your sins!*

How About 1 John 1:9

— There are *no* verses *after the cross* that command *Christians* to ask for God's forgiveness. Most, however, would cite 1 John 1:9 as the exception: "If we confess our sins, He is faithful and righteous to forgive us our sins and to cleanse us from all unrighteousness." But, folks, we are already cleansed from all unrighteousness; we *are righteous* in Christ (2 Corinthians 5:21). If we haven't been cleansed, we're in a heap of trouble, because there is no other Savior who can do the job. So how do we explain this verse?

The heresy of Gnosticism was a problem when John penned this letter to the churches around Ephesus. Gnostics held that all matter was evil; therefore, Christ could not have inhabited a human body. They viewed Him as a phantom. They believed that it was *not sinful*, but normal and good for ethereal, mental, pious, religious meditation plus sensual hedonism to be practiced simultaneously. John's letter contrasts true believers (wheat) against the Gnostics (tares) 31 times! Gnostics were not born again, and I believe you will see by a careful study of 1 John 1:1-10 that John is likely addressing this problem and clarifying his position on Gnosticism to the churches:

> If we say that we have fellowship with Him and yet
> walk in the darkness, we lie ... but if we walk in the

211

> light ... the blood of Jesus His Son cleanses us from
> all sin. If we say that we have no sin, we are
> deceiving ourselves, and the truth is not in us. If we
> confess our sins, He is faithful and righteous to forgive
> us our sins and to cleanse us from all unrighteous-
> ness. If we say that we have not sinned, we make
> Him a liar, and His word is not in us (1 John 1:6-10).

I believe that he is appealing to the Gnostic tares among the wheat to get saved. If, however, you disagree with this, you still must deal with the fact that John says to Christians, "your sins *are forgiven*" (1 John 2:12). Also, the word *confess* in 1 John 1:9 does not mean "ask for God's forgiveness;" it means "agree with God" (about the evil of any sins you commit). We must get our sins up on the table and let the light of day shine on them *for our own benefit*. Let me illustrate that.

Bubbles

When Anabel and I were first married, we had an old English bulldog named Bubbles. Anabel and I both taught school, and we would leave Bubbles in the house while we were away. Our homecoming was a grand reunion of jumping, whining, wiggling with joy, etc. (Bubbles, that is, not Anabel). The second order of business was to let Bub out the back door to water the grass.

On a couple of occasions when we came home, Bub didn't meet us at the door. We called for her. No Bub. We searched. No Bub. Then I looked under the bed. There was Bub. She appeared to be holding her breath with fear. I couldn't get her to come out. Then Anabel discovered what her problem was. There was a huge puddle by the kitchen door where Bub's bladder warranty had expired.

I play the role of God in this story, and Bubbles is the Christian. She could not understand that, since I knew her heart was pure, I had given her a blanket forgiveness if she had an accident on the kitchen floor. I knew that her heart did not think, *Oh boy!* as soon as we had left for school, and then she proceeded to trash the house and mark all the furniture. But *she did not know* she was forgiven. She felt guilty that she had done wrong, and "her sin had separated her from her god." She hid under the bed from her god. Folks, I wasn't mad at her. Her "sin" had not produced anger in me. I had not turned my back on her. I was not standing with my arms folded across my chest scowling at her. I loved her. I had already settled such problems ahead of time. But she did not understand this.

You, on the other hand, are not a dumb animal. You have the capability—indeed, you are accountable—to seek the truth from God about His method of forgiveness. ("My people are destroyed for *lack of knowledge*"—Hosea 4:6). "Bill, are you telling me that I am free to sin all I want to?" Tell me, how much do you want to? You don't *want* to! You're tempted by sin, but you don't want to do it. Why wouldn't you? *Because you have His laws written on your godly heart, that's why!* You desire to please your God. Now do you understand why God has taken you out from under the Law? What difference will this make in the way you live? May I make a suggestion? Why not begin by coming out from under the bed?

Your Heart Is Not Set on Sin

We are to base our doctrine of forgiveness upon passages like Colossians 2:13-14: "He made you alive together with Him, *having forgiven* us *all* our transgressions, having canceled out the certificate of debt consisting of decrees against us and which was hostile to us; and He has taken it out of the way, having nailed it to the cross." The "certificate of debt" was a contractual agreement between a debtor and a creditor. Such certificates were used in matters of commerce, law, etc., in that day. When a debtor paid his debt, the Greek word *tetelestai* ("paid in full") was written on the certificate of debt, then it was signed by the creditor and returned to the "payer" as his receipt. Similarly, when a man had been jailed, a certificate of debt upon which the charges against him were written was nailed to his cell door. Upon his release the word *tetelestai* was affixed to the certificate, and it was signed by the chief magistrate. It was then given to the man. So long as he had this in his possession he could never again be tried and convicted for those particular crimes. His debt to society had been paid.

John 19:30 records Jesus' final words on the cross: "... He said, 'It is finished!' And He ... gave up His spirit." Do you know what Greek word has been translated "It is finished" here? *Tetelestai!* Oh, my brother, my sister, how profound! How awesome! Preserve this moment—make it a special happening. Get a pen and a piece of paper. Write this heading on the paper: Certificate of Debt. Now write a number across the center of the paper in one-inch script indicating the estimated number of sins you will have committed in your entire life on earth (as in 10,000,000). Now take a red felt pen and in large block letters write the word TETELESTAI, cutting diagonally across that number from lower left toward upper right. Then at the bottom of the sheet write, "Dictated personally, but signed for Him in His absence," and then sign the name *Jesus*. Fold the letter and place it in an envelope for safekeeping. Anytime someone or the power of sin tries to convince you that you have not been forgiven of *all your sins*, take out that signed certificate of debt and stare at it for a minute or so. Then have a praise and adoration session.

So, does confession have its place for Christians? I believe it does (James 5:16). What are you to do when the Holy Spirit convicts you that you have sinned? Respond quickly and own up to it lest you hide under the bed!

Lord, I sinned (confession). I'm truly sorry (repentance). I don't want to live like that (godly sorrow). I wish I could be more consistent in my obedience (godly desire). Thank You, that based upon Your Word, not upon how I *feel*, I am a forgiven saint, that You're not mad at me, that You took out all of Your anger on Jesus. Once again, Lord Jesus, I "present myself to You as a living and holy sacrifice" so You can live Your life through me.

Then *act like* the forgiven saint that you are.

Pick a Son—Evidence of God's Forgiving Heart

God spoke to David through the prophet Samuel: "I will raise up your descendant after you, who will come forth from you, and I will establish his kingdom. He shall build a house for My name, and I will establish the throne of his kingdom forever" (2 Samuel 7:12-13). Of course, this spoke of David's son Solomon, who built the Temple of stone, but its deeper meaning references Jesus Christ, who gave birth to new men and women in Christ—the *spiritual* temple made without hands. One of Jesus' names was "son of David" (Matthew 1:1).

Let's say that you were living back in the day of King David, and God came to you to pose this question: "As you know, I intend to bring My only Son out of the lineage of King David. My problem is that David has 8 wives and 19 sons. I want you to name the wife whose son I should select." Seven of David's wives are legitimate. The eighth is the wife David stole after murdering her husband, Uriah, to cover up his affair with her by which he had gotten her pregnant. David had 18 sons via his legitimate wives, plus Solomon, his son by Bathsheba, Uriah's wife.

Although you might struggle to choose the purest and godliest of 18 of these sons, you would know to eliminate number 19—Solomon. There is no way that anyone would

215

have the effrontery to choose *Solomon!* No one but God, that is. *God chose him!* Why would He do this? I believe God chose Solomon just for *your* sake, if you are one of those folks who think you're too sinful to come under God's umbrella of forgiveness. What a God!

The Lion of the Tribe of Judah

Jesus is from the tribe of Judah (Hebrews 7:14; Revelation 5:5). Judah had a son named Er, whose wife was Tamar. Er died, and Judah violated the law by failing to give her to any of his other sons so that she might produce sons (Deuteronomy 25:5). Tamar subsequently disguised herself as a prostitute and opened for business along the road which Judah was to travel. When he saw her, he propositioned her, not recognizing her. He promised her a kid goat as payment, but as the animal was not with him, he gave her his seal ring, cord, and staff as surety. Later he dispatched his friend to take the kid to her and retrieve his surety, but she had discarded her disguise and gone home. When it became obvious that she was pregnant, it was reported to Judah and he gave orders to burn her alive. As they were taking her away, she sent the surety goods to Judah with the message, "I am with child by the man to whom these things belong." Judah repented and withdrew his order. She named her son Perez.

— Now Judah had many sons. Had you been asked by God to identify Judah's son through whom He should ultimately bring forth His own Son, Jesus, which son would you avoid choosing at all cost? Perez, of course. But, once again, guess who God chose—Perez (Matthew 1:3; Luke 3:33)! Why would He do such a thing? To prove His grace, forgiveness, and love to you ... that your sins are not so heinous that the blood of Jesus cannot wash them away and change you into a beautiful person. He's God—He gets to make the rules. He can do anything He wants to do.

Rahab was a common prostitute. She sold her body to pay the bills. Her kids grew up and produced families of their own. Centuries later a boy was born out of her lineage. His name was Jesus of Nazareth (Matthew 1:5). Why would God do such a thing? He wants you to know that you're not too soiled to be treasured and loved. His grace will wash away your sins in the blood of Jesus and purify you now and for all eternity. Ask Rahab.

How to Forgive Others the Easy Way

Mary had an affair. Oh, she didn't mean to. And afterward she regretted it with all her heart, but she had done it, she had fallen. Her husband, Bob, was busy with his profession. Although he provided well for his family, he was gone a lot, and she was lonely. All she had meant to do was just talk. Bob simply wasn't around enough. He had brought an out-of-town business associate home to spend the night. Sam just couldn't say enough nice things to Mary, and she found herself enjoying every minute of his attention. He began to phone her during the daytime when he was in town and Bob was at the office. Mary and Sam just seemed to hit it off. She found herself anxiously anticipating his calls. Then he asked her to meet him for lunch. It was an innocent thing, so she did. They had lunch together several times over a period of months. She began to anticipate these meetings. What fun he was! One thing led to another, until one day Mary agreed to meet Sam at a motel dining room. That's when it happened. When she got home and looked herself in the eye in her mirror, she was disgusted at what she saw. She hated herself and hated Sam. She wanted to blame Bob, but she knew that she was accountable. She had failed Bob, herself, and God. She knew she was forgiven by God, but how could she ever forgive herself? She *had* to come clean with Bob. Could he *ever* forgive her?

Of course, it rocked Bob to his shoe soles when Mary confessed her unfaithfulness. He not only struggled with what Mary had done, but the Holy Spirit had convicted him that *he* was not entirely innocent. Without Mary having said so, he understood that if he had not been so busy with his work and spent so much time either physically away from home or even *mentally* away at work even though his body was at home, maybe this would not have happened. He realized that he had inadvertently made Mary vulnerable. It was the Adam and Eve story over again, where Adam had apparently gotten so occupied with *his* work that he allowed Eve to become vulnerable to Satan's lie. Why else would she have been out there alone with the devil?

Trusting Christ, the Great Forgiver, to Forgive Through Us

Bob had been practicing trusting Christ to express His life through him in his work, but he had never brought Christ on-line to do so at home. He felt he didn't need to do that. *He* could keep the home fires burning himself. He could handle that on cruise control. Now he realized what a fool he had been. He had let the evil one blindside him. "Lord, I'm sorry. That was so foolish of me. Thank You that I'm forgiven. I'm going to trust You to forgive Mary through me. Jesus, You're the Forgiver who forgives all people. I'm going to trust You to repeat that through me to Mary."

So Bob went to Mary, took her in his arms, and held her—just held her—for about five minutes. Then, by faith, he whispered blessed words of forgiveness to her, *believing that Christ was doing it through him*. Bob did not *feel* forgiving; he simply *chose* to let Christ use him as a vessel of *His* forgiveness to Mary. Once Bob had whispered those words to Mary, he chose to *believe*, by faith, that he had *meant* them. His feeler did not agree with this decision, but he thought, *Rain on you, feeler! I meant every word that I*

said to Mary! When the power of sin stepped up the program of injecting thoughts and imagery of Mary and Sam in
that motel into his mind, Bob thought, *I know where that's
coming from! No! I refuse those thoughts!* And then he set his
mind on *Thank You, Jesus, that You have forgiven Mary
through me! What liberty to know that I don't have to handle
this!*

— That lasted about a minute before the power of sin
cranked up again. Then Bob cranked up his faith engine
again. *Oh, Jesus, this is difficult, but I know that nothing is
impossible with God. Thank You that You are more powerful
than the evil one. Thank You that those doubting thoughts
I'm having are not mine. Thank You for forgiving Mary
through me, for me.* And this lasted two minutes. Folks, Bob
is engaging in spiritual warfare here, but he knows that the
battle is not Bob's. "The battle is the Lord's" (Isaiah 17:47)!
He's going to win! Bob must continue to rebuff these thoughts
with those familiar first-person-singular pronouns for 5 minutes, 10 minutes, 15 minutes, until they ease up. When the
thoughts come back, Bob must bring Christ as life on-line to
overcome them for him again. Finally, Bob will enjoy good,
solid victory over the enemy, and his marriage will be saved.
Do you see the power in this? Do you see the vast difference in this technique as opposed to sucking it up and
trying to fight this battle yourself?

And what about Mary. . . . How did she respond to her
husband's godly behavior? First, she was relieved to know
that God had forgiven her when she had come to Christ ten
years earlier. Now she was so grateful to Him for giving her
a husband who could forgive her for making such a horrible
mistake. *Now,* if she could only forgive *herself!* She absolutely
hated herself for what she had done. Sensing that Mary was
struggling with this, Bob stepped up and became Mary's
loving counselor/confidant.

How to Forgive Yourself the Easy Way

Bob sat down with Mary and explained how she was to surrender her all to Christ to express His forgiving, loving life through her, even to forgive herself. He explained that it was not her responsibility to forgive herself; it was Christ's job, and He had already *done so*. All she needed to do was act like He had, by faith. If God had already forgiven her of all her sins at salvation (and Mary understood this to be true), then He would have no problem reinforcing this within her heart. Bob lovingly and sweetly challenged her that if she refuses to forgive herself when *God Himself* has already done so, then she has higher standards for forgiving herself than *God* has! Mary saw the folly of her position and repented of believing such a lie.

Mary went to a private place and began to pray:

> Thank You, Jesus, my great, forgiving Champion, for forgiving Mary through me. That sounds kind of childish, Lord, but I see the wisdom of it. I don't believe that I could have ever forgiven myself, but by letting You do it for me, I can see a light at the end of the tunnel. Thank You, Jesus, for doing this for me. Thank You for my husband and dear friend, Bob. What a treasure he is to me. Thank You for using him to explain how I am not to look to my feeler to determine if I've really forgiven myself. I'm simply to believe that I have done so by a choice of my free will, trusting that You have done so in Your power. Thank You, Jesus. Thank You.

That lasted about a minute before the power of sin cranked up again. Let the battle begin! "The battle is the Lord's!"

12 THAT THEY HAVE ALL THE FAITH THEY NEED

JIM WAS MILDLY SURPRISED. He realized it had been an unusually cool fall, but he didn't think the temperature had dropped *this* much. He thought, *The color is right. It feels right. The refraction of the light on the surface is right. I believe the ice is ready for skating! Man, oh man! I can hardly wait to glide across the ice and feel that fresh, cold wind in my face. I love the sense of freedom it gives me. Boy, is my wife going to be surprised when I tell her the good news.*

Jim took pride in his skill at assessing whether the ice on his lake was thick enough to support his weight. Although he was anxious to begin the skating season, he had learned that patience is the better part of valor when it comes to being the first one in the county to open the ice-skating season. The lake had been in his family for years, and when his folks died, Jim and his wife had built their home on the hill overlooking its cool, clear waters. He hurried back to the house to change clothes, dug out his skates from the closet, and trotted back down to the pier he had built. He plopped down on the boards, took off his boots, and slipped on the skates. The leather against his feet made him chuckle with anticipation. *As comfortable as an old shoe*, he thought. After tying the laces firmly to give his ankles good support, he walked expertly down to the end of the pier, sat down, took a little hop onto the ice, stood up, and with powerful strokes glided out to circle the perimeter of his own private skating rink. Such exhilaration! To Jim, this was really living!

Without so much as a warning groan, the ice gave way under his weight; off balance, he crashed through headfirst and disappeared beneath the surface. As fate would have it, he had been on the exhale stroke of his breathing rhythm when his body submerged. He choked on a mouth full of the frigid water, and the desperate, strangling cough, along with the weight of his wet clothing and skates, proved too great a handicap. He barely had time for a fleeting last thought, and it was over just that quick.

Why Faith Is Such a Big Deal to God

Sorry to begin this chapter by making your feeler react adversely, but I wanted to use the story to dash some cold water in your face. I wanted you to be wide awake so you won't miss the important point it illustrates. Stay in the right lane, because we're going to leave the freeway at the next exit. The sign over the exit ramp reads "Faith, Don't Leave Earth Without It." We'll stop and analyze Jim's fatal mistake, along with a second ice tale a bit later to help us grasp an imperative rest stop on God's freeway: "Without faith it is impossible to please Him" (Hebrews 11:6).

— Why does God place so much emphasis on our faith? It's because faith gives every person equal opportunity to deduce God's "invisible attributes, His eternal power and divine nature, [which] have been *clearly seen*, being understood *through what has been made* [by Him], so that they are without excuse [if they don't acknowledge Him]"(Romans 1:20). God, speaking through Paul, says about such people, "Even though they knew God [exists], they did not honor Him *as* God [submit to His authority], or *give thanks*; but they became futile in their speculations [about God], and their foolish [hearts were] darkened [unable to comprehend spiritual truth]. *Professing* to be wise, they became fools" (verses 21-22).

Jesus said about His identity, "I am *the* truth." The folks
who retreat from the world and go to the mountains to
"search for truth" could save their money by investigating
the claims of Jesus Christ with a teachable attitude. He's got
a monopoly on truth. Like C. S. Lewis's trilemma: *Jesus is
either a liar, a lunatic, or the Lord that He claimed to be.* He
can't be 99 percent truth and 1 percent questionable, you
see, or He would be a liar or a lunatic. Another C. S. (Lovett)
said that Jesus was *God in an earthsuit.* The person who
refuses to believe that God *is* truth, and thus *tells* the truth,
infers that he sees no difference between God and Satan.
Character *does* matter, gang. God's character is impeccable;
Satan has none. In addition, whereas "it is impossible for
God to lie" (Hebrews 6:18), it is *impossible* for Satan to tell
the truth, because "whenever he speaks a lie, he speaks
from his own nature; for he is a liar, and the father of lies"
(John 8:44). Thus, the man who rejects all or part of the
Bible tacitly indicates that he sees no difference between
God and Satan. While God tenaciously reveals His glory and
grace to man, Satan tenaciously impugns God's integrity.
Academia, the intelligentsia, and the liberal media swallow
the lie—hook, line, and sinker—because they trust in their
own intelligence and seek the respect (acceptance) of the
public and peers.

Although it looks like Satan is ahead on points, the fight
will end by a knockout in the final round, and the Winner
won't have a scratch on Him. Although many human
"judges" haven't discerned it, God has been catching all of
the devil's blows on His gloves. He's just toying with Satan,
carrying the fight to the final round. The fight is fixed, gang.
God has already written the account of round 15. He flips
His adversary into a fiery lake with one word, *Scat* (Revelation 20:1-10)!

Each person has the opportunity to believe this by faith.
God said that there is no other way (Hebrews 11:6). Man

must weigh the evidence, draw the correct conclusion (that God tells nothing but the truth), submit to His authority, and live his life accordingly. Man demonstrates his faith, or lack of it, by the way he lives. Every moment is "show-and-tell" time on earth. We all know folks who talk a good game, but never deliver. God addresses this through James: "Show me *your* faith *without* the works, and I will show you *my* faith *by* my works" (James 2:18). The "proof is in the putting" of action to your words.

A lover longs for a love "object." God deeply desires *your* love. He wants reciprocity. His tender, loving heart is not made of cast iron. If you are indifferent to His courtship, He's not going on about His business thinking, *Well, that's the way the cookie crumbles. There are more fish in the sea than that one.* No! Passionate love is not like that. People die to demonstrate passionate love. That's what *God* did for you—put on an earthsuit and died for you. God created you that He might pour out His *agape* love on you and receive your voluntary love in return. Think about it. This wonderful, intimate relationship with the Creator of the entire universe is available to *you*—His creation. The most loving, most important, most powerful, kindest, most generous, most compassionate Person in the universe—the One who spoke the entirety of creation into existence—*this* Person is madly in love with *you!* He has fixed it so that you will sit with Him on His throne forever and ever and ever.

An important aspect of this relationship is that it showcases God's glorious, altruistic nature in that He does far more giving *to* you than getting *from* you. His grace toward you continually demonstrates that He is worthy of the praise of all creation (see Ephesians 3:10; 2:7). Unbelief of what God has told us in the Bible tacitly accuses Him of being Satan's yokefellow. Saved though I may be and naïve though I may be, I forfeit my ability to please Him unless I choose to believe the entire Bible. Ask yourself how you would feel if *your* fiancée refused to take your love letters seriously.

All the "bad press" God receives, which begins, "How could a loving God . . ." is baloney. The bad things that happen on earth are the result of Satan and his servants rebelling against our wonderful, marvelous, altruistic, merciful, gracious God by declaring independence from His reign. *God* is the One in the white hat who graciously gave us Jesus Christ to save us from the mess *we* created and continue to aggravate. As that famous philosopher Pogo Possum once said, "We have found the enemy, and it is us." If someone refuses to get on board with Jesus, it's not *God's* fault that he reaps destruction from here through eternity. Indeed, He's done everything possible to rescue us from harm's way.

The first chapters of both Romans and 1 Corinthians state that those who opt for puny man's philosophy of the meaning of life and refuse to submit to God, by faith in Christ, are without excuse. We all get one shot at it, gang. They won't get the chance to plead their case: "He who believes in [Christ] is not judged; he who does not believe *has been judged already, because he has not believed* in the name of the only begotten Son of God" (John 3:18).

Do You Need More Faith?

Have you ever been in a situation where you believed that you had to get "more faith" by 7:00 the next morning? Or in the next hour? Or minute? It's impossible, isn't it? Let's get out of the car and sit on that bench to discuss this for a bit. I want to share some insight with you to defuse the devil's accusations that you don't have enough faith to make your Christianity fly. I think I'm not unlike most believers in that I struggled in my pilgrimage to "get more" of this mystical commodity called "faith." Most of us can identify with the dad who poignantly cried out to Jesus on behalf of his ailing son, "I do believe; help my unbelief" (Mark 9:24).

When the doctor announced to Anabel and me in 1963, "Your son is incurably ill and will be hopelessly mentally

225

retarded," we became extremely vulnerable to those who teach that if you just have enough faith, you can have anything you ask from God. She and I spent our share of painful days and nights crying out to God for enough faith to believe Him for the healing of our son, Mason, from Herler's Syndrome—but it didn't happen. Mason's "healing" came when he ejected from his faulty earthsuit in 1972 at age 12. He had lived in virtual solitary confinement in an earthsuit which had a faulty brain which could not process data, but he's OK now. He's been released from that earthsuit. We can hardly wait to see him so we can get to know him as he really is!

Some well-meaning Christians, even leaders, would say that our lack of faith was the critical variable that caused God to withhold His healing grace from our son. They would have us believe that a perfectly healthy son was just a faith away. Try to chin on that bar when the stakes are that high. I want to be kind here. Their advice was intended for our benefit. I do not fault *them*; I just disagree with their doctrine. Let's use the Bible and Jim's experience with the ice to reveal the fallacy of their claim.

Did Jim, the skater, lose his life because of his lack of faith? No, he had *more than adequate* faith. His faith was so strong that he bet his life on it. Not many folks have such faith. He had great faith in *his* ability as a judge, and he had great faith in the *ice's* ability to support his weight. Jim's problem was not a lack of faith; his problem was the fallibility of the *objects* of his faith: 1) *his* ability to judge ice and, 2) the *ice's* ability to support his weight. *He placed greater than average faith in two objects which were unworthy of such faith.*

— Faith is a way of life on planet Earth for both the lost and the saved. We flip switches and believe the light will come on, by faith. We place our faith in restaurant cooks that they will not poison our food. We have faith in the USDA seal of approval on our packaged food products, believing they're fit for our consumption. We place our faith in total strangers, trusting that they will obey the red-light as we sail through on the green. We pump colored liquid into the car's tank, trusting that a station owner whom we do not know is selling gasoline instead of amber water. Oh, we have *lots* of faith; we *continually* walk by faith. Here's something that many of us misunderstand: Faith *never* lets us down; the *objects* of our faith sometimes let us down.

Her Faith Did Not Let Her Down

Some years ago, a university professor was teaching her class the art of rappelling. This sport involves securing a stout rope at the top of a cliff, running it through a system of rings attached to a sturdy harness around your body, and then lowering yourself in a controlled descent to the base of the cliff. The instructor took her class onto the flat roof of a six-story campus building, secured the rope to a large steel grid embedded in the roof, threaded the rope expertly through her harness, stepped onto the parapet, pulled the slack out of the rope, and leaned backward over the eaves. Her technique was letter-perfect. But, to the horror of the class, the grid popped out of the roof, clanged over the edge of the parapet, and the professor plunged six stories to her death.

This is a true account of a woman who had faith in the strength of the climbing rope, faith in her ability to rappel, and faith in the grid's ability to support her controlled descent. The problem did not lie in her lack of faith, but in the fallibility of *one of the objects* of her faith. The anchor to which she entrusted her life was not worthy of her faith. It's imperative that man choose one Anchor on this planet if he hopes for a happy landing: Jesus.

The Object of Your Faith

Neither skater Jim nor the professor needed more faith; their faith was adequate. *They needed more knowledge of the objects of their faith.* Had Jim had more *knowledge* of the ice and the professor more *knowledge* of the grid, they would not have plunged to their deaths. The world says that what you don't know won't hurt you. That's never true in the things of God. He said through His prophet Hosea, "My people are destroyed for lack of knowledge" (4:6). *Knowing* God, the Object of your faith, what He has said about your identity, and how to trust Christ to "life out" that identity through you, by faith, are crucial keys to the peace that passes understanding.

A.W. Tozer said that nothing twists and deforms the soul more than a low or unworthy conception of God, and I believe he was correct.[1] But how can we obtain the truth about God? Well, as we saw in an earlier chapter, He lived in an earthsuit for 33 years—Jesus put a face on God. Hebrews 1:2 says, "In these last days [God] has spoken to us in His Son." Notice again that God did not say *through* His Son, but *in* His Son. Jesus Himself said, "He who has seen Me has seen the Father" (John 14:9). Colossians 2:9 says, "For in Him all the fullness of Deity dwells in bodily form." That's *a-l-l.* In some strange, mystical way beyond our ability to comprehend, the Father and the Holy Spirit indwelt Jesus' earthsuit with the Son, and yet these Two were exterior to it simultaneously. (I don't *understand* this; I'm just explaining it to you!) It follows, then, that if we want to know what God is really like, we must get to know Jesus personally.

Another Ice Story

There's nothing like ice stories to cool you off on a warm day of traveling on the freeway. Here's another one. In the nineteenth century, Sam and his wife, Betsy, lived on the west bank of a wide river on the American frontier. Across its half-mile breadth was a small trading post. There were no bridges, so they crossed the river by rowboat; in winter they traversed it on the ice. As it was not uncommon in that day to welcome overnight travelers, they had recently shared their cabin with one such man who unknowingly had shared something with them in return: a highly contagious disease which resulted in a rapid, painful death for its victims. Three weeks after the traveler's departure, Betsy awakened, feeling ill, and by late afternoon she lay dying. Recognizing the symptoms, Sam knew his wife had only hours to live. The antidote which would cure her was available at the trading post across the river. He cursed his stupidity for not keeping a bottle of it on hand, but times were hard and money scarce.

It was early winter, and the nights were unseasonably cold. But though the river lay frozen, Sam was sure the ice was neither thick enough to support his weight nor thin enough for his boat. But as he loved Betsy dearly, he determined that he would rather die trying to cross the ice to save her life than to live without her. He kissed her fevered brow, fully believing he would not see her again in this life, and dashed quickly down to the river. He stooped to his knees and pushed a large plank out onto the ice before him, hoping that by distributing his weight he wouldn't break through; but in his heart he believed that the ice would never support him. You might say Sam's faith would measure .0001 on the faith scale.

— Slowly he inched out onto the ice, praying as he slid the board before him. Things went well for the first hundred yards, but then the ice began to groan. Slowly he scooted— more groaning, more fervent prayers. His heart "shouted," *Hurry, hurry—Betsy's life depends on me!* A hundred and fifty yards, creaking, groaning. Then a crashing roar! The ice was breaking up! Sam clamped his eyes shut, bracing for the icy waters. The roaring increased, but he was still dry! *What's happening?* he puzzled. The source of the noise was behind him; he glanced over his shoulder. A man was racing a team and wagon across the ice! It roared by him, pulled up the opposite bank, and stopped at the store, where the driver dashed inside. He was after medicine, too.

Sam leaped to his feet, threw his arms in the air, and shouted, "Hallelujah!" He dashed, slipping and sliding across the ice to the store, got the medicine, hitched a ride back across in the wagon, dashed into the cabin, gave Betsy the medicine, and they lived happily ever after.

More Faith?

Now, it so happened that John and Nancy lived in the log house two miles downriver on a high bluff overlooking this panorama. John had been watching with considerable interest as Sam crawled across the ice. Although it was too far away to hear any sounds, John saw everything clearly through his binoculars. Nancy called him away for something, causing him to miss seeing the wagon race by. Imagine his surprise when he returned to the window and saw Sam leaping and slipping and falling in his dash for the store. What would have gone through John's mind as he saw this creeper-become-leaper? Somehow God had injected Sam with more faith, right? Wrong. Sam's faith had not increased. *Sam had acquired more knowledge of the object of his faith—the ice.* He had learned that the *ice* would not only hold *his* weight, but would even support a team and wagon! Coming to know the object of his faith radically changed Sam's behavior.

The Faith Required

Sam's circumstances were so dire that he chose to risk his life rather than risk his wife. One might argue that Sam needed more faith. But Jesus said that all the faith one needs is "mustard seed" faith (Matthew 17:20). Sam had enough faith—he staked his very *life* on it. Again, the *object* of Sam's faith is the critical variable. This is why God sometimes uses circumstances such as Sam's to conform us to the image of Christ. Romans 8:28-29 says, "We *know* [not maybe or sometimes] that God causes all things to work together for good to those who love God, to those who are called according to His purpose. For whom he foreknew, He also predestined to become conformed to the image of His Son, that He might be the first-born among many brethren."

Those verses don't teach that God *causes* pain and suffering, but that He causes every circumstance to be *used for our best good* according to *His* purpose. And the verses go so far as to reveal His purpose: to fashion us into the image of Christ. In such difficult times as I've presented, both real and fictional, we are to step out onto the "ice" of God—ice we come to know will support us. We don't need more faith; we need to get to *know the Object* of our faith: the Father, Jesus Christ, the Holy Spirit. As we learn that God is absolutely trustworthy, the behavior follows naturally.

It is best to not quote Romans 8:28 by itself because *it does not stand alone.* Quoting verse 28 and omitting verse 29 leaves an unnecessary question in the mind which begs an answer: *How could anything good possibly come from the trauma I'm experiencing?* When verse 28 is coupled with verse 29, however, our experiences on earth take on a glorious, purposeful new meaning. We have God's promise that the good, bad, and ugly experiences work together to conform us to the image of Christ.

Why We Suffer

This leads us to the subject of God's trustworthiness. What sort of God would place us on a planet where the circumstances of life so crush us that we determine that our only hope lies in *knowing* Him? Would He be a hostile God or an *agape* God, if He knew that it takes some deep-water days to bring a man to the end of *his* strength and into the glorious experience of *Christ's strength* in him and through

231

him? God is not the author of evil. "God is love" (1 John 4:16). And remember, James 1:13 says, "Let no one say when he is tempted, 'I am being tempted by God'; for God cannot be tempted by evil, and He Himself does not tempt anyone." Hebrews 5:8 says of Jesus, "Although He was a Son, He learned obedience from the things which He suffered." Amazing! Although I don't understand this completely, I see one thing clearly: Undergoing tough circumstances is part of our conformation process. Philippians 3:10 says, "That I may know Him, and the power of His resurrection and the *fellowship of His sufferings,* being conformed to His death." A sweet camaraderie is developed between you and Jesus as you undergo difficult times together. Romans 8:18 says, "I consider that the sufferings of this present time are not worthy to be compared with the glory that is to be revealed to us." At times, His *agape* love permits us to experience difficult times for our best good.

The "Measure of Faith" Versus the "Gift of Faith"

The Scriptures teach that in addition to the "measure of faith," which is "allotted to each" (Romans 12:3), there is the spiritual "gift of faith," which is given to a select few (1 Corinthians 12:7-9). Those who have it bear a heavy stewardship responsibility. The *gift* of faith is to be used to edify the church, not for personal benefit. It is not for getting our greeds supplied, but for getting the needs of the body of Christ supplied (1 Corinthians 12:7). Some well-meaning Christians apparently do not realize that they have the *gift* of faith, rather than the plain-vanilla variety.

— If believers with the "gift of faith" mistake it for the "measure of faith," they may mistakenly believe that God wants every Christian to have faith like theirs. So they establish a "faith" ministry on this hypothesis and begin to teach that if we have enough faith, we have a *right* to *guaranteed*

health, wealth, and even parking places, because this works
for them. God has no choice, you see. He *has* to do our
bidding because of our bold faith. Should you employ this
technique and it fails to work, the conclusion is one or both
of two reasons: You lack the faith to move God into action
on your behalf, or there is "hidden sin" in your life. Both of
these will leave you stranded at the "Emergency Stop Only"
exit on God's freeway.

Aggressive disciples of this Americanized "gospel" believe it's *agape* to point out to those in the midst of their
pain and suffering that if they will just exercise "enough"
faith, God will—indeed, *must*—deliver. We have God over a
barrel, you see. We can control Him! If He doesn't deliver,
the problem is our weak faith or personal sin. This can dev-
astate a Christian. My purpose is not to rail against such
counselors, but to be an agent of God's grace to hurting
people who may fall victim to their false counsel, regardless
of how well-intended.

Some teachers cite God's faith all-stars in Hebrews 11:17-
34—people who are hailed by the Bible as those whom
God miraculously delivered from their problems. What a
marvelous testimony of God's grace! This is good unless one
fails to deliver "the rest of the story," as Paul Harvey says;
they ignore God's equally strong, if not even more enthusi-
astic, endorsement of other faith all-stars who *were not* delivered, but given grace to endure:

> By faith Abraham, when he was called, obeyed by
> going out to a place which he was to receive for an
> inheritance; and he went out, not knowing where he
> was going. By faith he lived as an alien in the land of
> promise, as in a foreign land, *dwelling in tents* with
> Isaac and Jacob, fellow heirs of the same promise; for
> he was looking for the city ... whose architect and
> builder is God. By faith even Sarah herself received
> ability to conceive, even beyond the proper time of
> life, since she considered Him faithful who had

promised; therefore, also, there was born of one man, and him as good as dead at that, as many descendants as the stars of heaven in number, and innumerable as the sand which is by the seashore. All these *died in faith, without receiving the promises* ... (Hebrews 11:8-13).

And others experienced mocking and scourgings, yes, also chains and imprisonment. They were *stoned*, they were *sawn in two*, they were tempted, they were *put to death* with the sword; they went about in sheepskins, in goatskins, being *destitute, afflicted, ill-treated* ... wandering in deserts and mountains and *caves* and *holes in the ground*. And all these, having gained approval through their faith, *did not receive what was promised, because God had provided something better* [than earthly health, wealth, and deliverance] ..." (Hebrews 11:36-40).

These heroic Christians, obviously people with faith equal to or perhaps greater (13a; 39b) than others in the chapter who are more often cited, were *not delivered* from their predicament. Rather than deliverance, they were given *grace to endure*. They had to wait; they had to welcome God's promise "from a distance" (verse 13). Notice what God says about that sort of faith. He calls it *something better* (verse 40). Interesting. Such folks are not "weak-faith" people. Folks, the Christian who does not see this is vulnerable to having his faith decimated by the devil.

You Do Not Need More Faith
to Step Forward in Christ

We Christians do not need more faith; we need a growing *knowledge* of the *Object* of our faith: God the Father, God the Son, and God the Spirit. Paul says, "For my determined purpose is that I may *know* Him, that I may progressively become more deeply and intimately acquainted with Him perceiving and recognizing and understanding the wonders of His Person more strongly and more clearly . . ." (Philippians 3:10, AMP). *Knowing Christ intimately* was the primary goal of Paul's life, and God wants it to be ours as well.

God is dedicated to our everlasting welfare (Jeremiah 29:11). Christ on the cross is the only "statement" He need ever make to prove this to us. At times, it may become necessary for Him to *agape* us by allowing us to experience situations where we have little choice but to creep out onto Jesus Christ like Sam scooted out onto the frozen river. And when we do, we find that He is more than sufficient to meet our need. The supply to meet every need that man can experience on earth is Christ Himself. God spells relief: J-e-s-u-s. We need to *know* Him. This is how we are changed from creepers to leapers.

---

13   WHY HE ALLOWS US TO SUFFER

— AT THE HEIGHT OF THE Vietnam War, the *Wall Street
Journal* reported that the president and four other politicians
met weekly to make all of the decisions on how the war
would be waged for the coming week, and that not one
trained military mind sat in on these sessions, not even the
chairman of the Joint Chiefs of Staff. They reported that
these politicians made such decisions as identifying the targets for bombing, determining the *types* and *quantity* of
bombs, the number and types of planes to be launched,
even the military tactics to be employed. Politicians micro-
managing the war from Washington! Imagine the impact this
must have had upon our military who were fighting the battles. How would you like to have been one of Wyatt Earp's
deputies and be limited to carrying one bullet in your shirt
pocket, like the fictional Barney Fife on the "Andy Griffith
Show"? Meanwhile, the bad guys carried fully loaded guns,
and when they had emptied them at you, the rules that the
U.S. politicos agreed to permitted the enemy to yell, "Time
out!" run back into a safety zone, reload, and rush out to
attack you again. Many in our military felt they carried such
a handicap in the Vietnam War. Bob Dole, speaking in support of our military in that conflict, said, "The long, gray line
did not fail America; America failed the long, gray line."

You can easily see how such strategy, enacted by politicians back home in the safety of the White House, seeking
to placate both dove and hawk, negatively affected the
morale of the warriors who were risking their lives in battle.
Their loyalty and resolve for self-sacrifice were undermined

because *there was no consensual big picture embraced by both the warriors and their supreme commander*. Such a situation can have a negative effect on those who are required to submit to the authority who controls their destiny. They could get the idea that their supreme authority was insensitive, uncaring, and unjust. Their respect for him could turn into smoldering hostility, which is the attitude of some naïve, uninstructed, disenchanted Christians toward God.

Understanding the Big Picture

We Christians war against "the spiritual forces of wickedness in the heavenly places" (Ephesians 6:12). In the heat of these battles, you may have puzzled over why God allows bad things to happen to the people who are on His side and whom he professes to love. In times of suffering, having a clear understanding of and being in agreement with the big picture in which you and your Supreme Commander are involved will dramatically influence your morale regarding the purpose of your life on earth. If you're not in a pickle now, you will be sooner or later. The devil is not dead; he's just got a terminal case of tapeworm.

God told Adam that the world would turn sour on him if he took over and tried to run his own life. He did, it did, and it's still happening. Jesus said, "In the world you *have* tribulation, but take courage; I have overcome the world" (John 16:33). *Tribulation* is God's term for Satan's work. There is tribulation in this world, and it is all attributable to the devil and the Fall. But before we send Adam and Eve "down the river," who among us did not begin from day one to pursue a life of independence from God? We are rebellious by birth, and by rebirth in Christ were created with a high motivation to be obedient to God. But despite our rebirth, suffering and evil still buffet us. God says of the redeemed, "*When* [not if] you pass through the waters, I will be with you; and through the rivers, they will not overflow you. *When* [not if] you walk through the fire, you will not be scorched nor will the flame burn.... Since you are precious in My sight ... do not fear, for I am with you" (Isaiah 43:2-4-5). When you are in a fix, understanding:

- what God has stated about His commitment to your well-being

- that hard times are a product of the Fall, but are necessary for being conformed to the image of Christ

- that your sufferings are not always *caused* by God, but allowed by Him

- that your sufferings can be used by God to your eternal benefit

- the big picture will strengthen your resolve to stay in the fight with vigor.

Understanding the big picture is the key to producing Christians with a resolve to self-sacrifice. Conversely, a *lack* of clear understanding, or a disagreement with the big picture, erodes morale in spiritual warfare. This is especially true when you're suffering. Satan is more aware of this than we, therefore much of his strategy targets your mind during suffering. He seeks to deceive you through the power of sin to blind you from obtaining an accurate view of God's big picture and the role that suffering plays in it.

Religion Versus Christianity

What does all of this have to do with suffering? Let's begin by stating that Satan loves to get people—even entire countries—hooked on *religion*. Religion can effectively put blinders on people. The Bible says this was the case with Israel in the first century, and it yet remains: "Their minds were hardened; for until this very day at the reading of the old covenant *the same veil* [over their minds] remains, because it is *removed* in Christ.... but whenever a man turns to [Christ], the veil is taken away" (2 Corinthians 3:14-16). Religion is one of Satan's most effective tools. If he can keep people busy doing what they are deceived into believing are spiritual push-ups, he can divert them from being open to participating in God's grace through Jesus Christ. Religion is *man's* idea of how to approach God. Christianity, on the other hand, is God's gracious, *agape* effort to approach man through Jesus Christ. Oh, Satan dearly loves religion. The Crusades were fought over religion. Nazi guards who wore crosses in the death camps of World War II were into religion. Religion is far more effective at taking prisoners than street-corner hookers. Hookers take prisoners one at a time, while religion imprisons entire nations, cultures, and ethnic groups in one broad sweep of the brush.

— *Christianity is not religion.* Christianity is *relationship* with God through Jesus Christ. Christianity is more like a superb marriage relationship (sans the physical union, of course). And this is not this author's dogma, but God's biblical proclamation. The Bible teaches that God pursues you to establish an intimate, loving marriage *relationship* with you—someone with whom he can share His affection and receive your *voluntary* love in return. Many fail to understand this. Indeed, some "churches" are not churches at all, but merely institutions which have people jumping through religious hoops trying to earn something that cannot be earned: God's acceptance, which is available only through Jesus Christ. "No one comes to the Father, but through Me" (John 14:6). The majority of the folks who comprise their membership have not been reborn via faith in Christ. Their "christ" is often a tireless workaholic who set the curve for humans to emulate to make it to heaven. Or their "christ" is an indulgent Santa-Claus figure, who is powerless in a universe which is out of control or whose credo is tolerance for members of other religions (except zealous followers of

Jesus Christ), just as long as the adherents are "sincere."
Some of their leaders do not even believe Jesus Christ is the
virgin-born Son of God. These dear people have been *vacci-
nated* against getting a case of the real thing: an intimate
love relationship with the living God of the universe. Religion blocks them from Christianity.

God paved the way for such a relationship through offering His Son to die in our stead for our rebellion. What grace
(unmerited favor)! A human committee would never dare de-
vise a plan whereby God becomes a Man and "throws Himself
in front of a train" in order to melt our stubborn hearts with
such love so as to win our hand in spiritual marriage. He truly
is an awesome, merciful, *agape*, gracious, kind God!

The Problem with Being
"the Richest Man in Town"

By initiating His plan to become our spiritual Father, or
more intimately, our Dad (Galatians 4:6; Romans 8:15),or
even more intimately, our Bridegroom (Hosea 2:16-20), a
rub arose: how to re-create free moral objects-of-His-affec-
tion who would love Him for *who He is*, rather than for *what
He could do for them*. This is a problem for anyone who is
"the richest man in town," be he God or human. The richer
the person, the greater the possibility that those who *profess*
to love him simply cater to him in order to curry favor. Many
seek *benefits* from him rather than a personal relationship
with him. If he were poor, they would never seek his friend-
ship nor respond to his overtures to establish one, especially
if he insisted on being in control. It seems to me that rich
humans can never really know, beyond a doubt, that *anyone*
poorer than they are truly loves them. Unconditional love is
to be found in Christ alone.

God knows the intentions of our heart because He is
omniscient (all-knowing). We Christians, however, who *profess* to love Him can never be certain of our own love for

Him until we experience what we perceive to be undeserved suffering. When we are in the midst of such suffering, we have the advantage of *choosing* to continue to believe God is altruistic toward us, or to opt for Satan's accusations against Him—accusations the power of sin will submit to our minds in those first-person-singular pronouns (*I, me, my*, etc.) God has placed us in an environment which provides us with a *choice*. This way we can discern the depth of *our* love for Him. Tell me, can there be any other way? I don't think so.

Similarly, the *unbeliever* can either see earth as having evolved out of *nothing*, or he can consider the flora, fauna, sun, moon, stars, babies, eyes, ears, taste buds, *ad infinitum*, and think: *Someone is behind all of this, and I want to know Him. He deserves my homage.* Unregenerate man has been given the capacity to make such a choice. "For since the creation of the world [God's] invisible attributes, His eternal power and divine nature, have been *clearly* seen, being understood *through what has been made*, so that they are *without excuse*" (Romans 1:20). When a lost man acknowledges God, He will move heaven and earth to get the message of Christ to him in some manner.

Which Do You Seek: Heaven or Relationship?

Are you riding the glory train because you love the Engineer, or because you seek the train's destination? Do you have a passion for the King, or for His palatial, trouble-free environment (heaven) where He has promised you will dwell forever? Will He continue to receive your loyalty and devotion only so long as it pays off for you? Or do you murmur and grumble against Him when troubles come your way? Do you have God on a performance-based acceptance? If He performs according to *your* will, do you "pay Him off" by affirming your love for Him, hoping that in this manner you can keep Him under *your* control?

Of course, most of us don't overtly think of our relationship with God in this way. It's possible, however, that by our actions we are treating Him so. This is the dilemma that Job faced, and he flunked the test for most of the book. He thought God was unfair. He even demanded the right to defend himself in a face-to-face confrontation: "I would present my case before Him and fill my mouth with arguments. . . . When He has tried me, I shall come forth as gold" (Job 23:4,10). Job figured he merited God's best due to his yeoman performance. But unlike us, he had no Bible or teachers. Must God *earn* your loyalty and love? Sufferings will invariably yield the answers to such questions. Sufferings put the squeeze on a person, which enables him to know himself. God doesn't need such answers about your faith because he already knows. He doesn't have to test man to find out where his heart is. *We* need such answers about ourselves. How we respond to what we deem to be unjust sufferings will reveal this.

A "Heavenly" Hell

This will help you find out if it's heaven that you seek or a personal relationship with God. What if heaven were anything *but* a utopian environment? What if it were a dry and thirsty land where the temperature soared into the hundreds daily? What if the streets and buildings were terribly crowded? What if you had to work hard in the fields all day, and such manual labor were your eternal destiny? What if there were no beauty, no wildlife, no clear streams, only dry washes? There would be one bright spot in your day, however: your coworker would be Jesus Christ. You would get to visit with Him all day long as you labored side by side. He would be your dearest Friend and vice versa. There would be a scarcity of food, so you would receive only two meals daily—a subsistence diet; and you would go home to a noisy apartment which you shared with nine strangers and your one dear

Friend: Jesus Christ. You and He would develop a fantastic, intimate, loving, emerging relationship as He shared the secrets of His heart with you and answered all of the questions you've had or ever will have.

What if hell, on the other hand, had the idyllic climate of California? What if you and all of the people there had individual mansions, ate sumptuous meals, enjoyed glorious vistas with beautiful wildlife, trees, and wildflowers? And what if your choicest friends were there so you could fellowship to your heart's content? There would be the epitome of entertainment, vast libraries, exciting spectator sports, incredible fishing, skiing, hiking, biking, and other outdoor activities. Oh, and what if the devil had been banished to another environment forever, so he could not play havoc with your life-style there in hell? *You* would be completely in charge of yourself—a true lord of the ring. You could even sate yourself with hedonism if you chose. The only thing missing would be Jesus Christ because, you see, he would be living in "heaven." Make your choice before reading the next paragraph. Will you choose a hellish "heaven" which includes Jesus, or a heavenly "hell" without Him?

When the Lord laid this on my own heart some years ago, I was stunned. I could not respond. I was numb with doubt. I thought I really loved the Lord, but this threw me a curve that I couldn't hit. I had never considered such a thing. After days of soul-searching and prayer, He finally answered my dilemma by bringing these thoughts to my mind: What if the doctors told my sweet Anabel that she had a disease which could prove fatal? If she expected to live, she would have to move to the desert. (For this guy reared in the mountains of eastern Oklahoma, the desert is not my idea of a place to retire.)

Would I say, "Well, Sugar, you know that I simply have no leading to move to the desert. I'll tell you what—you move to the desert, and I'll stay here to keep the grass mowed, the canoe in shape, and take care of all the details that home ownership requires. I promise to phone you to deliver a 15-second monologue before each meal, and just before bedtime each night I'll deliver a final one-minute monologue. We'll also agree that once a week we'll fly to a site halfway between us where we'll sit on a hard bench together for one hour. We'll sing some hymns, you bring some special music, and I'll bring a teaching from the Bible. This way, it'll be very similar to the relationship we enjoyed before you got sick." Folks, this parody approximates what passes for the "relationship" some folks have with Jesus Christ. That's not even close to the fabulous, intimate relationship that Christ died to give us.

There's no way I would settle for this with Anabel! I would say, "Rain on California; I'm heading for the desert to learn how to eat real *sand*wiches!" I want to be wherever *Anabel* is because it's an emerging, intimate relationship with Anabel that I want, not a gravel-bottom valley full of pretty water! This is the way God solved my dilemma. He showed me that it's *Jesus* I seek, not His *home*. Make no mistake about it, I'm delighted that Jesus lives in a utopian environment called heaven, but I'm relieved to know that I would still want to live with Him forever if He lived in the desert. He could make that desert bloom. He specializes in making silk purses out of sows' ears. God wishes every Christian would choose a developing, intimate relationship with *Him*, not crave the environment where He lives.

Who Is in Control?

Another barometer of your relationship with God is whether or not you murmur or perhaps even rail at God if things don't go *your* way. By so doing, you are witnessing before men and angels that God does not merit your consistent loyalty and love. Although the angels constantly proclaim His worthiness, God is not *worthy* to hold down His job, in your opinion. You are tacitly saying that, given the chance, you could do a better job of running your section of the universe than He is doing. You're claiming that *you should have the right to be in control of your circumstances.* This is a lord-of-the-ring action. It's usurping His role. Dear one, the *only* way you can demonstrate that you love God *just for who He is* is to consistently praise Him, regardless of how your feeler votes, even when bad things happen to you—things that you don't believe you deserve. "Always giving thanks *for all things* in the name of our Lord Jesus Christ to God" (Ephesians 5:20). "In *everything* give thanks; for this is God's will for you" (1 Thessalonians 5:18)—*for* all things and *in* all things. Look at it this way: Earth is the last chance you'll ever have to suffer. Earth is the closest thing to hell we'll experience, but the closest thing to heaven the lost man will experience. Don't blow it. It's an important part of the big picture.

— What could be more motivating than to know beyond a shadow of a doubt that God, who cannot lie, has stated unequivocally that His beneficent, altruistic, gracious purpose is to take the circumstances of your life, the good, along with the bad, and use every one of these to accomplish the most glorious *agape* action on your behalf imaginable: fashion you into the image of Jesus Christ, the blessed One, the anointed One, the chosen One, the Lamb of God, the beloved Bridegroom, the King of kings, the Lord of lords, the first-born from the dead, the One who is high and lifted up, the One to whom all authority in heaven and earth has been given? The Christian who can't find reason in that to consistently praise the Lord through thick and thin simply does not understand the big picture. He doesn't "get it." God wishes we knew why He allows Christians to suffer. I do not appeal to your emotions on His behalf, but to your intellect. Your emotions will vote with the flesh every time suffering occurs. Will you allow something to control you that can't even think? Your mind and your will are the key players here; God has cast your feeler in the "walk on" bit part. Although *never denying* how you feel, *faith* (seated in the mind and brought on-line by the will) must *practice, practice, practice* dominating feeler, denying its insistence upon usurping the starring role.[1] Those who are armed with the big picture know that God is conforming us to Christ's image, and they have ample cause to lift consistent praises to Him, even through times of suffering. And remember, by understanding that the true definition of a hypocrite is "pretending to be something you are not," you can *know*, beyond a shadow of a doubt, that you are *acting like who you are*, not faking it, when you praise Him with sincerity, even though your emotions vote against it.

The Sacrifice of Praise

What parent does not like to be praised and respected by his children? And when Dad announces to the kids that he's decided to grant their hearts' desire and take the family to Disney World, what child would not shout his approval and pound ol' dad on the back while jumping for joy? Good ol' dad! Sure. We love to please our kids, and we love for them to show appreciation and respect to us. Why do parents like this? I think God made us this way because *He* is this way, and we are created in His image. Now try this one: What parents would not *really* appreciate it if their kids still praise, love, and respect them even when given a "no" answer? Such praise tells the parents that the kids' love for them is valid. It's not based upon whether the kids get their needs (or greeds) satisfied. This is what *our* Dad wants from us. It's called a "sacrifice of praise." Trusting that Christ is your Strength to manifest this *through* you is the key.

Hebrews 13:15 says, "Through Him then, let us continually offer up a *sacrifice of praise* to God, that is, the fruit of lips that give thanks to His name." By praising God in the midst of your personal adversity, or even calamity, you demonstrate to every observer that God would get your vote if He had to run for reelection every year, or month, or day, or minute. It's a snap to praise the Lord when you get an unexpected Christmas bonus; that's not a *"sacrifice* of praise."* What's tough is to believe that God *always* acts for your best good (defined as *agape* love) when He doesn't come through in the clutch as *you* would have Him do. It's hard to praise and honor and trust Him, perhaps even through tears or gritted teeth, when you feel like life has been dealing from the bottom of the deck. But offering up praise during such times as these demonstrates a *"sacrifice* of praise"* (Hebrews 13:15). Folks, I'm certainly not teaching the falsehood that I should smile and say a cheery, "Praise the Lord!" at Anabel's funeral. It would, however, be appropriate for me to tell God through my tears that it's OK—that this is not going to be an impediment to our relationship. And you know what? He will actually see to it that I become more conformed to the image of Christ for having experienced this heartbreak as I offer up "sacrifices of praise."

I have seen God work miraculously when a Christian began to offer a "sacrifice of praise" in a time of suffering. When I was a university professor, I counseled across the coffee table at home, as many of you doubtless do. Although "Mary's" husband sat in the pew most Sundays, I wouldn't have bet the homestead that he was saved. She had confided to Anabel and me that "John" treated her like a dog, even spanking her at times. What a guy! We had tried many things without seeing any positive results. I had been studying two passages on praising God: "In everything give thanks; for this is God's will for you in Christ Jesus" (1 Thessalonians 5:18), and "Always giving thanks for all things in the name of our Lord Jesus Christ to God ..." (Ephesians 5:20). Praise God *in* all things and *for* all things.... that was so illogical in a case such as hers, but the Holy Spirit seemed to be instructing me to ask her if she had ever praised God for allowing her to be caught up in such a situation. Sounds like a crazy idea, doesn't it? Now don't write and rag on me. I didn't want to mention it either! But it seemed like the Holy Spirit was insisting, so I timidly asked if she had ever tried praising God as John began to make one of his threatening moves toward her—then I ducked. She looked at me like I had fallen out of a tree. I wanted to crawl under the coffee table, but Anabel had beaten me to it!

The next day Mary called with one of these "you're-never-going-to-believe-what-happened" stories. John had become nettled over some small issue and had started toward her to do his usual. She had fled to the bathroom, slammed the door, locked it, and begun to praise the Lord and thank Him that He was her Deliverer. Meanwhile, John rattled the knob and shouted threats about what he was going to do when he got his hands on her. He finally gave up and roared out of the driveway. Mary heaved a sigh of relief, and then *really* began to praise God, only this time it was no *sacrifice!* You say, "Well, that's not such a hot story. He may have had an appointment." One thing I failed to mention: When Mary saw that the coast was clear to come out of the bathroom, she discovered that she had failed to lock the door! Furthermore, when John returned, he acted like the episode had never happened!

 Folks, God taught me a powerful lesson that day which I've used again and again in my own life and suggested to others. God wants us to praise Him *in* as well as *for* all things. That's a hard teaching, but God told us to praise Him through thick and thin. When you consider the alternatives the choice is a no-brainer. Are you praising God in and for all of the things that God allows to come into your life? I'm not saying God always *causes* your hard times, but He allows them. Folks, take it from one who practices praising

God *in* and *for* all things: Praising God in all things will enable you to see miracles.

> Consider it all joy, my brethren, when you encounter
> various trials, knowing that the testing of your faith
> produces endurance. And let endurance have its perfect result, that you may be perfect and complete,
> lacking in nothing (James 1:2-4).

> In this you greatly rejoice, even though now for a
> little while, if necessary, you have been distressed by
> various trials, that the proof of your faith, being more
> precious than gold ... even though tested by fire, may
> be found to result in praise and glory and honor at
> the revelation of Jesus Christ (1 Peter 1:6-7).

By praising Him *in* and *for* your circumstances, you
leave God two alternatives: Change the circumstance, or
give you so much grace that you'll actually become glad for
the experience. Either way, you're the winner.

God's Worthiness

Let's exit God's freeway at the sign that says "God's Worthiness." Park the car under that shade tree over there—I
want us to go for another ride in God's helicopter. As we lift
off, let's look backward even before the beginning of time to
better understand another way sacrifices of praise fit into the
big picture. As we view God creating His corps of angels,
you'll notice that He created one angel who was a cut above
the rest: Lucifer. I agree with those who teach that Ezekiel,
attributing superhuman characteristics to the "king of Tyre,"
was actually describing fallen Lucifer. He's described before
he fell as having the "seal of perfection," being "perfect in
beauty" and "full of wisdom" (Ezekiel 28:12). Either stunning
beauty or astounding wisdom can become curses when misused. When an individual has *both*, he becomes exponentially
more vulnerable to pride. Such was the case with Lucifer,

and it proved to be his downfall (Ezekiel 28:17). He apparently convinced many angels that he was more worthy to be God than God is (Revelation 12:7-9). He was ambitious for personal gain and personal power, so he initiated a hostile takeover of heaven (Revelation 12:7). It's important to see here that, like man, God instilled in Lucifer and in the other angels a freedom of choice. God didn't *cause* Lucifer and those angels to become rogues, but their rebellion certainly didn't shock Him. God is omniscient.

I believe Lucifer used the same seductive skills with the angels that he used with Eve to convince many of them to support his hostile takeover attempt. I believe he accused God of being unworthy of their homage and sold them on the idea. I can imagine him observing their daily routine of praising God and asking them how they can be certain there is not someone more glorious than God who is actually *more* worthy of their praise. You can see where planting such doubts might lead, especially if Lucifer enhanced them and presented them with half-truths as well as outright lies about how much better off their lot in life would be if *he* were God.

Use your imagination to speculate on the strategy Lucifer might have employed with these pre-fallen angels. He could point out their lack of self-actualization—that they were being restrained from developing into all that they could be; that they deserved to be placed in positions commensurate with their nobility; that God was restricting them, limiting them with unfair labor practices; that if *he*, Lucifer, were God, he would see to it that heaven would be straightened out. . . . He would guarantee a fair shake for all and rewards to those who would support him. After all, they had only to look at his beauty and listen to his wisdom to recognize his superiority and leadership ability. Whatever his strategy, the Bible implies that one-third of the angels fell for it: "And [Satan's] tail swept away a third of the stars of heaven, and threw them to the earth" (Revelation 12:4).

I believe these rebellious angels became demons. Jesus said concerning them, "Then [I] will also say ... 'Depart from Me, accursed ones, into the eternal fire which has been prepared for the devil and *his angels*'" (Matthew 25:41). Hell was "prepared for" rebellious Lucifer and his angels-cum-demons, not people. People must *choose* to live eternally with these demonic beings by stepping over the broken body of Jesus Christ. What a horrible, unnecessary waste of the grace of God, who loves sinner-humans!

God quickly extinguished Lucifer's rebellion. He could whip the devil blindfolded while wearing handcuffs and leg irons. He could whip him without even getting out of His recliner! So, "[the devil] was thrown down to the *earth*, and his angels were thrown down with him" (Revelation 12:9). You'll notice that with billions upon billions of planets to target, God threw this motley crew to a tiny speck of dirt called "Earth." Then, according to His plan, God created two humans who were to propagate the same Earth with millions of objects of His affection. But wait a minute. With mega-billions of planets available, look where God placed Adam and Eve: on that same planet called "Earth." It goes without saying that God was not shocked when Adam and Eve were no match for Lucifer-cum-Satan's deception and fell into sin. Is it possible that, as God was placing Adam and Eve on Earth, the remaining two-thirds of the angels in heaven may have thought: *Oh, no! Don't put them on Earth! Put them on Jupiter! Satan will eat 'em alive!* I think so. But God was simply initiating His divine plan whereby He would ultimately pour out His *agape* love and grace upon unworthy mankind in the Person of Jesus Christ. If that merciful, altruistic, gracious act does not *prove His infinite worthiness* to be praised, adored, and served as the God that He is, I don't know what more it would take to convince His creatures. Knowing all of this to be true, we, His creatures, can, by faith alone, enthusiastically submit to His authority, worship Him, and praise Him as our God.

Exploitation?

Understanding God's big picture answers the question I hypothesized that Satan has raised concerning God's worthiness. But a second question remains: Did God create man simply to prove His worthiness to be God? Are we mere pawns in His giant scheme to prove himself? Never! To do so would be exploitation, which is contrary to His identity. *Exploit:* "To use unfairly for one's own purposes." Just as it's impossible for a man to leap over the World Trade Center unassisted, *it is impossible for God to exploit man.* The Bible says there are some things that God cannot do. God cannot lie; God cannot back out on His promises; God cannot force people to love Him, etc. "God *is agape*" (1 John 4:8). And to do any nonaltruistic thing is out of character for Him. Remember, *agape* means "I will do the most altruistic, the most redeeming, the most constructive thing for you." *God cannot exploit man!* That's impossible.

Learning of His worthiness to be God by faith during our earthwalk accrues to *our* eternal benefit. Those who reject Jesus will learn of His worthiness by being slam-dunked to their knees by God's awesome presence at the judgment; "every knee shall bow" simply because of His overwhelming Persona. His presence will flatten them just like it prostrated rebellious Saul of Tarsus (Acts 9:3-4). God could accomplish such homage immediately, but this is not in keeping with His plan to woo us to Himself as free moral agents. As my friend Jay Kesler teaches, God could awaken us each day with fiery-red skywriting that says, "REPENT!" But this would *intimidate* us into submission, not woo us by His grace and loveliness, and would not accomplish His purpose of proving His worthiness. Instead, it would be possible to view Him as a tyrant.

253

— Thus, He patiently waits. And even by waiting, His patience and tolerance of man's abuse of His good name (reputation) validates His worthiness of our love. He even tolerates the indignation of hearing His and His son's names used as profane expletives. Do you realize that in the United States of America where the politically correct god is named "Tolerance," the only god who is not tolerated is the *true* God? Is it coincidental that neither Buddha's name nor Allah's name are insulted or used as an expletive? No—Satan targets only the *true* God and His Son. How incredibly patient God is!

Tomorrow's Forecast Calls for "Reign"

Wasn't it an uplifting experience to see eastern Europeans rush through the Iron Curtain to freedom after years of political slavery? Being released from suffering, especially undeserved suffering, increases a person's appreciation of freedom by an exponential factor. Imagine such a person who is placed in a leadership role over others who need sympathetic understanding. Do you suppose he would have an extra measure of compassion and tenderness toward those over whom he reigned? I think so. You and I will reign with Christ. (We'll visit this rest stop later.) I believe it will enhance our ability to reign with greater *agape* by having experienced the softening-up process of Earth, where we become convinced of His worthiness to be God and our own unworthiness to be sharers in His grace. Suffering accompanied by His gracious comfort (2 Corinthians 1:3-4) are key players in this equation.

My friend Jack Taylor says that suffering will either make you bitter or better, and I believe he's onto something. Since God is *agape* and we're being conformed to the family image, you and I must go through many struggles as we allow Christ's *agape* life to be expressed through us. Earth is our training ground for this. This is an essential part of equipping us for our eternal reign with Christ. Praising God will make you

better. Griping over your circumstance will make you bitter.
Our eternal reign will be as yokefellows with Christ over a
social order where *agape* is supreme. If we have not
allowed ourselves to become at home in such an environment, how effectively will we reign in it eternally? You and I
won't reign with an iron hand, gang, so we would do well
to avoid practicing such behavior.

Sanctified Behavior Equips Us to Reign with Christ

Only a work *of* God is acknowledged *by* God. And the
only credible way we can participate in God's work is by
allowing Christ to do it through us (Romans 15:18). Apparently, the more diligently we allow Christ to *agape* and serve
other people through us on earth, the more authority we'll
be entrusted with for eternity. Jesus says of the obedient
servants in the parable of the talents, "Well done, good and
faithful slave; you were faithful with a few things, I will put
you *in charge* of many things; enter into the joy of your
master" (Matthew 25:23). Folks, the good servant's faithfulness in earthly authority was greatly rewarded in another
venue. This is an analogy of the correlation between the
Christian's behavior on earth and his future role in heaven. It
has to be because it's certainly not addressing the future of
lost folks. Christ is an *agape* lover, and we're being conformed
to His image (Romans 8:28-29). Our ability to *agape has* to
play the primary role in our reigning training. Since Christ is
agape personified, how could it be otherwise?

The Bible seems to hide the details of our future reign,
dropping a note here or there. For instance, Paul sarcastically
pierces the presumptuous Corinthians' balloons: "You are
already filled, you have already become rich, you have become *kings* without us; and I would indeed that you *had*
become kings so that we also might *reign with you*" (1 Corinthians 4:8). Even as he chastens them, he makes it clear

that *our future reign in heaven* is a fact. "He who overcomes, I will grant to him to sit down with Me *on My throne*, as I also overcame and sat down with My Father on His throne" (Revelation 3:21). No mistake about it: You and I are being trained to reign, and apparently these Corinthian Christians were not taking their training seriously, because Paul is castigating them for their attitude.

Heaven will be a very active place. Indolence erodes all of the good qualities in a person. Man does not thrive on self-absorption, self-indulgence, or laziness. We're not going to be sitting in recliners in a huge coliseum, cheering for Jesus and the Father 24 hours per day for all eternity. Indeed, we will be doing lots of cheering, praising, and worshiping, but God's got other exciting, proactive plans for our future. The Bible is not clear about exactly what or over whom we will reign, but that makes no difference. We're better off not knowing, or God would have told us. Suffice it to say that there is reign in tomorrow's forecast. So, as far as exploitation is concerned, one could hardly accuse God of that when we consider such a glorious future. We are the bride of Christ; we will reign with Christ—it's incredible!

— It's absolutely critical that we choose to praise Him through the bad as well as through the good times in order that we might demonstrate that, in our opinion, He *is worthy of the continual praise of all His creation for eternity.* What an honor it is to lift one small voice of praise to God with an Okie accent from the wee, dinky piece of dirt in the universe called Texas and play a bit part in God's grand scheme! Our praise refutes Satan's accusations that God is an egomaniacal, high-maintenance, temperamental Person who requires our continual praise in order to keep His sagging ego pumped. God's revelation explains *why* it is important for me to praise Him in all things. It tells me *why* planet Earth was never intended to be a combination Disneyland/ Wal-Mart Supercenter. It reveals *why* Christians experience all of the difficult things that lost folks experience, such as cancer, fatal accidents, drownings, layoffs, crushing disappointments, unfaithful mates, or (fill in the blank). By praising God *despite such adversity* or in the midst of it, and remaining loyal to Him by the grace of Christ through us, and verbally affirming His worthiness to be God, He uses us as examples to all creation that He is worthy. To God be the glory!

14 THAT WE ARE BEING TRAINED ON EARTH TO REIGN IN HEAVEN

I WALKED INTO A STORE THAT WAS owned by a Christian and his wife and was surprised that her office appeared to be vacant. Even the family photos had disappeared from the wall. "Is Mary OK?" I asked her husband John.

John seemed hesitant, as if he were pondering his response. "Well, Mary isn't with the firm anymore. We've been separated for several months . . . and we're getting a divorce."

"What!"

"Oh, it's my idea. Mary and I want such different things out of life. Always have. We've never had the same goals. We probably shouldn't have married in the first place. We were young and thought we were in love, but you know how that goes. I've tried to make a go of a bad situation for years. I think a clean break is best for both of us. The kids will be better off. There's always a lot of tension in our home. It'll take them a while to adjust, but frankly, I think everyone will welcome the change. No one knows how rough it's been. You know . . . you keep going . . . hoping things will get better, but they don't. I'm going to let her have the kids. You know, kids are better off with their mother." And on it went. . . . this man is a Christian, but shoot, you're not shocked. You could tell me similar stories from your hometown or church or even your own family.

"Bill, what does a chapter on reigning with Christ have to do with divorce?" Folks, there's little or no difference in the divorce rate among the Christians and the unbelievers in the United States of America. That alarming statistic tells me that we are beginning to act more and more like *them*. We're to be known as marching to a different Drummer. I believe that Christians who divorce their mate without biblical justification are but one evidence of the casual attitude many Christians have today toward living an exemplary life which has *everything* to do with our future reigning with Christ. Look what Christ says: "He who overcomes, I will grant to him to *sit down with Me on My throne*, as I also overcame and sat down with My Father on His throne" (Revelation 3:21). This motivates me to want to live an overcoming life.

Good News and Bad News

Turning off God's freeway at the "Training for Reigning" exit will give us a chance to look at the relevance of holy living on earth. I don't enjoy reminding people of biblical principles that might inflict pain on my spiritual relatives, but this will be a liberating rest stop for some who are divorced, while convicting others. We're going to discuss how to play the hand that was dealt to us (or perhaps that we dealt to ourselves) so we can get on with our training-for-reigning.

I believe that Christians fall for the devil's lies and blow it like John did for two main reasons:

- They naïvely believe that Jesus Christ's death served merely to provide us with a ticket to heaven and an escape from hell.

- Satan has removed the social stigma from divorce to such a degree that divorcers are able to garner tacit approval from the church.

You will notice that I used the term divorcer. John is a divorcer, the *instigator* of a biblically unjustified act against God, his wife, and his family; John is sinning. Mary, on the other hand, though doubtless not a perfect wife, was not a willing participant in this divorce. Indeed, she did everything within her power to dissuade John. She is a *legitimate, biblical divorcee*, victimized by a *divorcer's* action. Hear me now—I am not referencing people who divorced their mate for a *biblically justifiable* reason (i.e., infidelity), but rather those who divorce merely because they are unhappy, weary of the relationship, have found a new love, etc. Although it's possible for both participants in a divorce action to be divorcers, obviously there can never be two divorcees. One (or perhaps both) must *initiate* the action.

Do You Seek an Environment, or a Person?

Although I doubt that he would verbalize it, I believe that at the core of John's unsound doctrine lies the perception that Jesus is sort of a "Celestial Environmentalist" who died to save us from a bad environment (hell) that we might live forever in a utopian one (heaven). "Do you want to go to heaven? Just ask Jesus into your heart." A pleasant *environment* is the goal of such slipshod theology, rather than experiencing an intimate relationship with God. Obviously, everyone would like to go to heaven. This is a precious promise from God, via faith in Christ. But it's common for believers to so concentrate on heaven (the environment) that they put the Bridegroom who awaits them on the back burner of their minds. The biblical goals for the believer must be:

- to develop an intimate love relationship with our Father, Christ—our Bridegroom, and God's Spirit.

- to mature in Christ.

- to live a life which brings honor to God's reputation.

- to prepare to reign with Christ through eternity.

261

The narrow scope of the "get-into-heaven" view of salvation is fertile soil for the Deceiver to cultivate the lie that once the Christian gets his celestial retirement plan in place, it's pointless to become overly concerned about rewards for holy living. *After all, one day we'll cast all of our crowns at Christ's feet anyway, so why bother with maturity?* I was stunned when I heard a respected Bible teacher compare attaining heaven to an event in a track meet and say, "We're all going to finish in a dead heat anyway." What a tragic, unbiblical misunderstanding of our eternal roles. I believe that many Christians hold that view and are *naïvely throwing away a significant portion of their eternal future in heaven.*

Admission Versus Maturation

Of course, *admission* to heaven is based solely upon faith in the finished work of Christ, and every new creature in Christ will attain that equally; that will be a "dead heat." A saved divorcer—even a murderer who comes to Jesus with a repentant heart—will experience this. After salvation, however, each Christian plays an active role in his maturation—an ongoing process which requires *obedience* coupled with a well-toned *faith* (Romans 6:13b; 12:1). There is no way this will be a "dead heat." The degree of maturation will make a *huge* difference in each believer's eternal future. Christians are *active* participants in this process. Faith without obedience won't accomplish Christian maturity. If Jesus had *believed* He was to die for our sins, yet never *obeyed* by submitting to the cross, we would have no Savior.

We are the bride of Christ and will reign with Him forever. A fiancée who played no ongoing, active role in the relationship would contribute nothing to that relationship, and it's no different with Christ and His betrothed. God desires a relationship with saints who are reciprocating, free moral agents, not robots! And it's through this interactive, intimate relationship that we grow. Here is what Anabel and

I believe is Paul's "life verse": "[For my determined purpose is] that I may know Him [that I may progressively become more deeply and *intimately acquainted* with Him, perceiving and recognizing and understanding the wonders of His Person more strongly and more clearly], and that I may in that same way come to know the power outflowing from His resurrection [which it exerts over believers]" (Philippians 3:10 AMP). Once you begin relating to the Lord, believing that all of the barriers have been let down, intimacy becomes the name of the game.

Obedience is critical in our maturation process. God says through Peter,

> Now for this very reason also, *applying all diligence*, in your faith *supply* moral excellence, and in your moral excellence, knowledge; and in your knowledge, self-control, and in your self-control, perseverance, and in your perseverance, godliness; and in your godliness, brotherly kindness, and in your brotherly kindness, love. For if these qualities are yours and *are increasing*, they render you neither useless nor unfruitful in the true knowledge of our Lord Jesus Christ. For he who lacks these qualities is blind or shortsighted, having forgotten his purification from his former sins. Therefore, brethren, be all the more diligent to make certain about His calling and choosing you; for as long as you *practice* these things, you will never stumble (2 Peter 1:5-10).

Notice my italicized portions; they deal with diligence in obedience.

Perhaps a couple of analogies will be helpful toward understanding just how critical a diligent devotion to maturing in Christ is. A student was *admitted* to Harvard University. He celebrated the event with friends and family; his mom dropped a word to the society editor of the local paper, who ran a feature along with his photo; his dad had it framed for his bedroom wall. Over the years, when someone noticed the hanging, he enjoyed retelling the old, old story of the day he was *admitted* to Harvard. But he never followed through on his pilgrimage to Harvard University. He didn't know that he was required to enroll in classes, or that he must be a resident student on campus while enrolled in a minimum number of hours. He never heard about required courses, never learned how to use a library or how his experiences at the university were intended to play a vital role in equipping him for his future.

As a middle-aged man, he remained oblivious to the future he could have enjoyed through obedience and perseverance following his admission to Harvard. He had naïvely believed that admission to the university was an *end* instead of a *means* to an end—a fallacy which carries some similarities to those who subscribe to the limited view that the purpose of salvation is to attain heaven. And the Bible doesn't indicate that there will be a chance to correct such a mistake once we arrive there.

Lest I be misunderstood, I am not teaching that new creatures in Christ who waste their opportunities for potential growth on earth will be subject to depression as they cohabit the halls of heaven with the more spiritually mature. God is big enough to solve that problem. After all, He must make some provision for erasing certain data from our memory, or most of us would spend eternity grieving over loved ones whom we knew to be suffering in hell. Perhaps a second analogy will help to clarify this.

— Suppose you and I won a trip to the Rocky Mountains, which neither of us had visited. You are a geologist, while I simply enjoy the great outdoors. They gave us a rental car in Kansas City for the trip. After driving across Kansas and eastern Colorado, we see what we mistake for blue clouds on the horizon, but it dawns on us that those are the Rockies. Excitement sets in. Finally, we top a hill and the mountains appear in all of their majesty.

Soon we're in the foothills, and throughout the day we drive higher into the mountains, stopping at points that interest one or the other of us. You marvel at what you are experiencing, as do I. But each of us would have experienced a different level of enjoyment because of our experiences *before* we arrived. As a geologist, you would have enjoyed the environment at a deeper level, knowing much more about what you were experiencing; my delight, while nonetheless exhilarating, would not be so complete. However, since the level of our delight would seem to be equal, neither of us would be aware of either a deficiency or a superiority of our appreciation of the Rockies.

Analogies break down when compared to the real thing, but I think what I'm conveying is clear. Admission to heaven is wonderful beyond words and is a promise to those who have believed by faith in the saving grace of Jesus Christ. But *admission* is only our *introduction* to Jesus, our open door to the pursuit of *knowing* Him (Philippians 3:10). Experiencing the "Rockies"—heaven and its inhabitants—will doubtless be wonderful in and of itself, but will you be a "geologist," having enjoyed a growing, intimate relationship with Jesus? Or will you walk through the door to meet Him, really for only the second time? Progressing no further than an introduction is hardly the way to build a "marriage" relationship with the Bridegroom!

You Are Determining Your Eternal Role

Both Jesus and the scope of the Bible in general teach a diversity of eternal roles for Christians. This goes far beyond admission to heaven in its ramifications and is based upon our *faithfulness* to allow Christ to live and reign *in* us and *through* us during our earthwalk. Folks, this is not an offensive, burdensome fact of the Christian life. We *desire* to obey our Savior (Hebrews 10:16). We *like* God's ways (Romans

7:22). Although much of our future life in heaven is a mystery, Jesus implied that *there is no general-admission seating in heaven* (see Matthew 20:20-23). "Oh, Bill, who cares where we'll sit! Just so I made it; that's all I care about." Folks, I'm telling you, that attitude is coming from the power of sin who wants to block you from discovering the marvelous opportunity you have while on this planet to prepare yourself for eternity. He hates your guts and is hard at work to minimize your effectiveness both here and there. That's falling into the same mentality trap that deceived the wanna-be Harvard man.

Although the Bible clearly documents that we *shall* reign with Christ (Revelation 22:5), the specifics of who or what we'll be reigning over are sketchy. I believe God did this to afford us time to be strengthened "in the inner man" so we wouldn't succumb to the flesh's desire to compete against the brethren for eternal position. What a flesh trip that would be!

Our level of spiritual development and the role in which God will place us in eternity are interdependent. Although you and I are key players in the process, God already sees the results from the helicopter. Remember now, this is not fatalism, but simply understanding that God is omniscient. Although you may make the decision to change for the better before you finish this page, it won't come as a shock to the One in the helicopter. He won't say, "Well, would you look at that! Ol' Sam decided to get with the program!" It isn't that He forces your eternal role on you, but that He's known what choices you would make from before the foundation of the earth. Gang, when you're omniscient, you know all the dates, times, and places that everyone on earth is going to trim his fingernails! Although Satan will seek to make us chafe at this, God intends that we find rest in it. It's fantastic to know that the One who's the most powerful and who loves you most is the One who has everything under control.

Let's postulate some key points as we examine Revelation 19:7-8, a passage which reveals our *proactive* role in preparing ourselves for our celestial wedding. Your preparation for this wedding serves the double function of developing your spiritual maturity as well as preparing yourself for your eternal role.

"The marriage of the Lamb has come and His bride has *made herself ready.* And it was *given* to her to *clothe herself* in fine linen, bright and clean; for the fine linen is the *righteous acts of the saints."* In light of what we've discussed in this book, I'd like to make seven points from this passage:

Point Number 1. God gives all saints the opportunity to perform a *particular work* which is to *our own benefit.*

Point Number 2. This work is *making us ready*—clothing ourselves.

Point Number 3. The *fine, clean linen* with which we clothe ourselves is comprised of *our righteous acts.*

Point Number 4. This is different from the instantaneous sanctified identity we experienced through salvation. This involves developing into a mature version of the saint you already are.

Point Number 5. This work is performed *before* we get to heaven, so we get only one opportunity: our tenure on planet Earth.

Point Number 6. God alone can perform a righteous act.

Point Number 7. There is but one way that a saint can participate in a righteous act: We must let Christ perform it *through* us, by faith.

Folks, in some marvelous way you might say that you are sewing your wedding gown by allowing Christ to express life through you on earth. I believe the wedding gown

—is a metaphor for your level of spiritual maturity. What else could "His bride has *made herself* ready" mean (Revelation 19:7)? Of course, *God* is the One who grants the increase; maturity can never come about through fleshly effort (Galatians 3:1-3). But God has granted you *the marvelous privilege* of being a participant in your maturation process—the process which prepares you to reign with Christ in what Paul Billheimer called the "eternal social order."

Revelation 21:1-11 describes your brilliance, your radiance, your beauty as you, along with your fellow saints, "made yourself ready" (Revelation 19:7) for marriage to the Lamb (Christ). Obviously, salvation is the initial source of the bride's brilliance. Without salvation there would be no brilliance for any man. But the statement "it was given to her to *clothe herself* in fine linen, bright and clean; for the fine linen is the *righteous acts of the saints*" (Revelation 19:8) indicates that earthly obedience plays a significant part in this glorious scene. The factor being addressed is the *development* of the saint, not his birth.

"And I saw the holy city, new Jerusalem, coming down out of heaven from God, made ready *as a bride* adorned for her husband" (Revelation 21:2). Perhaps you're puzzled at how a city can be comprised of saints. New Jerusalem is the dwelling place of God, where omnipresent God dwells in the saints. God says, "The temple of God is holy, and that is what you are" (1 Corinthians 3:17). God refers to Christians as "stones" who make up the temple of God: "[Christians are] living stones ... being built up as a spiritual house for a holy priesthood, *to offer up spiritual sacrifices acceptable to God through Jesus* Christ" (1 Peter 2:5). God's work alone is acceptable to Him. Therefore, the spiritual sacrifices spoken of here *must* be the works of Christ *through* us, by faith, not *our* works for Him. Christ *produces* the acceptable works; we are the vessels through whom He does so. The *exercising* of our faith is the key here.

God's description of what we'll be like in heaven is elaborated upon further: "And one of the seven angels ... came and spoke with me, saying, 'Come here, I shall show you the bride, the wife of the Lamb.' And he ... showed me the holy city, Jerusalem, coming down out of heaven from God, having the glory of God" (Revelation 21:9-11a). That's the church, gang (see Ephesians 2:20-22; 2 Corinthians 3:9,16; Galatians 4:26; Revelation 3:12). "Her brilliance was like a very costly stone, as a stone of crystal-clear jasper" (Revelation 21:11b). This describes you and me in heaven in our glorious state. The remainder of the chapter and the first part of the next continue to describe the church in heaven. It culminates with "and they shall *reign* forever and ever" in Revelation 22:5.

It's beyond the purpose of this book to explain in detail the reasons that Mormonism is not a branch of Christianity. Just because a man wearing a white smock is seen walking down the hall of a hospital doesn't mean that he's a physician. Just because a group of well-meaning folks worship a being they call "Jesus" doesn't mean he is the risen Jesus Christ of Christianity. This is the case with Mormonism. Why introduce Mormonism into our discussion? It's because Mormonism teaches an eternal hierarchy and man's ability to improve his position in the heavenly chain. I want to dispel any notion that I am a Mormon in disguise. I totally disagree with their doctrine. I reiterate that *I am not challenging us to compete with one another* for a higher position on the celestial ladder. Actively pursuing a higher position would not be a righteous act. Such positions are meted out according to *righteous* acts, not *fleshly* ones. Obviously Christ through me would never compete with Christ through you to jockey for eternal position. But it's a fact of the Christian life that a hierarchy *will* exist in eternity.

James and John said to Jesus, "Grant that we may sit in Your glory, one on Your right, and one on Your left" (Mark

269

10:37), to which He replied, "To sit on My right or on My left, this is not Mine to give; but it is for those for whom it has been prepared" (Mark 10:40). Favored positions in eternity are not available through political patronage. They are available to every saint through faith and obedience by allowing Christ to express His life and will through them (1 Corinthians 3:10-14).

The kingdom of God arrived when God humbled Himself to indwell us by the Spirit of Jesus Christ, who is in each born-again person (Luke 17:21). If you are saved, Christ is living in you; but the question remains: Is He *reigning* over you? This is the key to your sanctified performance on earth, as well as to your future reign with Him. Although He indwells each Christian, He obviously is not reigning over some of us. Each Christian is in moment-by-moment control of this, and the judgment seat of Christ will reveal whether we used His power to submit to Him, allowing Him to be Lord of our ring, or whether we offered our members to "[the power of] sin as instruments of unrighteousness" (Romans 6:13).

Two Judgments

— In addition to the judgment seat of Christ that I have referenced, the Bible speaks of a second judgment, commonly referred to as the great white throne judgment (Revelation 20:12). While the judgment seat of Christ reveals the eternal reward or lack thereof for each *saint's* earthly performance, the great white throne judgment deals with the degree of punishment for each *sinner's* sins. There are two important facts that each unsaved person should understand about his identity and his earthly performance.

- *Sinner-man identity*—The unregenerate man's *spiritual identity* by birth (sinner) will *condemn* him to hell. His earthly performance is of *no consideration whatever* in

270

this issue. He will not go to hell because of his sins, but because of his sinful nature. His "sinner-man" identity banishes him to everlasting hell. "He ... who does not believe [in Christ] has been judged already, because he has not believed in the name of the only begotten Son of God" (John 3:18). Each person who has failed to place his trust in Jesus Christ's vicarious, sacrificial death and resurrection for him has *already* determined his own destiny. There will be no judgment day to determine this. By *not* making a choice, he *made* his choice. The unrepentant sinner-man will have zero opportunity to plead his case before God, as he doubtless believes he'll do. God's Love Letter is clear that he will never get such a chance. After all, it would be fruitless because a person can never get his spiritual identity changed post-death.

• *Sins of the sinner-man*—The great white throne judgment is a judgment day which is exclusively for the man without Christ. Sinners already in the realm of the dead will be raised; sinners killed in the holocaust of the end time will be caught up. At the great white throne judgment, God will determine each sinner's *level of everlasting punishment.* His everlasting punishment *will be determined by his earthly performance* (sins). Apparently, the graver the sin, the more intense the punishment. There will be no happy hour, festive atmosphere—reunion of old friendships that lost folks sing about and anticipate. God's Love Letter says that there will be "weeping and gnashing of teeth." The latter indicates extreme anger. My take on this is that many of these folks are religious people who were never born anew, but who sought eternal life through ritual. They are angry at being misled by false shepherds. How tragic that these dear people never bothered to read God's Love Letter with an open, seeking mind.

271

In the Books or in the Book?

/ "I saw the dead, the great and the small, standing before the throne, and *books* were opened; and another *book* was opened, which is the *book* of life; and *the dead were judged from the things which were written in the books*, according to their deeds" (Revelation 20:12). God cites *multiple* books and *one* book, the book of life. The multiple books contain God's unedited journal entries of each lost person's millions of sins. It's all there, gang: every act, every thought, even every sin of omission. Wow.

The *single* book, on the other hand, is not such a journal. It contains *no record of sins* committed, *only the names* of those who have claimed Jesus Christ as their personal Lord and Savior (Revelation 20:15). Jesus was judged and punished for their sins (Isaiah 53:1-12). Their sins were paid for by Jesus Christ on the cross, and they have been forgiven. God deleted those sins from His hard drive (Psalm 103:12).

The great white throne judgment for those without Christ is a *penalty phase* judgment exposing every one of their millions of individual sins. Not a pretty picture. It's frightening, for example, to imagine the degree of punishment being accumulated by high-profile role models who flaunt their sinful lives before the impressionable youth of the world. Or for those who propagate the politically correct holocaust of infants by supporting abortion rights, including those who do so for political gain. Jesus said, "It would be *better* for [them] if a millstone were hung around [their necks] and [they] were thrown into the sea (Luke 17:2). Why would it be *better* for such folks to die prematurely? Wouldn't it seem like if they're going to hell anyway, they would be better off to remain on earth as long as they could? No, because the longer they continue to lead young people astray, the *heavier the eternal punishment* they accumulate. Their only hope lies in repenting and appropriating Jesus Christ's sacrifice while there is yet time.

God Acknowledges His Work Only

Abraham and Sarah's struggle to produce a son gives us insight into what will be involved at the judgment seat of Christ, where each Christian's works will be evaluated by God. When his son, Isaac, was about 25, God said to Abraham, "Take now your son, *your only son*, whom you love, Isaac, [and offer him as a living sacrifice]" (Genesis 22:2). What an astounding commandment! To Abraham's credit, he *immediately* set out to obey the Lord (verse 3). But have you ever wondered why God referred to Isaac as an "only son"? Why did He exclude Ishmael? The answer to this question reveals how imperative it is that we accept as factual that *we can do nothing* until we embrace Christ as our very life. The Good Housekeeping Seal of Approval on a product influences shoppers to purchase it. Well, God has *His* seal of approval. If the sticker don't say "Christ's work through me," He ain't buyin'! We must continually embrace the truth that Jesus taught: "Apart from Me you can do *nothing* [of eternal value]" (John 15:5). God wants to be involved moment by moment, and the Christian who trusts in even a smidgen of his own power loses: game, set, match. God hates independence.

God, you see, had waited to deliver on His promise to Abraham until he aged enough to be "dead" as far as getting Sarah pregnant goes. And as for Sarah, she couldn't ovulate when she was a teenager, let alone at 90. Our dear sister was decades past menopause! Ishmael was the do-it-yourself son that Abraham, Sarah, and Hagar produced through the flesh. Ishmael was *their* work. Isaac was *God's* supernatural work. *God acknowledges His work only*, whether it be on earth or in heaven; everything else is rejected. Even Jesus adhered to this maxim: "The words that I say to you I do not speak on My own initiative, but the Father abiding in Me does His work" (John 14:10). Jesus never did anything independently. I don't think most Christians understand that when through Isaiah God said, "All *our* righteous deeds are like a filthy garment" (Isaiah 64:6), he did not limit this to the unsaved's inability to merit heaven via good works. It also applies to the Christian's inability to merit God's approval via *his* good works. This is why we must allow Christ to work *through* us, by faith, if our work is to have any eternal significance (Romans 15:18a).

God Wishes Christians Knew That They Will Not Be Judged

Forgive me for being so redundant about the judgment seat of Christ issue, but I believe it is misunderstood. Many well-meaning Christians threaten other believers with God's judgment to keep them in line. This is not God's method. The devil loves for us to sing this song:

> You better watch out; you better not cry;
> You better not pout, I'm tellin' you why,
> Jesus Christ is coming to town.
> He knows when you've been sleeping;
> He knows when you're awake;
> He knows when you've been bad or good,
> So be good for goodness sake!

How often do we hear that we're going to face an angry God who is going to skin us alive for the "unforgiven sins" in our lives at that final judgment? Folks, I'm happy to report that the Bible says it ain't gonna happen like that. You could hardly be "seated in the heavenly places" already, with un-forgiven sin (Ephesians 2:6). You're forgiven, period (Colossians 2:13-14)! What's going to happen at the judgment seat of Christ is that what we have trusted Christ to do *through* us will be acceptable to God; everything else we have done, even *for God*, will be burned up because it was independent effort. The Bible speaks of God as a consuming fire:

> He has promised, saying, "Yet once more I will shake not only the earth, but also the heaven." And this

expression, "Yet once more," denotes the *removing of those things which can be shaken,* as of created things, in order that those things which cannot be shaken may remain. Therefore, since we receive a kingdom which cannot be shaken, let us show gratitude, by which we may offer to God an acceptable service with reverence and awe; for our God is a consuming fire (Hebrews 12:26-29).

I believe that the "things which can be shaken" refers to the things the flesh produces which will be burned by "God [who] is a consuming fire."

Acceptance Versus Approval

I believe that many Christians, ranging from the high-profile to the low, will see their earthly efforts go up in flames because their *method* was wrong. Their method was human *independence*. In speaking of our works that will be judged, God says, "Let each man be careful *how* he builds ..." (1 Corinthians 3:10). Look at that; He's talking about our *method*, gang. In verse 13 He says, "Each one's *work* will become clear; for the Day will declare it, because it will be revealed by fire; and the fire will test each one's work, *of what sort it is*" (NKJV). The phrase that I emphasized is a literal translation of the Greek. The good news here is that it will be the Christian's *work* that will be judged, *not the Christian,* since Jesus was judged for us. We're home free! The bad news for some Christians is *of what sort the work is.* Was it *man's* work or *God's* work? Was it work that *man* did *for* God, or was it work that *God* did *through* man? The fire at the judgment seat of Christ will reveal that our *method* by which we produced our works is the critical variable. The judgment will not be based upon a sliding scale, with Jesus having set the curve. It will be a higher, a stricter grading system than that, and it will be an easy call for God to make. The judgment will be based upon *whose work it was*—man's or God's. You can see that this will require a pass/fail judgment. No subjective evaluation whatever. If it's God's work, it passes; if it's man's work, it fails.

You and I are to bring honor to God, to allow Him to enhance His reputation through us on earth. He calls this "glorifying His name." The *only* provision for our accomplishing this is to "offer ourselves as living sacrifices" to Christ to let Him express His life through us to do His will on earth (Romans 6:13; 12:1; 15:18). No one teaches Sunday school *for* Him, preaches *for* Him, goes to missions *for* Him, rears children *for* Him, is kind to his spouse *for* Him, loads the dishwasher *for* Him, mows the lawn *for* Him, or is courteous at the four-way stop *for* Him. Though the motive may be admirable, the work is unacceptable wood, hay, and stubble because it's the product of independent human effort. God's method is that we trust Christ to accomplish these *same, identical things* through us, by faith. In this manner, God can showcase *His* worthiness to mankind, not ours.

Let's dispel some false notions about the judgment seat of Christ. *You*, as a believer, will not be judged! A careful study of 1 Corinthians 3:10-15 reveals that your *method* of producing works ("*how*" you build, verse 10), *of what sort your work is* (verse 13), your *motives* (4:5), and your *words* (Matthew 12:36) will be judged. *You will not be judged:* "If any man's work is burned up, he shall suffer loss; but he himself shall be saved, yet so as through fire" (1 Corinthians 3:15). Though your works will be judged, you will apparently stand before God as an intensely interested observer while your earthly performance is being reviewed. Knowing this truth can take a huge load off your back. Such knowledge is a beautiful rest stop, as there are many well-meaning Bible teachers who teach that Christians must be "kept in line" by the threat of facing an angry God's future judgment. I'm happy to tell you that this cannot be documented by *post-cross Scripture*. I don't fault the *motive* of these teachers;

I'm sure they mean well, but their position is unbiblical. Obviously, God does not approve of sin—but His acceptance of us is unchanging. *He never smolders in anger at new creatures in Christ. He took out all of His anger against us on Jesus at the cross* (Isaiah 53:2ff). But as far as our performance goes, remember what we learned through Abraham's experience: Only a work *of* God is approved *by* God. He rejects all human, independent products or efforts. "All *our* righteous deeds are like a filthy garment" applies to *saints* as well as sinners (Isaiah 64:6).

A Pass/Fail Judgment

Keeping in mind the truths we've covered so far, let's look at the judgment seat of Christ in 1 Corinthians 3:11-15:

> For no man can lay a foundation other than the one which is laid, which is Jesus Christ. Now if any man builds upon the foundation with gold, silver, precious stones, wood, hay, straw, each man's work will become evident; for the day will show it, because it is to be revealed with fire; and the fire itself will test *of what sort each man's work is* [literal translation of italicized phrase]. If any man's work which he has built upon it remains, he shall receive a reward. If any man's work is burned up, he shall suffer loss; but he himself shall be saved, yet so as through fire.

Whereas your old foundation was in Adam (fleshly), your new "foundation" spoken of in the passage above is Christ (Spirit), and the building itself (your individual spiritual maturity level) must be constructed of the same *spiritual material* as the foundation, "which is Jesus Christ" (1 Corinthians 3:11). That is huge, folks. Be sure you get that last point. The *building material* will be the criterion by which each work will be judged. The building materials are of *your choice*, and they are obtainable from only two sources: the Holy Spirit or self. At the judgment seat of Christ, God's refining fire will examine your building (level of maturity) to see "of what sort" it is (1 Corinthians 3:13). This will clearly be a dichotomous judgment. He will either reward you or deny you reward according to the *method* you employed on earth. Did you trust Christ as life through you? Or did you live independently, even trying to "help God" at times? What is your building made of: Christ or self? Those parts of your building that are of the same spiritual material used for its foundation (Christ) will pass with flying colors (1 Corinthians 3:12-13). Any part which is *your* independent work, regardless of how "successful" it was on earth or how "religious" it was, or *even how much God used it to His glory on earth*, such as leading folks to Christ, will be condemned as wood, hay, and straw and thrown into the fire (verses 12-15). Yes, God *will* use even fleshly service to accomplish His will on earth, but the servant himself will receive no reward.

The judgment seat of Christ is not a judgment of whether or not a person is saved. The very fact that a person is at the judgment seat of Christ proves that he is saved. Salvation is *God's* work, and *it never goes on trial*. Our salvation is as sure as God's Word. The judgment seat of Christ is a *pass/fail* judgment based upon "of what sort" *your* work was, God's or man's. (Gold, silver, jewels versus wood, hay, straw—1 Corinthians 3:12. That's pass/fail.) The Word does not support the notion of a sliding scale or bell-curve judgment which factors in circumstances, ability, condition of earthsuit, heritage, environment, or even spiritual gifts. Your *faith* (in Christ as life) and your *obedience* in following through with action on that faith will be the determining criteria. And don't receive the accusation from the power of sin that you don't have enough faith to pull this off! You employ the same faith you used to get saved with. Simply add Christ as life to Christ as Savior and Lord and start acting like it's true. Finally, following the judgment seat of Christ, even a new creature in Christ who loses every single reward will still be saved because *salvation is a work of God*. Salvation can obviously *never* be a work of the flesh.

— Check out the parable of the talents in Luke 19:12-26, where Jesus tells the story of a nobleman who departed to claim a kingdom for himself and entrusted his precious treasure to ten slaves. Those who proved trustworthy were told, "Well done, good slave, because you have been faithful in a very little thing, you are to be in authority over ten cities" (verse 17), implying that obedience to God's will on earth correlates with our eternal reigning role. As Ron Blue taught me: "God owns it all; you and I are stewards who are responsible to do the Owner's will. Stewards can't own anything." Hey, you don't even own your toenail trimmings. There are but two ways to live (handle God's resources entrusted to you) on earth: in the Spirit (allowing Christ to live through you) or after the flesh (independently, trusting in your own ability). *How* you live will determine the level of your eternal reigning role because apparently trusting Christ as life will be our strategy for reigning eternally. Why would there ever be any other? Since this is the way God is training us on earth, why would He change this Christ-centered method in eternity?

You Are Being Finished at the Quarry

The Bible portrays earth as a finishing school in which God works to refine us: "For I am confident of this very thing, that He who began a good work in you will perfect it until the day of Christ Jesus. . . . For it is God who is at work in you, both to will and to work for His good pleasure" (Philippians 1:6; 2:13). God is diligently working to conform us to the image of His dear Son. "For whom He foreknew, He also predestined to become conformed to the image of His Son, that He might be the first-born among many brethren" (Romans 8:29). Remember that God has used the metaphor of describing us individually and corporately as "living stones" in the heavenly temple (1 Peter 2:5). The construction strategy for Solomon's physical temple in the Old Testament was a foreshadowing of the heavenly *spirit/soul* temple, which is "not made with hands" (2 Corinthians 5:1). "We heard Him say, 'I will destroy this temple made with hands, and in three days I will build another made without hands'" (Mark 14:58). Jesus was speaking of us! *We are those living building blocks in the temple not made with hands!*

There is an intriguing fact about the Old Testament Temple (God's dwelling place) constructed by Solomon which is a significant foreshadowing of the level of spiritual maturity you reach before death. God says, "The house ... was built of stone [*finished*] at the quarry, and there was neither hammer nor ax or any iron tool heard *in the house* while it was being built" (1 Kings 6:7). Each building block was *finished far away from the Temple site*. Likewise, *we, the stones*, are being perfected on earth, which is the "quarry" where the chisels ring, the dust flies, and the storms blow (1 Kings 6:7). We will depart from our earthsuits at death and be transported directly to the temple site (heaven) where each "living stone" in the "temple made without hands" will be slipped *perfectly* into its designated, individual place. That is worth a second read as you trust the Holy Spirit to show you how significant this is to your eternal future.

I believe this is an allegory of the plan God has for the development of our eternal reigning role, which is determined by the degree to which we "offer ourselves to Him as living sacrifices" on earth, cooperating with the Holy Spirit as He chisels away our fleshly patterns for living. It seems obvious to me that such equipping will not be a slow, individual process in heaven, but will be revealed through the judgment seat of Christ as *having already been accomplished or not accomplished* on earth. "Godliness ... holds promise for the present life and *also for the life to come*" (1 Timothy 4:8). How? If heaven is a great coliseum where we're all kicked back in recliners, then why should we concern ourselves with maturing in Christ? Why even bother? Indeed, why should *God* even concern Himself with working night and day to lead us to spiritual maturity (Philippians 1:6; 2:13)? Are your eyes open, my brother, my sister? This is huge for your eternal well-being.

Gang, the misconception of heaven being a place of eternal lazy relaxation is from the Deceiver, not the Holy Spirit. We would go nuts under such a condition! God did not even create the lost man for such a life, let alone re-create the saved for it. The construction technique used for Solomon's Temple indicates that you and I (the temple "made without hands"—Mark 14:58) are presently locking ourselves into our eternal roles from which we will never, never budge one fraction of an inch. Although *corporate* growth of the entire body of Christ will doubtless occur in heaven as we bask in sweet fellowship with the Lord and sit under His marvelous wisdom, *we get one shot at maturing into the spiritual state that we will possess eternally, and it all happens on earth.* This is where the chisels and hammers ring against the living stones. "There was neither hammer nor ax nor any iron tool heard in the house while it was being built." All of the shaping and conforming of Christians to the image of Christ takes place on earth, not in heaven.

— I'm reminded of a time during my number-one son Preston's teen years when, visiting an Ozark Mountain craft park, we were watching a wood-carver hew an Indian out of a log. "How in the world does he do that?" I marveled.

"It's easy, Dad. He just chips away everything that doesn't look like an Indian."

This is what God is doing to us in the earthly "quarry"— chiseling away our old flesh patterns, conforming us to the image of Christ. Our role is to cooperate with Him in this process. Isn't that exciting?

God uses each and every circumstance we experience to conform us to the image of Christ (Romans 8:28-29), and He accomplishes this via a dynamic mix of love, persecution, joy, anger, being struck down, euphoria, tragedy, satisfaction, success, stress, crushing disappointment, "undeserved" calamity, inexplicable pain, ecstatic hope, etc., "always carrying about in the body the *dying* of Jesus, that the *life of Jesus* also may be manifested in our body" (2 Corinthians 4:10) Christ is our life, gang. God uses all things to crowd us toward weakness, to a recognition of our inability to make life work independently. It is through personal weakness and disenchantment with self that a Christian is best prepared by the Holy Spirit to discover how to let Christ do it all *through* him, *for* him. Jesus is the only One who has ever lived the overcoming Christian life, and *just as He was totally dependent upon the Father, we are to give up on our own strength and be totally dependent upon Him working through us*. It's our choice.

Divorce Revisited

Consider once again John's divorce. The Bible teaches that John is already forgiven for his sin. We've covered that in chapter 11. But unlike forgiveness, depending on Christ as life isn't an automatic call with our salvation; it must first be embraced, then *practiced*. Some Christians rebel against the circumstances in which God seeks to weaken them, taking a giant step backward in their spiritual maturity program and, consequently, in God's heavenly social order. This describes John's action. What a price to pay, both here and there. Many married Christians, who have not been instructed about the significance of earth's role in training them for reigning or who feel life is passing them by and they're not getting enough gusto, receive the power of sin's lie with those first-person-singular pronouns: *This marriage is so tedious and stressful. Why not dump* my *marriage and family "phase" and get a fresh start with no entanglements? I know I don't have a valid, biblical justification, but God will forgive me. After all, I know I'm on my way to heaven, so what difference does it really make? I think I'll just do it.* What a tragic mistake. This is like dropping out of high school. Read the following verses and see what our reigning role involves. I believe you'll conclude that the way we live on earth *does* make a difference.

"You have made them ... a kingdom and priests to our God; and they will reign *upon the earth*" (Revelation 5:10). There's reign for us in tomorrow's forecast, gang. Christians will reign with Christ over the (apparently) repopulated earth during the millennium.

"And they shall rule along with Him a thousand years" (Revelation 20:6, AMP). The Crusades began in 1095. Had you begun reigning with Christ over the earth in 1095, you would still have more than an earthly lifetime left to reign. Is that a bird in the hand worth preparing for? Will you kick and fuss and waste your sorrows during this mega-brief time on earth, instead of allowing God to use them to drive you deeper into being made more like Jesus, even on the anvil of adversity?

"And they shall reign ... forever and ever [through the eternities of the eternities]" (Revelation 22:5, AMP). Whoa! How's that for tenure in office? No term limits! Those over whom Christ reigns *now* will reign *with* Christ in whatever future social order He plans to create *forever and ever and ever and ever and . . .*

Reigning over What?

— I don't know (and I don't care) what sort of critters we'll reign over, but He says, "If we endure [cooperate with God and His workings in us, instead of fighting for our independence], we shall also reign with Him" (2 Timothy 2:12a). God says we will reign, so it must be for our eternal good or He wouldn't plan it for us. Reigning-through-submission-to-Christ's-authority courses are available only on earth, not in heaven. *Christians can either take them for credit (conformed to the image of Christ), or you can audit them, but you **will** be enrolled in them and you **will** attend class.* And if you audit the course, you will be enrolled in another similar course for credit. Endurance in trials is eternally significant to your future reigning role. And here is God's grace: *You* don't have to endure! You're not even *supposed* to endure! *Christ* will do the enduring *through you.* It's so foolish for a Christian to buy the lie and blow off his entire life (or a significant portion of it as John the divorcer did), making up his own rules as he goes, thinking that it's no big deal to do so.

Who is it that has a love/hate relationship with you? He *hates* you so much that he *loves* to see you compromise your faithfulness in light of these glorious plans God has for your present and future. Satan! Remember how faked-out the would-be Harvard man was! Remember how deceived Esau was who swapped his eternal future for a bowl of stew! The Harvard man is fictional; Esau is still alive as we speak. Think about what you will be doing in the year 2172, or 6589 or 15758. Does that seem so far removed that you can put off getting started today? Remember: You can be in God's presence in a heartbeat, and *maturity comes only via proper mellowing on earth.*

Do you identify with John?[1] Confess it to God and thank Him that He's not holding it against you. Jesus absorbed that hostility on the cross. If you haven't already done so, ask any who were wounded by your sin to forgive you.[2] If reconciliation would not create *worse* problems, perhaps God will make a way for this. Tell Him that, by His grace, *you are willing* to let Christ live through you for your reconciliation if *He* wishes.[3] If *He* does not open this door, then move forward in God's grace. It's never too late for a new beginning till you eject from your earthsuit.

15 THE FOLLY OF SELF-GENERATED SELF-ACCEPTANCE

"AL, WHERE'D YOU GET those shoes?" I asked the rich young senator from southwest Oklahoma. I represented the education lobby with the Oklahoma legislature at the time, and my friend was sporting the first pair of alligator loafers I had ever seen—on anyone other than an alligator. Man, it was lust at first sight when I saw those shoes. I could just visualize how cool I would look in a set of them. Al told me where he had bought them. "How much?" I queried.

"Oh, about 100 dollars." Hey, we're talking about preinflation dollars. A hundred dollars would have bought shoes for my entire family! I immediately experienced what Bill Gothard calls "the death of a vision."

Months later, a friend that I grew up with dropped by my office near the capitol building. He was superintendent of schools in a prestigious school district and enjoyed a comfortable income. He drew up a chair, leaned back, crossed his legs, and began to jiggle the toe of his shoe up and down. You guessed it: 'gator hide! Arrrgh! Just when I had about overcome my lust for Al's loafers, here came my old boyhood friend flashing the same brand, up and down, up and down, playing peekaboo behind the lip of my desk! I recalled the old Quaker's prayer, "Lord, it's no wonder You have so many enemies, the way You treat Your friends."

"Did you give 100 dollars for those loafers?"
"Yes."
"How can you afford to pay 100 dollars for shoes?"

Now, you need a little background to better appreciate the rest of this story. George had grown up in an extremely poor home, so you can see how he might not have sterling-silver self-image flesh. The members of his school board were powerful, well-to-do individuals in his city. It's fairly easy to see how George would be particularly vulnerable to the temptation of developing fleshly techniques to compensate for his low self-esteem.

When George was a little anxious or emotional, he would wag his head as he talked, and at my question he switched from wagging his toe to wagging his head. "Bill, let me tell you something. (*Wag, wag.*) When I meet with my board, I can put on my alligator shoes and one of my Hickey Freeman suits and feel like I'm as good as any one of them! (*Wag, wag.*) I feel like I can whip 'em all!" I had never heard of a Hickey Freeman suit, but when I checked it out some time later, I found that they cost 300 dollars—about one-fifth the price of my family car! George had obviously sacrificed *greatly* to get those clothes.

Wood, Hay, and Stubble Games

The games we play seeking to enhance our self-worth ... And even if we "win" via using such games, it becomes "wood, hay, and stubble" to fuel that great wiener roast in the sky. "If any man's work is burned up, he shall suffer loss" (1 Corinthians 3:15); so we lose in the final analysis. Satan loves to make us unhappy with our lot in life and then get us chasing our tails looking for a solution. My lust for gator loafers was a compensating technique generated by the flesh so I could feel "cooler" than the unwashed masses who had to wear cow leather ... poor wretches.

Gang, we are wise not to base our self-worth upon our flesh. We need to opt for eternal criteria, which insulate us against earthly inflation. We can't let our self-image become tied to our earthsuit, for no matter what we do, all of us eventually become what my teen friend Kathryn calls "gravitationally challenged." Gang, gravity ultimately makes the earthsuit run down into our shoes. How about your self-image? Are you building a row of dominoes where one flick of Satan's finger will do you in? Are you building a house of cards where one bump of the earth's shaky table will wipe you out? In two-thirds of the earth, the greatest shame is to be an embarrassment to your family. But what about God? What is *His* opinion? Fleshly self-acceptance can disappear faster than you can say *stock market* or *car wreck* or *cancer* or *divorce*.

Sand Castles

Every subculture has its self-worth poker chips that must be anted up and all of us are players as we begin our earthwalk. Only Christ can liberate us from the game, but we've got to know how. Among western Kentucky corn growers, a guy has to have the "right" gimme cap from the "right" seed company to feel acceptable at the grain elevator. Just about anywhere you go, there is an understood hierarchy of automobile models—a scale by which folks quantify their worth or value. These come with various bells and whistles which set you apart as a person of worth.

How about the way your self-worth spikes when you raise your car's power radio antenna as you're in the crowd waiting for the light to change? Imagine how envious the poor lackeys must be who suffer through life with a fixed antenna. Who is the motivator behind a three-year-old girl entering the "Little Miss fill-in-the-blank" contest: the child or the mom? A woman in my state actually hired a hit man to take out the mother of her daughter's chief rival in the upcoming middle-school cheerleader tryouts just so the poor child's grief would adversely affect her performance. This woman has such a self-worth problem that she was willing to kill to solve it.

Our Needs Are God-Given

Do you suppose God understands the intensity of the need we have for self-worth? Of course. It's part number S-W 7 in His build-a-human kit. Implicit within what Jesus called "the second greatest commandment" (we're to love others as much as we love ourselves) is the premise that we were created to experience positive self-worth. The question is, What or who is the source of my self-acceptance? Is it the flesh or is it the Spirit? God says, "Whatever is not from faith is sin" (Romans 14:23). If my self-acceptance is the result of my own work, using the criteria of the world, I already "have my reward" and none awaits me at the judgment seat of Christ in heaven, where my works will be evaluated to determine their origin: flesh or the Holy Spirit (1 Corinthians 3:13-15).

— Let's take the next exit ramp off God's freeway, labeled "Fleshly Self-Acceptance." You'll notice the steaming radiators and exhausted motorists as we move slowly through this area. We'll not stop here, but I wanted you to see what it's like so you can avoid it. Before we can savor the sweetness of the "Biblical Self-Acceptance" rest stop to the fullest, we must understand that we all build our self-acceptance out of the flesh in the beginning. Learning through contrasting the right way against the wrong is very effective.

Psychotherapy

As we pass these stalled cars and frustrated drivers, let's discuss the way the world deals with a low self-image. I believe psychologists have made some helpful discoveries during the relatively brief tenure of this discipline. I taught the subject for several years, so I suppose it's all right to make a few comments about the profession. To me, the problem does not lie with psychology, but with psychotherapy. Psychology is the *study* of human behavior. Using the discoveries of psychology and perhaps some medication to help a hurting person play lord of the ring more effectively is psychotherapy. *Psychotherapy seeks to help folks develop more trust in themselves.* It seeks to increase *self*-confidence, *self*-esteem, *self*-reliance, etc. The basis for each of those is *self*. The *Christian's* confidence, on the other hand, is to be placed in Christ alone (Romans 15:18). And not in Christ to "help" me, as if the more I can contribute to the equation, the less of Christ I'll need. Psychotherapy seeks to build a firmer house of cards—even so-called "Christian" psychotherapy.

The psychotherapist portrays you as potentially capable of shouldering the load of living *independently,* and for big bucks he/she will seek to teach you how to do it. A lot of this is packaged as Christian counseling and being marketed on Christian radio stations as well as at pastors' conferences across America. They simply add the phrase "along with God's help" to the equation. Its practitioners typically seek to classify as many forms of aberrant behavior as possible with a medical label (i.e., bulimia, anorexia, obsessive-compulsive). Is it coincidental that most insurance companies only pay for treating a *medical* problem?

I was listening to a Christian radio station and heard some of these practitioners label Christians with an uncontrollable temper "rage-aholics." They spoke of how common the "rage-aholic" problem is, and addressed one another as "Doctor" this and "Doctor" that, "What do you think, Doctor?" It sounded like General Hospital. I interpreted this as an effort to convince the naïve that frequent loss of temper is a *medical* problem. Nonsense. It's sin. *These* folks must embrace their true identity in Christ and learn how to let *Christ* overcome their temper for them. Learning to develop greater self-control through therapy is long-term, tedious, temporal, expensive, and will be burned up at the judgment seat of Christ. Go figure.

Psychologists and psychotherapists can draw a decent historical road map of a person's lord-of-the-ring pilgrimage leading up to his present fix, but their ideas on how to fix his fix are based upon *self*. God says we are to "put *no* confidence in the flesh" (Philippians 3:3).

Boon or Bane?

Much of what passes for "Christian" counseling in most churches and seminaries is merely attaching Scripture to humanistic, self-help, psychotherapeutic models, which does not warrant the notion that they are anointed with God's blessing. The original behavioral models are generated by unregenerate humans' ideas on how to maintain independence; so, we must be mega-discerning when selecting a "Christian" counselor. *True Christian counseling is discipleship*, which leads the counselee to abandon all trust in himself and opt for his identity in Christ, along with dependency upon Christ as life through him.

If a person were to seek my help and I taught him unbiblical, self-strengthening techniques to help him *feel* better, have I helped him, or have I taught him how to develop more effective flesh? It's the latter, and since God exhorts us to "give no opportunity to the flesh," I would be working against the Holy Spirit, instead of in conjunction with Him.

Christian Is Not an Adjective

Does a Christian plumber use "Christian" wrenches, or does a Christian physician perform "Christian" surgery? Obviously not. I believe we must avoid using the word *Christian* as an adjective. Today the church abounds with well-meaning staff counselors, seminary-trained in psychotherapeutic techniques that seem to correlate with selected Scripture in order to "help strengthen" hurting Christians. Such folks would be best referred to as "counselors who are Christians," as such counseling techniques are not according to God's plan. God seeks to lead Christians to abandon their trust in self and place all confidence in Christ, who indwells us (John 15:5). I do not fault the counselors' motives; I credit them as well as their seminary mentors for meaning well. However, I fault their *method* as unbiblical. Such counselors may be compassionate, godly Christians, but if they naïvely equip Christians to play lord of the ring more effectively in order to help them *feel* better, they are not only failing to do God's work, they actually hinder the work of the Holy Spirit by strengthening the flesh.

— God's goal for us is *not* that we always *feel* good, but rather to conform us to the image of Christ (Romans 8:29). Every Christian desires to be Christlike. Jesus demonstrated *agape* love, patience, mercy, goodness, boldness when appropriate, compassion, generosity, understanding, silence when appropriate, wisdom, integrity, self-sacrifice, etc. My friend Frank Friedmann asks: Where did Jesus get the power to manifest such glorious characteristics? If you answered that *Jesus was God*, that's not how Jesus got His power. He laid that aside to become a man (Philippians 2:7; 2 Corinthians 8:9; Hebrews 2:17). If you answered that Jesus got His power from the Father, you are correct (John 14:10,24; 5:19). Jesus was the most *dependent* sound-of-mind-and-body Man to ever walk planet Earth. John 14:10 says that He depended solely upon Another who indwelled Him: His Father. Learning how to abandon all *self*-reliance and cast ourselves upon *Christ's* sufficiency for us and through us is mandatory to maturity in Christ. Trusting in oneself is folly. If Jesus never exhibited an ounce of self-reliance, it's a no-brainer that we must abandon all such trust. *God is diligently working to bring us to the end of trusting in ourselves* (2 Corinthians 12:9). God loves relationship; He hates independence. Godly counsel always takes our focus off self and places it upon Jesus Christ and His finished work for us.

It's one thing to take your car to a mechanic who uses world-system wrenches to tune your engine, but quite another to use a counselor who employs world-system counseling techniques to tune up your soul. *True Christian counseling is essentially discipleship*:

1) discipling Christians to *abandon* playing lord of the ring

2) discipling Christians to embrace *Christ* as Lord of their ring

3) discipling Christians to abandon their world-system identity

4) discipling Christians to embrace their true identity in Christ

5) discipling Christians to embrace their unconditional acceptance in Christ

6) discipling Christians to embrace Christ as life through them

7) discipling Christians to claim forgiveness for *all* their sins

8) discipling Christians to allow Christ through them to forgive any wrongs done to them by others

9) discipling Christians to give God permission to allow anything to come into their lives that He wills in order to best be conformed to the image of Christ.

Does that last one bother you? Who would you prefer to be in charge of your future: you or our merciful Father? Are you not convinced yet that He is far more able to pour out *agape* and blessings upon you than you are? Give it up! Embracing these truths enables hurting believers to cast their burdens squarely on Jesus Christ and let Him weather the storms of life *for* them, *through* them (Psalm 55:22).

Self-Acceptance

Remember that man's need to be loved comes from God. Since God is love, He created us to *need* love, because if we didn't need to be loved, we would have no need to know God personally. Since we began life with no knowledge of God, we each sallied forth as lords of the ring, seeking to be loved by *people*. People do not give love freely—we must *earn* it the old-fashioned way. We must merit it in their perception. Although it's not precise, I'm going to use the terms *love* and *acceptance* as synonyms.

Psychology has made some helpful discoveries. One hypothesis teaches that acceptance (love) can be attained if we believe three things:

- We must believe that we *belong* to at least one other person.

- We must believe we have *value*, that the world would be a bit poorer if we were to die.

- We must believe we are *competent*, that we can do at least one thing well.

Belonging, worth, and *competence.* This hypothesis implies that maintaining these three factors will produce a sense of being loved. It's very helpful, but our *method* for satisfying these needs is of critical importance. God's plan is that we learn how to "[accomplish] all things through *Christ* who strengthens [us]" (Philippians 4:13). The world's plan is that we tackle this as a do-it-yourself project.

We'll examine some *fleshly* techniques for satisfying these three needs. In chapter 16, we'll discuss how they are to be satisfied through *Christ.*

Our Need to Belong

The Team

If we are to bestow acceptance upon ourselves, we must believe that we *belong*. When I grew up in Oklahoma, the

293

high school all-star football game was an annual event of great significance. The north all-state football players were pitted against those from the south. It was a very prestigious Saturday-night contest in August that kicked off the fall football season, and enthusiasts turned out en masse. If a tornado had struck, it would have wiped out more macho flesh than the Red Sea when it sank the Egyptian army.

As you looked into the stands across the field, you could spot coats of many colors: red ones, green ones, purple ones, identifying football lettermen. If you've never been to Oklahoma in August, let me assure you that in terms of heat it's one of the nearest things to (as Radar O'Reilly says in "M.A.S.H.") *"h-e-double toothpicks"* that a person can experience on earth. You can believe that the *last* thing an Okie needs is a football jacket to protect his body from the evening chill. Those kids with the jackets wore them at great physical sacrifice. The sweat was rolling down their rib cages! Why would they punish themselves so? They wore the jacket to satisfy their need to *belong*.

These were kids with macho hang-ups, the kids who have a low masculine self-image. They needed others to see them in their jackets so they could fantasize that they were perceived as *belonging* to this machismo scene. The jacket helped to alleviate their *feelings* of masculine self-depreciation. They felt that they were not "as male" as they would have liked. Their worst nightmare would be to *feel* like others were speculating that they might play in the band. Trust me; I was once one of them. So, you see, the critical variable here is *others*. Without other people, this flesh trip becomes meaningless. Place the kid on an abandoned Pacific island, and he'll use his jacket for a minnow seine.

The Sorority

I was a psychology professor at a secular university in Oklahoma before God called me into the ministry. A middle-aged woman there worked as a lay helper of one of the campus sororities, and she took the job seriously. She was rarely seen without her sorority pin gleaming in the sunlight. I was curious as to why this lady wore the pin all the time. I concluded that she had a need to *feel* attractive and popular, a need to *feel* that she *belonged* to the group on our campus, which was noted for overflowing with those endowments. She wanted others to see her pin so she could fantasize that they were associating her with popularity and beauty. Would she wear her pin on that Pacific island? No. Maybe for homecoming, right? Hey, without people to impact, she would use it for a fishing lure. Remove *others* from the equation, and the game becomes unproductive.

Our Need for Self-Worth

The Roar of the Crowd

Like our need for belonging, our need for self-worth was built into us by our Creator. He could easily have eliminated this need, but He designed us this way. Like all of our needs, "[He will] supply *all* your needs according to His riches in glory in Christ Jesus" (Philippians 4:19). But like a bunch of hammerheads, we gobbled the world's bait and sought to satisfy our need for self-worth via the flesh.

King Saul was a plain-vanilla guy before he made it to the top. When he tasted the heady power of public adoration, he became addicted to the roar of the crowd. In the end he was more obsessed with maintaining *public* acceptance than with resting in *God's* acceptance. Samuel told Saul, "Isn't it true that though you were little in your own eyes, God made you king over Israel?" (paraphrase of 1 Samuel 15:17). Saul had a self-esteem problem, and he had made the acceptance he received from people his source of self-worth, rather than the *intangible* acceptance of our Father.

Following yet another of Saul's failures to obey God, Samuel told him that he was being cut from the starting lineup. Saul's response? "I have sinned; but oh, at least honor me *before the leaders* and *before my people* by going with me to worship the Lord *your* God" (1 Samuel 15:30 TLB). No godly sorrow; the man begged Samuel for one more curtain call. "Let's just act like it's business as usual in front of the crowd, Sam. Just the two of us superstars and *your* God." It's interesting to me that when the Old Testament kings are confronted by a prophet for being disobedient to God, they refer to God as *your* God, not *our* or *my* God. They seemed to instinctively know that *God is not real* to those who refuse to at least *try* to obey Him.

Creative Alternative

King Solomon was on an obedience roll, and God's material blessings were being poured out on Israel. He ordered 200 large gold shields, plus 300 additional gold-plated shields for his guards to carry when he went up to the house of the Lord (2 Chronicles 9:15-16). Pretty impressive. Imagine Solomon, surrounded by these 500 guys sporting the gold shields, pulling his chariot up beside you at the stoplight while you're making your power radio antenna go up and down to impress the other drivers. Sort of makes you want to stow your antenna in its sheath, doesn't it?

Eventually, his son Rehoboam became king and, within a few years, ol' Reho had turned Israel back to the party-god, Baal, whose worship featured sexual orgies. This resulted in God's bringing in the latest southern *rock* group called "Shishak and the Egyptians," who pounded Israel, stole all the gold, including the 500 shields, and then caught the red-eye back to Africa (2 Chronicles 12:1-9).

Rehoboam came up with what the Washington power brokers call a "creative alternative." He had his metal smiths construct *bronze* shields for his guards to carry when he went up to the house of the Lord (2 Chronicles 12:10-11). He played like nothing had changed! "I feel your pain, people! But, God is still blessing. Gold is out this year; it's too ostentatious. Bronze is the politically correct metal of choice. We donated the gold to our African mission outreach to boost their economy. Follow me—we're on a roll. God is blessing us!"

Rehoboam Revisited

You've gotta love the way the Bible lets us see the warts on some of the folks it describes. Even though he was reared as a rich kid, Rehoboam had a self-worth problem that he tried to solve via the flesh. His self-esteem was running two quarts low, and he sought to shore it up with a façade of manufactured blessing. Man, I can identify with him. I've danced to that tune. And I don't have to convince you that this game is alive and well, even in the church. I know of a church which enjoyed glory days under the leadership of an anointed pastor. A few years later, in the throes of a steady membership decline, his struggling successor began to proclaim the need to build an expensive new building. The reason given was "overcrowding" (God is blessing!). But the real agenda was the hope that the members would become excited about building a shiny new facility, get involved in the project, and pack the pews (and the building-fund envelopes) on Sunday.

The two Sunday-morning worship services were consolidated, and chairs were placed in the aisles to "prove" that the church was bulging at the seams. The pastor regularly apologized for the "temporary overcrowding" and enthusiastically encouraged the people with: "When we're settled into our new building, we'll be comfortable again—God is blessing us" statements. But not only were there empty chairs, there was still plenty of room in the pews at the single service.

The new-building wanna-be was a bronze shield—an attempt to generate and maintain self-worth.

Cars, Houses, Titles . . .

Like my boyhood friend George's love affair with snappy clothes, the world system offers us all sorts of ways to generate and maintain self-worth. You can get the "right" set of wheels to shore up your perceived shortfall. For a yuppie it's an Audi, a Mercedes, or perhaps a sport utility vehicle at this writing. For an over-the-road trucker, it's a gleaming tractor-trailer rig with plenty of running lights. For males in some subcultures it may be a "low-rider" pickup with dark tinted windows. For the country club geezer group, it may be a Lincoln or a Caddy. For certain others, just add whitewalls and some chrome. And, of course all of these things are subject to a yearly updating.

I sometimes attend the rodeo because I live in Fort Worth, and that's what you do when you live in Fort Worth. I'm amazed at the bull riders. A Christian friend of mine was a world champion bull rider, and when you take hold of his arm, it feels like a clothesline pole. I never do anything to upset this man. Me? The only thing I ride is my red lawn mower, the "Red Heifer." I love to don my straw cowboy hat, my shades, and ride her around the yard. It's an acceptance thing, don't you see. . . .

I think the bull riders unwittingly play an acceptance game. Prior to the bull riding, the cowboys hunker down, shoulder to shoulder, against the wall on the arena floor near the chutes, waiting for a bull to come charging out. As the bull bursts out—1500 pounds of muscular, spinning fury, flinging dirt into the air—the unspoken point of the "acceptance game" is to see which hunkerer blinks first should the bull decide to go after some of that cowboy meat at the edge of the arena. They look like a long sub sandwich to him. The loser in this little game is the first man to flinch from his seemingly casual, relaxed hunkering—just another day at the office, you see—and climb the wall to safety. It's an adrenal experience, an acceptance and self-esteem thing, gang. The amateurs in Spain who run down the streets in front of the charging bulls do so for the same reason: acceptance. Guys die for it. Women give their bodies to men for it. We *need* to feel like we're significant—valuable. *God* put it in us. But He never intended for us to satisfy it independently.

— You can seek to enhance your self-worth by getting a house in the "right" part of the city and take pleasure in having sales clerks ask for your address so you can say, "I live at 222 Divine." Oooooooo, the sweet sound of success. *You* know that *they* know that Divine Place means large American dollars. And you hate to shop out of town because these clerks are unaware of the *worth* of folks who live on Divine. As we cruise through this rest stop, look over there to your left. See the lady in that Lincoln with the hood raised? She just learned that her husband is leaving her for a younger woman. Her car, her jewels, her big house which were so special mean nothing to her now. She feels like her life is not worth living. She's a Christian who has placed all her self-worth eggs in the wrong basket.

Or you can have a title like "Doctor" or "Reverend" or "*The* Reverend," or retain an old military title such as "Captain," even though *your* war's been over for decades. Ahhh, the sweet sound of that title on a cool summer evening. (I thought about resurrecting my old title of Gunner's Mate Third Class, but it didn't fit on my business card.) There are some guys—even preachers—that you dare not call by their given name. It's an aura that they've either built or which has been built up around them that they make no effort to dispel. You've gotta wonder if some of these guys even have a given name. It's "Doctor Smith," or in the case of some preachers, "*The Reverend Doctor Smith*." Their kids call them

299

"Doctor Daddy." You wonder how their mom called them to supper. I know—I've been there and my flesh still enjoys the melodious, wonderful sound of *"Doctor* Gillham." Hot dawg! Don't you know that God is impressed? Then one time the Holy Spirit showed me that if Jesus goes by *His* first name, I had better start practicing up. I've been answering to "Bill" ever since. It's a self-worth thing, gang.

And then there's gold. Ahhh, gold. Nothing quite like a Mr. T. starter set to make you *feel* better about yourself as you face the world each day. Or knowing that your wife's diamond is the largest in the church.

Hey ... houses, cars, and gold are not evil. Anabel and I live in a nice house that is on loan from the Lord, but He's welcome to take it away tonight if He wishes. He'll just move us into another one. If, however, you *have* to have the amenities the world offers, you have a self-worth problem— and you're so much more valuable than all of this stuff that "moths and rust corrupt" or that can disappear before you finish reading this page. I assume you have noticed that in order for this game to satisfy, it must be played out before *others*. Again, it won't work on the deserted island. The bull rider wouldn't hunker against the pasture fence while the bull was racing toward him if he were the only spectator.

Our Need to Believe We Are Competent

Performance-Based Acceptance

If we are to bestow acceptance upon ourselves, we need to believe that we perform well—that we are competent. Other people are perceived by peers as "stores" in which the shelves are stocked with love/acceptance. Performance is a currency with which you barter for love. One must pay a price to acquire the product from these stores. Proprietors don't give their love away; they dole it out for a price, even within their own families. Most folks don't love unconditionally;

they deal in *conditional* love. You must *perform* to merit their love. You must be *competent*. This is called *performance-based acceptance*. If you perform to suit them, they will offer you their love. Oh, yes—love really does make the world go around. Many folks kill for it; even more die for it. Though it's called by many names, it's still the same: the need to be loved by both self and others.

"Let's You and Him Fight"

That subheading is an old southern, grammatically incorrect colloquialism that I grew up hearing. It means "I'm bored, so you two entertain me by pulverizing each other." But this was recorded in the Bible long before Oklahoma became a state. In 2 Samuel 2:14, Abner and Joab, a couple of Jewish generals, were visiting. Abner said, "Now let the young men arise and hold a contest before us." And Joab said, "Let them arise." Great idea, Abner! Let's order in some pizza and watch these young idiots save face by slaughtering each other just to impress us. And two teams of 12–24 young men who loved life, whose parents loved them and were proud that they were in the army defending the homeland—*killed each other to the last man* so these two old geezers could alleviate their boredom! There was nothing on TV that night, so they created their own entertainment.

Why would these young men senselessly kill one another? I believe it was to generate and/or retain acceptance from peers and self. Think of the price that would have been paid by a young man who spoke out against such madness or walked away from it: rejection by his closest macho peers and authority figures! Twenty-four young men chose death to avoid rejection. This same dynamic caused the soldiers of the Confederacy to march into the face of certain death against the entrenched Army of the Potomac at Gettysburg. According to soldiers' journal accounts, the attack was madness. The Japanese kamikazes and the hara-kiri casualties of World War II were pressured into these acts of stupidity by what's called "saving face," which is nothing more than retaining acceptance from peers and self—the politically correct word for it is *pride*. This is Satan's strategy that we humans foolishly adopt.

Folks, the Lord called me into the ministry of discipling believers into walking in victory over their flesh. Part of His equipping has been to make me sort of a flesh expert. I haven't ordered a T-shirt with "Flesh Spotter" emblazoned on it, but when I state that our need for acceptance is a *powerful, powerful* motivator, it's not a wild guess. The reason it is so powerful is because the need to be loved was built into us so we would respond to *God's* love through Christ. I believe it's critical that Christians comprehend this. How are *you* satisfying your intense need to be loved? Do you stand by God's freeway with a "Will Work for Love" sign? Who do you look to as the source from whom you seek to satisfy this intense need: spouse, parents, your kids, people, self, pets? If it's anything but God, what price are you paying to gain acceptance from your source? How do you satisfy your intense need for self-acceptance? Should your source(s) disappear tonight, would your life be over? Is such temporal, conditional love worth it when you *already have* the unconditional love of God in Christ?

Performance-Based Self-Acceptance

Not only do we shop at the love stores of our fellows, but we also trade at our *own* store. We make *ourselves* pay a price before bestowing acceptance upon ourselves. *We* must believe that we are competent. We must perform "well enough" to merit love from our own store. Most of us actually sell our commodity to others at a cheaper price than we demand from ourselves. Witness the perfectionist who must perform *perfectly* in order to win his *own* approval. He performs primarily for self, not others, and he *never* measures up to his own lofty standards. Thus, he typically does not like himself very well. While most of us wholesale our love to others, we exact retail prices from ourselves! And we have a sign in our store window: "Open Seven Days a Week—Closed Only for Sleeping." Not only is operating and shopping at love stores exhausting work on earth, but at death you discover that the fruits of your labor will be down the toilet. Double drat!

Whew! Let's pull back onto the freeway and get away from this depressing place. There, that's much better. You do understand that what we discussed at this rest stop has nothing to do with gaining or retaining your salvation, right? Christians are accepted into heaven based upon their faith in Jesus Christ—that's a done deal. God uses a pass/fail grading system here. The man who approaches God through Jesus Christ passes; the one who approaches God alone fails.

Look—the sign ahead says "Biblical Self-Acceptance—Exit Two Miles." That's the rest stop we're anticipating. Here is some exciting news. God has already met those three needs I postulated—your needs for belonging, self-worth, and competence—and wouldn't you know that He did it through Jesus Christ? Much of His grace, however, is like radio or television waves in that even though it surrounds us, we must be aware that it exists and know how to receive it before we can embrace it as our own.

16 A CHRIST-GENERATED SELF-ACCEPTANCE

"BILL, I ENJOYED YOUR LECTURE on self-acceptance, but that's something that I've never had a problem with. I realize that some people struggle with that, but I've always had a good self-image." The speaker was an attractive, smiling, genteel, pleasant, middle-aged woman, who demonstrated the truth that revelation can only come by what its name implies: truth that is *revealed* by the Holy Spirit, not by human deduction. This dear sister missed the point that, apart from embracing our identity in Christ, *every* self-generated self-image on earth—whether positive, negative, or in between—is a house of cards, a do-it-yourself job built by human effort. All of them have been generated by lords of the ring. Some are simply more productive, more socially acceptable than others and thus have a longer shelf life and greater acceptance payoff for effort expended. This lady had apparently been well-liked all of her life, and had thus learned to love herself. She understood perfectly well why folks invited her to their parties. She thought they had made a good decision. She had a self-generated, positive self-image that we discussed in the previous chapter.

— God, on the other hand, intends for each Christian to trash trusting in his fleshly self-image and begin to nurture his new, eternal, spiritual self-image (Galatians 3:1-3; 2 Corinthians 5:16-17). I reiterate: You and I are spirit critters who indwell earthsuits, not physical critters with a spirit. We are not mammals, but spirit critters who live in a mammalian vessel. Our basic, true identity is rooted in the spirit and soul (personality), while our physical component is temporal and expendable; it's a throwaway container. Our spirit and personality eject from the earthsuit at death to be clothed in our promised eternal "dwelling from heaven" (2 Corinthians 5:1-2). Enjoy the temporal blessings God provides by installing us in an earthsuit, but it doesn't take a rocket scientist to see the folly of gathering your self-image eggs in an earthsuit basket that's destined for the compost pile. It's going to become Miracle Grow, gang.

In the last chapter we exited God's freeway into the "Fleshly Self-Acceptance" rest stop, which proved depressing because we all recognized that we've spent much of our time crawling up a ladder of success that was leaning against the wrong wall. Now that we've analyzed some of our common fleshly attempts at generating self-acceptance, we're more motivated to understand how to embrace our *true* self-acceptance—a self-acceptance that will withstand all the storms of life on planet Earth. Let's begin by reiterating that psychology teaches that in order to generate positive self-acceptance, we need to believe three things:

- We *belong*.

- We have *worth*.

- We are *competent*.

Since God has said in Philippians 4:19 that He "shall supply all [our] needs according to His riches in glory in Christ Jesus," let's see how we can satisfy these three needs from our Designer's Resource, rather than from the shifting sands of the flesh, upon which psychotherapy bases its teaching. There's the sign up ahead for the exit ramp, "Biblical Self-Acceptance." Let's pull in and stop under those lovely shade trees so we can study the way that Christ has met these needs for us. Smell the fresh air and the aroma of

A Christ-Generated Self-Acceptance

the flowers? The travelers who have pulled in here look quite a bit different than those at the last rest stop, don't they? They have a peaceful appearance.

Our Need to Belong

First, let's tackle your need to belong. If you could choose anyone in the entire universe to permanently, inseparably *belong* to forever, whom would you choose? Of course, it's He . . .

- who chose *you* before you chose Him (Ephesians 1:4).

- who lovingly and tenderly re-created you through a planned spiritual pregnancy (2 Corinthians 5:17; Ephesians 2:10).

- who has personalized both your present and your future *for your best good* (Jeremiah 29:11, TLB).

- who guarantees that He will never leave you nor forsake you (Hebrews 13:5).

- who gave up His only Son to purchase you, slave that you were (1 Corinthians 7:23).

- who alone is wise enough to know what is the very best for you (Jeremiah 9:23-24).

- who is committed to accomplishing His very best on your behalf (Psalm 40:5).

- who has *infinite resources* by which to satisfy all your needs (Isaiah 40:28-31).

- who knows what you need better than you do (Proverbs 16:9).

- who is powerful enough to *abundantly*, not barely, meet your every need (Ephesians 3:20).

- who is powerful enough to keep His promise that no one can snatch you out of His hand (John 10:28-29).

- who loves you enough to have sacrificed His life while in His prime to rescue you from yourself (Romans 5:8).

- who is currently fashioning the dream home where you will live with Him forever (John 14:3).

If you belong to Him, then you *belong*, period. God says, "The earth is the Lord's, and all it contains, the world, and those who dwell in it" (Psalm 24:1). He further says, "For you have been bought with a price" (1 Corinthians 6:20). Our five senses, however, argue with us that God is so intangible, while people, on the other hand, can give us hands-on, measurable, concrete acceptance. The problem is that when we're targeting *humans* to satisfy our need for love—our need to *belong* with them—the specters of rejection, disappointment, or disenchantment invariably make this a high-risk venture. And boy, it's painful when someone we deeply love fails us or rejects us. *It's not wrong for us to desire and enjoy human love;* it's a matter of priority. God insists that we embrace *His* unchanging acceptance of us through Christ as our *primary Source* for satisfying our need for belonging. This alone guarantees that we can ultimately overcome the pain of any human loss or rejection. If it doesn't, then God was stretching the truth by claiming that He can and will supply all our needs in Christ. Let's see how this can work for you.

Game, Set, Match!

Let's say that four of the women in your Sunday school class meet each Saturday morning for breakfast, have a Bible study, then play tennis doubles and are back home by lunch. You've not met anyone at work that's your type, and these women seem like the neatest gals. Ever since you and your hubby moved to the city three years ago, you've wished tennis were a five-woman game. One of them often shares a special insight in Sunday school that the Holy Spirit showed them last Saturday during their study. Arrrgh! How you would love to have been there—to *belong* to that group.

One day you hear that one of the women and her husband are moving away; this means the Saturday foursome will be inviting someone to replace her. "Oh, God, it's such a little thing to want so badly, I realize that. But, Sir, if You could *pa leeze* see Your way clear, I would so *love* to be invited to join that group. Please . . ." Oh, how you pray. You're sort of embarrassed that you are praying so diligently about this matter, but nevertheless, you forge on. As far as you can see, you are probably the most likely candidate available to them. You know your Bible well; you play a good game of tennis; they seem to really enjoy your company and have each confirmed this to you; your husband gets on well with theirs; the math adds up.

You're up bright and early on Saturday, dressed in your tennis duds, racket in the trunk, and you just "happen" to drop by the restaurant where they eat breakfast, hoping the Lord will have them ask you to fill their foursome. When your eyes adjust to the interior lighting, there they sit, the three of them and, and, and S-U-S-I-E S-M-I-T-H! *What is she doing with them? She doesn't know Genesis from genetics! She rarely even stirs herself to darken the door of our Sunday school class. Furthermore, if she even cares for tennis, I'm not aware of it.* You manage to throw them a little wave and a weak smile as you head for a corner booth to cry in your Granola. One of them excuses herself and comes over to your table to ask you to pray for Susie, explaining that the Holy Spirit has led the three of them to reach out to her. That's *some* help, but now you're sort of angry at God. There are times when He just doesn't seem to care.

Overcoming Your Feeler

Most of us can identify with painful disappointments such as this. You've been rejected; you've just suffered a setback in satisfying your need to *belong*. This sort of experience can ruin your day, or week, or life. Can Jesus overcome it for you? You bet He can!

If you were a slave on the auction block and someone made a bid to purchase you that no one could match, when the auctioneer's gavel crashed down, would you then *belong* to that buyer? Of course. God, in His mercy and love, purchased you. First Corinthians 7:23 says, "You were bought with a price. . . ." There were two bidders at the sale that day—God and Satan—and *you* were the merchandise. Satan offered the glitter of the world system; God offered His only Son. You took God up on His offer. Whether you realized it or not, when you accepted Jesus Christ as your personal Savior and Lord, the Father bought you, so you *belong* to Him. You do not own yourself. You belong to the One who purchased you.

Setting Your Mind on Reality

Whenever such crushing rejection strikes, you must *instantly* begin to pump this fact through your mind over and over and over: "Thank You, Lord, that I *belong* to You! Oh, thank You, Sir, that I *belong*. Lord, I don't *belong* to those women, but *I sure do belong to You!* I *belong!* Praise You, Sir, I *belong!*" You must supersaturate your mind with thoughts like these for 5 minutes, 10 minutes, 15 minutes—you flood your mind with the *fact* that you *belong* to the most important Person in the entire universe. You've got to keep flooding your mind with this. Getting your feeler to cooperate is God's problem. You can't do that.

Knowing that you belong is *not* a feeling. This is a fact! God said so. Your *feelings* made you comfortable enough to

310

believe that you had a good chance to belong to the four-some, but your feelings were *wrong*. So now you are forcing your mind to concentrate upon the One who loves you more than you love yourself. You have spent a lifetime targeting others and self as sources of your love supply. Now you're going to target God. You're pumping truth through your mind. And do you know what will happen? Even though your emotions may not zero out, they *will* ultimately begin to ease off somewhat. Yes, they will. You're being "transformed by the renewing of your mind" (Romans 12:2). By targeting God first, people second, and yourself third, you'll be changing the way that you *think* and *believe* about the issue of *belonging*.

As your feeler begins to calm down a bit, shift your thoughts to praying for Susie and asking God to bless the efforts of your three sisters. You say, "Bill, I couldn't do that! I'd be a phony if I tried!" No, here you must remember that God doesn't expect *you* to do it. *Christ* is your life, and *you must bring Him on-line to pray for the four women through you*. You do this by thinking, "I'm going to let the Holy Spirit use me to pray," and by faith you choose to trust that the prayers you formulate for the new foursome are actually *Jesus'* prayers through you, or if God has given you a special prayer language, this is an appropriate time to bring it on-line either silently or quietly whispered. If negative emotions or thoughts begin to creep back in, then you immediately start praising God for how much you *belong* again. You stay at it, exercising faith and obedience, and the Holy Spirit will begin to ease your feeler and give you victory over your flesh.

This isn't mind over matter—a mere fleshly imitation of God's method; this is biblical obedience. You are "[setting] your mind on the things above" (Colossians 3:2), on the way things actually are in the heavenly places *where you live*: "Even when we were dead in our transgressions, [God] made us alive together with Christ ... and raised us up with Him, and seated us with Him in the heavenly places, in Christ Jesus" (Ephesians 2:5-6). You are not on your way to heaven; you're *already* in heaven from the helicopter view! You are canceling out other people as the prioritized target in your quest to belong and replacing them with God's guaranteed, after-the-fact acceptance through Christ. This is an exercise in spiritual maturity; this is doing spiritual push-ups, "getting in spiritual shape" as He conforms you to the image of Christ (Romans 8:28-29). And the bonus is that you will receive a reward at the judgment seat of Christ for the way you handled this little episode, because your victory is based upon Christ alone, not upon your own flesh.

Our Need for Self-Worth

Is it possible that Jesus can satisfy our need for self-esteem? Yes! It's not only possible, it's the only foolproof technique available to us. Years ago Bruce Narramore planted the seed in my mind from which the Holy Spirit has developed the following illustration. You tell the value of anything that is for sale by its cost. If a buyer is in the market for a used car and is willing to pay 10,000 dollars for the model he selects, *in the buyer's estimation*, the car and the money are interchangeable—one is *worth* the other (see Figure 16A).

Equal in Value in the Buyer's Estimation

$10,000

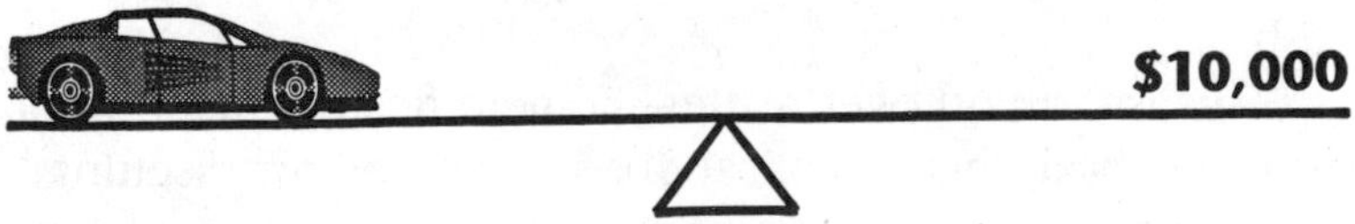

Figure16A

With this in mind, let's return to that slave-auction block. All those who are without Christ are "slaves of sin" (Romans 6:17); the rest of us have voluntarily enslaved ourselves to Christ and, having done so, are now "slaves of righteousness" (Romans 6:18)—another evidence of your true identity. You can identify this by the fact that you long to live a righteous life. That's a ten! See there? You *are* a slave to righteousness. Those without Christ are slaves to unrighteousness (Romans 6:16). Independence is a myth. When you were on that auction block, there was one Bidder who loved you enough to offer the winning bid: God. Since He gets to make the rules, His assessment of your worth is incontrovertible, as His opinion is the only valid reference point in the universe. You've heard it said, "God said it; I believe it; that settles it." My friend Jack Taylor says it better: "God said it; that settles it—whether you believe it or not."

How to Determine Your Real Worth

As you climb up onto the block, imagine the auctioneer calling out, What am I bid for this slave of sin?" God *could* have said, "I'll bid one set of used snow tires for that one."

"Sold to the Lord God Almighty for four used snow tires!"

Then the next slave of sin steps onto the block. He's a slender, lanky 16-year-old boy from North Carolina named Billy Frank Graham. God *could* have looked him over and, knowing his potential, said, "I'll bid the Florida peninsula for him."

"Sold to the Lord God Almighty for the State of Florida!"

This is the image that many of us have of ourselves before God. Indeed, God would have been justified to have made either of those two bids had He chosen to, because He is God; He runs things, remember? But human opinion had nothing whatever to say about the price He would pay for each of us. *God* determined that.

What value did Almighty God place upon you—a help-less, hopeless slave to the power of sin, a prisoner of war with the bleakest possible eternal future, a person devoid of loveliness, a rebel, a person destitute of any good work which might stand him in good stead? God said, "I'll bid My most precious Possession for that slave. I'll pay my beloved Son, Jesus. Although He's the only Boy I've got, My only Namesake, and I love Him with an immeasurable passion, I'll give Him up to buy that particular, unique slave, even though the tag on the slave's neck says "As Is—No Returns." I intend to edify that person to the lofty position of younger sibling to My only Son, Jesus. I'm going to sacrifice one Son to spawn another child" (John 1:12; 1 Corinthians 6:20; 7:23).

Your Fantastic Value

Let's put you (the product) on one end of the scales and Jesus (the "pearl of great price") on the other (see Figure 16B). Remember what we learned from the car illustration? In the buyer's estimation, the price that God is willing to pay determines the value of the object that's for sale. My dear, beloved relative in Christ, *God . . . our Father, opened His wallet and took out His most precious possession—Jesus—and laid Him on the auctioneer's desk to purchase you! God paid one Son to get a second child. There's an accurate evaluation of your present and eternal value.* What are you *worth* to your Creator—the God of the universe? *Jesus!*

— Don't misinterpret what I am saying. In no way am I devaluing Jesus, our blessed Savior, Lord, and life by saying that you are worth Jesus. God is showing you *your* value here. He's upgrading you to show you your true value in His eyes. My intent is to convince you to trash the fleshly criteria by which you have sought to enhance your self-worth in favor of your literal, fabulous value to the only One in the universe who ultimately matters: God. Here is self-worth that is set in eternal concrete, where neither moth nor rust can corrupt. This is so unbelievable that only God would dare to think it up. Certainly, a committee of our peers would never do so. But praise God, it's true! Jesus would have died for you had you been the only sinner on earth. This is how valuable you are.

Equal Value in the Buyer's Estimation

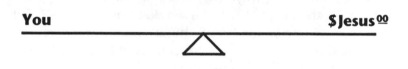

You   **$ Jesus $\frac{00}{}$**

Figure 16B

Experiencing Your True Identity

Now, let's see how you can make this truth become more than rows of black print on white paper. Let's say you were caught in a layoff two years ago; you took your pink slip home to your wife on your twenty-fifth wedding anniversary. Some celebration! Since then, you've been diligent about submitting résumés, but without success. You, your wife, and your kids are born-again and active in your church and are trusting the Lord to open His door of opportunity for you, but still no job. Women's clothing styles have changed, and your wife has only one presentable dress. It's been a humiliating, humbling experience. You've even had to plead with the utility companies just to keep the home fires burning, so fashionable clothing is just one of many things that have become a lower priority in your home.

Although your wife is very supportive, your heart aches as you see her wear that same old blue dress to church Sunday after Sunday. Each time she does, your heart cries out to God. This is heavy on your mind as you sit with her in the opening assembly amidst all the happy Sunday school chatter, when suddenly you overhear a woman behind you speak the word *blue* in conversation. Not one to miss such an opportunity to deliver a punch to your solar plexus, the power of sin—using those first-person pronouns—suggests to you that these women are criticizing your wife's dress. What's left of your self-worth gushes out like air from a ruptured balloon. You're surrounded by the stylish clothes of the class members, and the emotional pain is almost a physical sensation. "Lord, why? Why are You letting this happen to my wife and family? What did we do to deserve this?" You try to concentrate on the lesson, but it's no use. You are dominated by your thoughts and feelings of failure, which add to your already low sense of self-worth.

To see how God's victory strategy works, let's rewind the tape to the point where you heard the *b* word. When a painful stimulus like this strikes, you must instantly "shout" in your mind,

> No! I am not worthless! I am a man of infinite worth! Oh, thank You, Lord, that I am worth the fabulous price of Jesus—wonderful, wonderful Jesus. That's who You "spent" to purchase me. Thank You, Lord, thank You for the picture of those scales in my mind—such a graphic illustration of my personal value to You. And You make the rules. Your opinion is *reality!* Lord, although I long for a new job, my personal worth does not depend on what I *do,* but on who I *am,* upon what *You* say about my *value to You.* My self-worth is fabulous.

If you were alone, I would recommend that you utter these statements orally and vigorously for several minutes until the pressure begins to ease off. If you're in a group, supersaturate your mind with this truth for 5 minutes, 10 minutes, 15 minutes. You can do this and carry on a conversation simultaneously. I do this at times. You stay at it until the pressure begins to ease. I would also recommend that you type out, in your own words, a statement of your value according to God, or draw a small set of the scales depicting you and Jesus on the ends. Put copies on your mirror, your desk, or your dashboard. Saturate your mind with this truth. And, above all, teach this fantastic truth to your family so they'll not "waste this sorrow," as Paul Billheimer says.[1]

Now (you guessed it), as soon as you can, trust Christ through you to begin praising the Father for providing so well for your classmates, and for the fact that you and your family are not naked or starving. He has clothed you just like He promised: "Consider the lilies, how they grow; they neither toil nor spin; but I tell you, even Solomon in all his glory did not clothe himself like one of these. But if God so arrays the grass in the field, which is alive today and tomorrow is thrown into the furnace, how much more will He clothe you ..." (Luke 12:27-28). If the power of sin begins triggering the resentful or self-depreciating thoughts again, let those thoughts serve to remind you to generate more thoughts of praise, concentrating again on the true foundation of your self-worth. Turn the tables on the devil; use his thoughts as your wake-up call to crank up the praise. Stay at it.

— By doing this, you are effectively crossing out the opinion of others as your barometer for determining your self-worth and are prioritizing *God's* view. Are you being a phony by taking this stand against your emotions? Well, last time we looked, the true definition of a hypocrite is someone who "pretends to be something he is not." Did God consider you worth the "bid" of Jesus? Yes. So which one is lying to you? Your feeler or God? You're acting like something is true that *is* true, and rain on what your feeler says! It's lying! That solves your self-esteem problem.

Our Need for Competency

Have you ever blown it? I mean blown it publicly, so there is absolutely no doubt in anyone's mind that you are a candidate for the "Delbert Dumb of the Decade" award? Or have you done something like informing your friends that you are about to pull off a feat that will prove to be one of the greatest accomplishments of your life, only to fall flat on your kisser in front of everyone? Or have you allowed your name to be placed before the church in the elder or deacon election and gotten swamped?

Acknowledged Personal Weakness: the Secret to Personal Competency

If your answer is a sigh and a nod, you can identify with a smorgasbord of emotions during such episodes, one of them being a *feeling of incompetence.* Lay enough of those experiences end to end, and they'll invariably lead you *to* the end: depression city.

As soon as we get old enough to breathe, all of us seek to place our confidence in ourselves. Consider how a two-year-old knocks his mom's hand aside, spoon and all, so he can get *his* hands into his plate to feed himself. You've been there, done that. You figured that if you took control, you could do it at your own speed as you willed. Lords of the ring don't know any better.

― Before you came to Christ, who did you think had your best interests at heart? *You!* Who better to place your confidence in? As my Anabel has said, "Who was always there, omnipresent, Johnny-on-the-spot when you needed help, except *you?* If you didn't do it yourself, nobody was going to do it *for* you."

You can immediately see the problem with this. God tells us to "put no confidence in the flesh" (Philippians 3:3). "Cursed is the man who trusts in mankind and makes flesh his strength" (Jeremiah 17:5). Since the flesh is precisely where we've all learned to put our confidence, He must bring each Christian to the end of trusting in himself. It's only from this position of brokenness, of acknowledged, personal weakness, that most of us ever give up on our resources and opt for Christ as our *sole* Resource. That's why God says, "My power shows up best in weak people" (2 Corinthians 12:9 TLB).

Giving up on yourself is *mandatory* to spiritual growth and maturity. All other perceived "growth" is not growth, but merely a product of the flesh. Giving up on your so-called "strong" points and acknowledging your weaknesses is the key to welcoming Christ as your strength. Most people will never embrace Christ as their strength so long as they believe they are strong. An encounter with our powerful, *agape Father* in the midst of pain, or problems, or grief, or confusion, or extreme need, or (fill in the blank) will dissipate our puny attributes and turn our eyes toward Him.

Financial bankruptcy is loathed by investors the world over, but spiritual bankruptcy (brokenness) opens a treasure house of God's resources. Once a Christian begins making deposits into *this* investment account, he wonders why in the world he trusted in his own strength for so long. The Old Testament records more accounts of personal spiritual histories than does the New, and several of these reveal God's plan for removing all confidence in the flesh.

God chose Gideon to defeat Midian, but in reality Gideon wasn't to defeat them at all. God would defeat Midian *for* him. He spells this out as He is preparing Gideon for battle in Judges 7:2: "The people who are with you are too many for Me to give Midian into their hands, lest Israel become boastful, saying, 'My own power has delivered me.' " The flesh loves to claim credit for a piece of the victory action. If you don't believe it, do a replay of your own history.

319

Gideon began with 32,000 soldiers; the Midianites had 135,000. That's 4-to-1 odds against Gideon, which would cause most generals to try Plan B. But God said, "Nope. Too strong. Too much danger of you guys taking the credit when I whup up on 'em for you." So He kept reducing their numbers till only 300 had survived the cuts. God increased the odds to 450-to-1 against them! As if this didn't make them vulnerable enough, check out their role in God's battle strategy. Each man carried a torch in one hand and a trumpet in the other (Judges 7:16). Do you detect a slight problem here? *They had no free hand to hold sword or shield!* God whipped Midian *for* them in such a way that He could get the *total* credit for it. He wanted them to go home and say to their friends and families, "You're not going to believe this! Wait till I tell you what happened to me last night!" And God received the glory.

No Lifeguard on Duty—Swim at Your Own Risk!

Moses had a similar experience. As Ron Dunn says, "He sought to deliver Israel from their oppressors by killing Egyptians one at a time" (see Exodus 2:12). Although Moses' intent was noble, he was ignorant of God's rescue plans. God intended to wipe out the entire Egyptian army by inviting them for a swim in the Red Sea. He whipped them without Israel even owning a sword! His first move was for His future general, Moses, to set a new record for the hundred meters, wearing sandals and a dress, as he skipped town to beat a murder rap. Then He put Moses on a desert shelf until he lost all of the self-confidence he had developed from 40 years in Pharaoh's palace, having been trained by Egypt's finest in the art of strategic warfare. Believe it, this guy wore a black belt on his robe.

Finally, to paraphrase the account in chapters 3 and 4 of Exodus, God said, "OK, Moses, I believe you're finally *weak* enough for Me to deliver Israel through you." Moses' reaction proved God correct.

"Who, *me?* 'Scuse me, Sir, but You need to check Your play book again. I might have helped You out 40 years ago when I looked like Charlton Heston in the movie of my life and was a powerful man in the Egyptian government, but not now! Who am *I* that *I* should go to Pharaoh?" Moses saw his weakness as impotency, but God saw it as a signal that he was ready to be used. Again, I believe it was Ron Dunn who said, "When Moses thought he was ready, he wasn't ready; when he thought he wasn't ready, he was ready."

Some Things Never Change

— Folks, God hasn't changed His methods. Anytime we're concentrating on *our* resources, we're not ready. When we're concentrating on *Christ's* strength through us, we're ready. God still does business in exactly the same way. That's the reason He says we are to learn from Israel's experiences (1 Corinthians 10:11). In case you whizzed by those last few lines, may I respectfully suggest that you read them again? God's method for dealing with our independent strength has not changed. Every disciple who would walk with God must be weaned off trusting in his own physical or psychological strength (Habakkuk 1:11). I reiterate God's statement: "My power shows up best in weak people" (2 Corinthians 12:9 TLB). God desires the glory for the victories He bestows upon us; it's always accomplished by God's grace— sometimes working through us, sometimes working without us, sometimes working in spite of us. Since most of us are slow to recognize this, we have to be convinced of our impotency through personal failure. *Such brokenness is mandatory in our pilgrimage if we are to be conformed to the image of Christ.* There are no shortcuts.

Now, don't fall for the devil's lie that God delights to receive glory at our expense. God doesn't get a buzz out of bringing us down. No way. God enjoys the part where He gets to pick up the broken pieces and lovingly hold us while He bears our burdens. God is *for* us, and Christ on the cross constitutes all the proof anyone ever needs of this. Ignore the bad press God gets on this planet. That's Satan's doing.

God Gets Honest with Abe

Consider Abraham, whose fleshly self-competence provides a stark contrast to our competency that's available through Christ. When he was about 75 years old, God promised him a son. Meanwhile, he and his wife, Sarah, got tired of waiting for her to announce that she was feeling "different." After waiting several years, it seemed logical to the human mind that they should help God out, so Sarah had the grand idea for Abraham to sleep with her maid, Hagar. He thought that sounded like an exciting plan, I'm sure, and he and Hagar soon produced Ishmael. "Ain't God gooood! He gave us the boy that He promised us!" Yeah, right.

As you know, that independent effort turned out to be anything but a success story. Ishmael was the product of their flesh trip. God didn't need them "helping" Him out. *Twenty-five years* after His promise, God—knowing that Abraham's ability to produce kids was deader than a hammer and that Sarah was decades post-menopause—determined the time had come. Hey, if there was any strength left in those two *before* the pregnancy, I guarantee you they were weak nine months later when they were at up 3:00 A.M. rocking that screaming kid! To make it worse, their rocker was sitting in the sand! While their friends were all checking on their IRAs and tending the family burial plot, they were changing diapers. A part of them must've been thinking, *God, please don't help us anymore. No more promises, OK?*

I don't intend to come down hard on these dear folks. They are our parents in the faith, and they had no Bible to read, no preacher or Christian friends to give them godly counsel. They were trailblazers who blazed a spiritual trail unmarked by previous travelers. They were people of fantastic faith, to whom we owe a great debt of gratitude. I'm simply attempting to give meat and bones to the rows of black print in the Bible—words that describe their pilgrimage and make them as real as that sweet old couple in your church. They were just plain-vanilla folks like us. When we meet them, I'm sure they'll agree that all the honor and glory for their roles in our lives should go to our fantastic Creator.

Never Trust in Yourself

Jesus never trusted in His own ability, but placed His complete confidence in the Father. Now we are to place our complete confidence in Christ. Do you doubt that He could have turned the stone into a loaf of bread? Of course not. Do you doubt that He could have survived a dive off the pinnacle of the Temple? Of course not. Why didn't He do it? After all, what's the big deal about creating a loaf of bread or abstaining from doing so for the One who created both the stone and the wheat from which we make bread (John 1:3)? And what's the big deal about the free-fall from the Temple roof? Remember what we discussed earlier: Doing either of these would have been an *independent* act. It would have been sin. Jesus never committed an act independent of the Father: "The Father abiding in Me does His works" (John 14:10).

Has it ever been revealed to you that Jesus Christ did not raise Himself from the grave? Doing so would have constituted an *independent* action. The *Father* raised Jesus from the dead (see Acts 2:24,32; 3:15,26, et al). "But after I *have been* raised, I will go before you to Galilee" (Matthew 26:32). This makes His willingness to be crucified for us all the more precious, because when He stepped forth to sacrifice Himself, He knew in His marvelous heart that *He would never raise Himself!* He stayed on that cross and died, knowing that His Father had rejected Him as unclean (Mark 15:34). He had no ace in the hole as He stayed on that cross and died—He wouldn't simply *raise Himself* from the grave. No, sir! Jesus *became sin*, folks (2 Corinthians 5:21). He had one hope: *His Father's integrity to do as He promised.*[2] Satan must have had a fine time harassing Jesus and taunting Him that the Father was going to back out on His end of the agreement and leave Jesus in Hades. Oh, the magnitude of our dear Savior's sacrifice! His only hope lay in His Father's integrity. This is our one hope as well. We are to learn to be as dependent upon Christ as Christ was dependent upon the Father—His character, His integrity as the Promise Keeper. Paul says, "I will not presume to speak of anything except what Christ has accomplished through me" (Romans 15:18). Consider just three of Paul's statements which either directly or indirectly allude to Christ expressing His life through the Christian. These statements are made by the man who is inarguably the most intelligent, articulate, talented, gifted Christian in the New Testament:

- "When I am weak, then I am strong" (2 Corinthians 12:10).

- "For we who live are constantly being delivered over to death for Jesus' sake, that the life of Jesus also may be manifested in our mortal flesh" (2 Corinthians 4:11).

- "For I will not presume to speak of anything except what Christ has accomplished through me" (Romans 15:18).

My Breaking

As I said earlier, when I speak of God "breaking" us of self-reliance when it comes to generating self-worth, it's not a matter of God delighting in our humiliation. Never! The

One who gave His Son for us would never grind us under His heel with a grin on His face. He loves us and *always* works for our best good. "He who began a good work in you will perfect it until the day of Christ Jesus" (Philippians 1:6). That's *agape*. He has re-created us to "live in vital union with him" (Colossians 2:6b TLB). He hates personal independence, self-reliance, self-confidence, *ad infinitum,* because that mentality cuts Him out of His own big picture. Self-reliance is not noble, it's sinful. It's *Satan's* strategy, and it's deceiving the Christians who believe that personal strength is admirable, that self-competency is the ultimate goal. God seeks personal involvement and intimacy with us. He designed the new you in Christ so that dependency upon Him is what is best for you. Paul, writing to the Corinthians about his travails, says, "Indeed, we had the sentence of death within ourselves in order that we should not trust in ourselves, but in God" (2 Corinthians 1:9). Trusting in yourself is sin, pure and simple.

We learned very early to trust in our own strength and did not acknowledge God as our Source. This is the competency which the world system says we must have. Pro athletes say it's imperative; CEOs say it's imperative; movie stars say it's imperative. But God says we must place our trust in Christ alone (Romans 15:18). So an important page in God's cookbook as He conforms you to Christ's image reads, "Stir in two cups of personal failure and allow to sit until bubbles begin to form on the surface. Place in medium oven and allow to bake until done. Then remove and allow to cool." What better way to motivate the believer to abandon his fleshly strength than being whirled around and scorched by the stress and heat of this microwave world?

My "breaking" began in earnest soon after I stepped off the stage at Oklahoma State University with my doctoral hood resting on my shoulders; a signed contract as a new associate professor of psychology at Southeastern Oklahoma

State University tucked away in my desk; a Victorian home purchased for my family; a new Ford in my driveway; and an eagerness to stamp out ignorance in southeastern Oklahoma. My goal was to be a good professor so I could gain credibility and then win kids to Christ on campus—a worthy goal. The problem was that I thought I was such a hot dog that McDonald's didn't have enough mustard to cover me. *"Doctor* Gillham. Hoo-weee! Mercy, mercy! Make way, academia! Here comes God's man with the plan!" I hadn't the foggiest notion that I was setting myself up for Satan to demand permission to "sift me like wheat" (Luke 22:31), and that God had given him permission to do exactly that. God had to allow the devil to bring me down—cause me to "put no confidence in [my] flesh" (Philippians 3:3)—before He could initiate the next "step up" in conforming me to the image of Christ.

A surprise party never stunned the guest of honor any more than when I was nonplussed as Satan sprang "stage one" of his sifting project on me. I was lecturing to the 60 students in my Abnormal Psychology section, when my notes went stone-cold. I mean, I did a mime of a human freeze-frame. Each tick of the clock was an eternity as I struggled to get my thoughts together, but my mind was absolutely blank! I dashed off a 911 prayer, but all I got was, "I'm away from My desk right now ... at the tone ..." He had left for Mars and wasn't expected back till Monday. "God! Help! Remember—I'm Your man with the plan! Your saved psychology professor has turned into Delbert Dumb!" SILENCE. The embarrassment was horrendous. My face lit up like the town Christmas tree. I was devastated, humiliated. After what seemed like a lifetime, I somehow began lecturing again. Finally, the bell saved me. I gathered what little pride (ugh) I had left, stuffed it into my briefcase, and retreated into my beautiful paneled office where I locked the door, laid my head on the desk, and literally melted before the Lord, begging for mercy.

God's Provision Was in Me All the Time

I didn't log this experience in my journal because I was afraid that someone would find it after I died. I was so embarrassed! My self-esteem plunged to zero. I can only speculate on how often this horror story was repeated in the classroom—suffice it to say, many times. But, brother, I can remember the feelings of failure, desperation, lost dreams, hopelessness, embarrassment, and low self-worth like it was yesterday. I had no idea that God was *allowing* this in order to bring me to the end of my love affair with my flesh. When I was convinced that there was absolutely no hope, that my contract would not be renewed and I would suffer the humiliation of crawling back to ask for my old, less-prestigious job, God began to reveal to me that Jesus Christ was in me to teach psychology through me. I was to teach my classes with a *new method*, trusting in Christ who indwelled me instead of in myself.

In my bedroom I prayed, "Lord Jesus, I don't understand this, but I see in the Word that You are my life (Colossians 3:4). Frankly, I'm terrified to face my classes; I've lost all confidence in myself. If the classes get taught, You're going to have to do it. I can't. I am going to trust You to do it all *for* me. It's going to be my body, my personality, my knowledge of psychology (what little there is of it), and my Okie accent, but I, by *faith*, am believing that You are the Vine and I am a branch. Only You can do Your work through me. I give up. I quit. If I flop, it's your burden, not mine. I have just become *Your* problem. You take over" (or something like that).

Putting Feet to My Faith

And then I did a very important thing. I didn't stay by my bedside waiting until I *felt* Him take over. I *acted like* Christ was living through me despite the fact that *I didn't feel Him* take over. *I felt fear, doubt, and insecurity.* Did you get that? I *felt* fear, doubt, and insecurity. If you could have asked my feeler for its opinion, it would have sworn that I was *faking* it! I acted *contrary to my feelings. I* got up (a *feeling* didn't get me up); *I* went down the stairs; *I* went up to the university to study my notes, but all the time I *believed* with barely a thimbleful of faith that Jesus Christ had and was doing it all *through* me. Folks, I did not feel filled with new courage or confidence. I felt like this wasn't going to work and that I was doomed to fail once again. I simply kept repeating in my head that the burden was on His back, not mine. I was casting my burdens on the Lord as He *commanded* me to do (Psalm 55:22). And, gang, it began to work! Tell the world that a miracle was taking place! I got through the day. And another day. And another. It continued to work. Oh, there were testing times when it looked like I was going to blank out again, but I immediately prayed (in a microsecond), "Lord, here it comes; You've really got a problem here; I'm sure glad *I* don't. It's going to be really interesting to see what You do with this. Let me flop or carry me through. The ball's in Your court. The burden is Yours."

Folks, He brought me through! To Christ be the glory! I now have a pen set on my desk inscribed "Professor of the Year," which was awarded to me a couple of years afterward. Guess who gets the glory for that! I see it as a memento to Christ's faithfulness to me in one of my darkest moments. Through allowing me to experience colossal failure by trusting in myself, then spotlighting Christ as life within me, God had shown me that *Christ* alone is my competency. Wow! What a fantastic relief! What a burden-lifter!

Biblical Competency

Competency? Absolutely, but your eternal competency is not as the world sees it. While the world scores your competency based upon the *results* of your performance, God scores your competency based upon your *method* of performing. Is your effort independent self-effort, or dependency upon Christ? Are you placing your trust in yourself, or giving it the "ol' college try" while trusting in Christ as life? So long as you are *diligent* and are trusting Christ as life moment by moment, *He gets the glory for the good result and carries the responsibility for your "perceived" failures.* Yes—absolutely. As stated earlier, He's not grading you by the *results* of your work, but by your *method*: your faith in Christ as life. If your method is faith in Christ as life, your effort will receive God's approval at the judgment seat of Christ: "Well done, good and faithful servant." As you shift your focus onto resting in God's acceptance and meriting *His* approval by trusting Christ as life, you are gently and lovingly crossing out "others" and "self" as your primary sources of competency, replacing them with God's evaluation—which is the only valid assessment in the universe (1 Corinthians 4:3-5). Folks, this is the only way for any man to win on this planet! We've got to read from the same page that God's reading from.

God says to wise Christians, "Do not be conformed to this world, but be transformed by the renewing of your mind" (Romans 12:2). It is in embracing God's method for both acceptance and approval that your need to be loved is satisfied on a moment-by-moment basis. This is paramount for you to learn during your pilgrimage. Before coming to Christ, all of us went astray by seeking to establish and maintain a positive self-image through conforming to the world's (and psychology's) tenets. We targeted others and self as the twin sources for meeting our need for love and acceptance. We sought to bring our performance into line with whatever the shifting winds of the culture required to generate and maintain self-acceptance. That's what is happening in our world.

— Even though we know that "God shall supply *all* our needs through Christ," most Christians apply this promise to physical needs only. Thus, they continue to satisfy their psychological needs in the same way that lost folks do, trusting in their own flesh. Even the church has gone on a feeding frenzy in its love affair with secular psychology. Most psychologists who are Christians, most professors in seminary counseling departments, most radio and television programs featuring Christian counselors, and indeed, most pastors select "the best and most wholesome" from the world's smorgasbord of psychotherapeutic techniques for building "positive" self-worth, telling us that embracing these teachings is godly when, in fact, it is simply "wood, hay, and stubble" destined to add fuel to the fire at the judgment seat of Christ (1 Corinthians 3:14-15).

Examine Your Prayers

How much of your personal prayer life involves asking God to maintain the self-image *you've* built by your own flesh? How much of it is spent pleading for Him to restore a facet of it which is threatened or has been lost? Perhaps you're angry at God because He let something happen to you which reduced or even removed the source of your former "positive" fleshly self-image: job loss, the kids leaving the nest, your earthsuit degenerating, poor health, baldness, professional titles losing their clout, the dream house has depreciated due to demographic changes, folks don't give you the respect that they once did, *ad infinitum.*

Since God says, "From now on we recognize no man according to the flesh" (2 Corinthians 5:16); since Jesus knew who He was and thus never embraced a do-it-yourself, fleshly self-image; since God has stated that He is working hard to conform us to Christ's image (Romans 8:29;

Philippians 1:6; 2:13), what must His attitude be toward our petitions to shore up our fleshly self-acceptance? Such prayers break His heart. God wishes Christians would embrace a *Christ-generated* self-acceptance which is set in heavenly concrete.

By sacrificing His son, God made it possible for us to embrace the identity change that He has already given us—an identity which is as indestructible as Christ Himself! Most Christians never embrace it for their own personal enjoyment on earth; they anticipate doing so when they die. That is the power of sin's lie. Look at the truth from the window of God's helicopter.

The Twin Pillars of Biblical Self-Acceptance

Identity and performance—these are the twin pillars upon which we humans build our self-image, our self-worth, our self-acceptance. Lost folks (and alas, most Christians) seek to satisfy these via the flesh. Perhaps you now realize that your true identity is *spiritual*, and that you are totally accepted by God because of your identity in Christ. That takes care of number one: *identity*. Hopefully, you now realize that your performance always passes with flying colors when you allow Christ to express His life through you to do His will. That takes care of number two: *method*. There you have it: a self-acceptance that this world cannot tarnish. You *are accepted*, and as you cooperate with Christ to let Him live His life through you, your method is *approved*. Why not bow your head right now and sell out? Agree to trash that old self-image that you've either treasured or abhorred. Toss that house of cards now and avoid seeing it consumed at the judgment seat of Christ. You're going to love it.

17 "God's Rest" Foreshadowed by Israel's Experience Beyond the Jordan

GOD KNOWS THAT ONE OF THE best ways to spike the interest of a potential consumer is to give him a sample of His product. He ought to, since He designed us. Joshua's leading of the people of Israel across the Jordan River and into the promised land is replete with "tasty samples" of God's plan, which became available to man through Christ. God often intends for Israel's experiences to whet *our* appetites. First Corinthians 10:11 says, "Now these things happened to [Israel] as an example, and they were *written for our instruction.*" That's us. Two things God is "marketing" to us in the Book of Joshua are our new identity in Christ, and Christ as life through us. It's also helpful to understand that He often treats Israel as if she were one individual. Thus, it's sometimes appropriate to apply her experience to ourselves as individuals.

The Significance of the Jordan River

Some of the "samples" God gives us through Joshua's leading Israel into the promised land amaze me. If these won't light a man's fire, his wood is wet. Joshua 3:1 says, "Then Joshua rose early in the morning; and he and all the sons of Israel . . . came to the Jordan, and they lodged there before they crossed." Let's zoom in on a freeze-frame of this river in order to study some samples.

The Hebrew word *Jordan* means "descender." The river descends some 2500 feet on its journey from its headwaters

to the north end of the Sea of Galilee, which it then exits on
the south and flows to its termination at the Dead Sea, 1300
feet below sea level. The sample we'll study involves the
final 20-plus-mile segment from the city of Adam to the
Dead Sea (see Figure 17A).

I find it far more than a curiosity in God's Word that:

- from a city named *Adam*
- flows a river named *Descender*
- which ends in a sea named *Dead*.

Because:

- from a man named *Adam*
- a "life" of spiritual death *descends*
- which ends in everlasting *death*.

Wouldn't you agree this is worthy of asking the Holy
Spirit to show us what He wishes to reveal to us through this
amazing allegorical sample?

Death River

The 20-plus-mile section of the Jordan River, which flows
from the city Adam to the Dead Sea, is a sample of the "life"
of lost humanity, all of whom *descended* from Adam from
birth and are doomed to a "life" which God calls "dead" (Ephesians 2:1). This spiritually dead-to-God "life" ultimately *descends* to everlasting *death* in hell. So, it's no stretch to call
this portion of the Jordan "Death River," and the Dead Sea
"hell." The Dead Sea contains no life forms, period. This is
no accident of nature, gang. God choreographed this scene
as a sample. He runs things. That's His job description.

One definition of the word *baptize* is "to become identified with." As you know, Jesus was baptized in the Jordan
River. But *where* in the Jordan River? In the *Death River* section! In fact, He was baptized at the very spot where Joshua
led Israel across the river.[1] Why would Jesus walk some 90

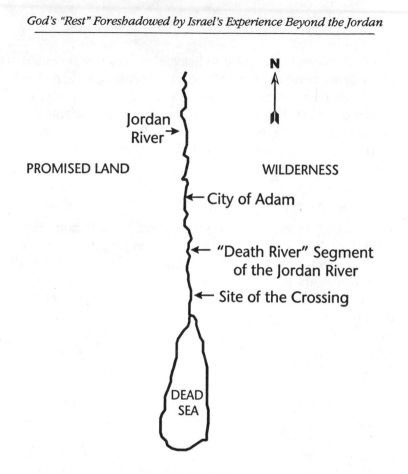

Figure 17A

air-miles south (much further by land, due to the mountainous terrain) from Galilee to the "Death River" segment of the Jordan, when He could have walked 15 or so miles east and been baptized in it upstream? By being baptized in Death River, Jesus became identified with us so we could be identified with His crucifixion and resurrection (Philippians 2:7).

West of the Jordan

Crossing the Jordan River to the promised land, which is west of the river toward the Mediterranean Sea, does not symbolize dying and going to heaven, despite what certain hymn lyrics teach. The promised land harbored God's enemies, and there were wars to be fought over there, which hardly describes heaven. The promised land represents the Spirit-controlled, Spirit-empowered, Spirit-filled life where God wins victories for and through His people. It is an Old Testament sample of knowing Christ as life in our day.[2]

Crossing Death River

Joshua 3:15 says, "Those who carried the ark came into the Jordan, and the feet of the priests carrying the ark were dipped in the edge of the water (for the Jordan overflows all its banks all the days of harvest)." You don't have to be a rocket scientist to figure out that if you are leading a million-plus people across a river, you don't try it at flood stage! Unless, of course, you are God and have a hidden agenda: developing an Old Testament sample which foreshadows New Testament reality. The torrent of Death River is a sample of humanism (man trusting in self), which sweeps down to everlasting death and destruction in hell (the Dead Sea).

Looking at Joshua 3:1-2, notice what Joshua was instructed to have Israel do when they reached the river: "Then Joshua ... and all the sons of Israel ... came to the Jordan, and ... it came about *at the end of three days* ... [that they would be ready to cross]." God let those folks sit and stare certain death in the face for three days. It looked impossible to cross that torrent. Picture this scene. They must have believed that many of them would not make it to the other side. They must have wondered, *Am I a dead man just waiting for it to happen?* Who else spent three days in the grave? The One who said, "Take up [*your*] cross, and *follow* me" (Matthew 16:24). Israel's experience here is God's sample to us of the New Testament believer's thoughts as he ponders his own crucifixion with Christ. Even though this is an accomplished fact for us (Romans 6:6), the Christian who desires to *experience* this intimate walk with Christ must agree to the terms: "Take up *your* cross and follow Christ." Deliberately choosing death on a cross is a sober, serious decision that many Christians resist. Yet, it is the key to experiencing the life that overcomes.

Israel's feeling of hopelessness as they stared at those floodwaters is an important part of the sample. The cross which Jesus exhorted us to pick up is an instrument of death. You don't enter into the Spirit-empowered life by skipping across the river, strewing rose petals. You do it by first contemplating what this implies: death to attaching your primary significance to your fleshly identity, such as engineer, housewife, athlete, pastor, Texan, African-American, white, too small, too tall, just right, homely, popular, beautiful, winner, loser, *ad infinitum;* death to seeing *yourself* as your source, whether you have a positive self-image, an average one, or a negative one; death to seeing the identity with which you were first born as still being your present identity; death to all personal rights (as if someone on a cross has any rights); death to all of the above; death to (fill in the blank), saying, "Lord, I choose to pick up *my* cross. I give up on myself as my source and claim Christ, not only as Savior and Lord, but as my life. I now choose to offer myself as a living sacrifice, holy and acceptable to God (Romans 12:1) through whom Christ can do His will on earth." You get the same deal Jesus got when He agreed to the cross: no plea bargains. Jesus said it this way, "Whoever wishes to save his life shall lose it; but whoever loses his life for My sake shall find it" (Matthew 16:25). Take the step I've described and an amazing thing will happen. You will find life—*real* life. Folks, I'm not referencing getting saved here, but experiencing the abundant life Jesus promised.

Obviously, the first step for the person who seeks a relationship with God is claiming Jesus Christ as his personal Savior and Lord. I believe this explains why God had Israel stop three-fifths of a mile short of Joshua, the ark, and the priests, who were down by the river (Joshua 3:4). Joshua means "The Lord is salvation"; the ark stands for God; the priests stand for Jesus as man's Intercessor with God, all of which will open up a new life for God's people. By keeping the people back more than a half-mile, God guaranteed a clear line of sight to the "savior" for each person. It's the same today for both the man *coming* to Jesus for salvation (John 14:6), and for Christians (Hebrews 12:2). Although a person (such as the crucified thief) with a limited understanding of what Jesus accomplished for us can be saved by faith, we must have a *correct view* (understanding) of who God is, who Jesus is, and what He accomplished for us to travel in the fast lane to maturity in Christ. Christianity is not blind faith, folks.

A Miracle That Forecasts a Greater Miracle

— Then, "when ... the feet of the priests carrying the ark were dipped in the edge of the water ... the waters which were flowing down from above stood and rose up in one heap, a great distance away *at Adam* ... and those which were flowing down toward the ... [Dead] Sea, were completely cut off. So the people crossed . . ." (Joshua 3:15-16).

The miracle where Death River stopped flowing from Adam is a sample of what happened for us through Jesus at Calvary where He stopped Adam's life in its tracks. "The priests who carried the ark of the covenant stood firm on *dry ground* in the middle of the Jordan while all Israel crossed on *dry ground*, until all the nation had finished crossing the Jordan" (Joshua 3:17). That dry ground represents God's accomplishment for us in Christ. Your old identity was eliminated—"dried up"—by your crucifixion in Christ (Romans 6:2-8; Galatians 2:20; Colossians 3:1-4). There was no moisture remaining in Death River. This sample forecasts that there is not a trace of Adam's life in new creations in Christ.

Just as God cut off the source of Death River at Adam, the city, *He cut off Adam's life as your source at Calvary.* Then, when you were *re-created* in Christ, God gave you a *new life—Christ as life.* Eternal life is not a mere extension of *your* life. Eternal life is Christ Himself (1 John 1:1-2). Adam is no longer your spiritual ancestor—Christ is. You've been spiritually reborn from Christ's spirit "gene pool," to use a metaphor. You now have not only a new spiritual present and future, but a new spiritual *past!* Christ, not Adam, is now and always will be your *spiritual Ancestor.* Everything that happened to Christ on the cross happened to you because you were *in Him.* "He chose us in Him *before the foundation of the world,* that we should be holy and blameless before Him" (Ephesians 1:4). Don't let the devil tell you this is fatalism. Remember the helicopter.

You ask, "Bill, how can this be possible?" *I haven't the faintest idea.* But then, we don't have the faintest idea why the blood of Christ cleanses us from all sin, either. We just *believe* it because God said it. *That* truth is just as unbelievable as far as human reasoning goes as the death of your sin nature. The reason forgiveness of sin is not difficult for you to accept is because you've heard it and read it in your Bible for years. So *use the same faith* to believe that your old sinful nature was executed when you died in Christ. If you've read this far, surely you've seen enough Scripture to be convinced. God gets to make the rules, remember? We're simply to believe Him, by faith. If your mentor did not teach you this, perhaps it's because he/she simply has never seen the pieces of the puzzle fitted together yet.

You are now and always have been a spirit critter who indwells a suit made of earth, not a physical animal endowed with a spirit. The new *spiritual* past you have been given in Christ is of far greater importance than if you could be reborn as the *human* of your dreams—a world-system view. "For [you] are *His* workmanship, *created in*

Christ Jesus for *good* works, which *God* prepared *beforehand*, that we should *walk* in them" (Ephesians 2:10). This says concerning all who are in Christ:

- First, you were crucified in Christ (Romans 6:2-8).

- You were then born anew through His resurrection, refashioned by the greatest, most altruistic One who will ever exist, and elevated to be God's child *by birth!* Your Dad is the Founder and Owner of the universe.

- You were re-created in *Christ*, not in your mom. You are *literally* a new creature (2 Corinthians 5:17). Dismiss the baloney that "God just sees you *as if* this were true." The Greek text doesn't support that view.

- *Good* activities have been planned by your spiritual Parent which are tailor-made for *you*. These things are not intended for your destruction, but for your ultimate best and the ultimate best of those in your sphere of influence. " 'For I know the plans I have for you,' says the Lord. 'They are plans for good and not for evil, to give you a future and a hope' " (Jeremiah 29:11 TLB). Even the so-called bad things which happen to good people (saints) are *intended* to produce good results (conform you to Christ's image—Romans 8:28-29). That's your Father's wonderful, philanthropic plan for you.

- You should walk in these plans, not in your own independent plans that you may deem to be superior to His. *Your* plans for yourself are inferior to His plans for you. They're simply not good enough for you. If you could see the view from the helicopter you'd understand, but just take His word for it because He can't lie. God actually knows what is the epitome of good for you and has already planned it. He is rich enough and powerful enough to see these plans through. But God will not violate your will. *You* have the privilege

of choice (Romans 6:13). Although God will autono-
mously cause *some* of these good plans to become
reality, you must cooperate with Him to bring many of
them on-line by faith and obedience.

God Erects a Grave Marker

"Then Joshua set up twelve stones in the middle of the
Jordan at the place where the feet of the priests who carried
the ark of the covenant were standing, and they are there to
this day "(Joshua 4:9). God had a purpose for this rock-
toting and piling. Why did He have Joshua gather 12 rocks,
and why pile them at the feet of the priests?

The New Testament often answers questions which are
left hanging in the Old Testament. I believe the 12 stones
which Joshua gathered and placed "at the feet of the priests
who carried the ark ... and ... are there to this day" represent Christians' old spiritual identity in Adam.[3] Jesus said,
"You did not choose Me, but I chose you" (John 15:16).
Joshua (Jesus), not the people, chose those stones. I
believe:

- These stones represent all 12 tribes (completeness),
  which translates to the complete body of Christ.

- Joshua's placing these stones at the feet of the priests
  in Death River represents your crucifixion in Jesus.

- These stones that were later inundated in Death River
  would seem to be an Old Testament sample of the
  burial of the old man (baptism).

- The phrase "[the stones] are [in the bottom of Death
  River] to this day" foreshadows that God would crucify
  the old man in Christ because the metaphor fits perfectly with the New Testament (Romans 6:6).

The New Man—Created in Christ

"Command them, saying, 'Take up for yourselves
twelve stones from here out of the middle of the Jordan,
from the place where *the priests' feet* are standing firm, and
carry them over with you, and lay them down in the
lodging place where you will lodge tonight' " (Joshua 4:3).
Here we see the foreshadowing of the believer's role in
salvation. Joshua (the savior) does not pick up *these* stones;
a believer from *each tribe* does so, indicating completeness
(every Christian) and individual free choice. God does not
force anyone to become a new creation in Christ. Each individual is accountable to choose or reject Jesus Christ's
gracious gift of eternal life. A person must *want* to be transformed into a new creation to *be* so transformed. Joshua
did not pick up *these* stones; the people did. Jesus doesn't
make sinners get saved; they *choose* to respond to Him
(John 3:16-17).

The second group of 12 stones which were taken *from
the priests' feet* (Christ's intercessory role on the cross) have
no part of Death River. These 12 stones came *from the foot
of the cross* and represent all who are born anew with
Christ's resurrection life. Allegorically, they emanated from
Christ in His Savior/intercessory role. These represent the
believer's new identity, that person who by faith in the finished work of Christ has "crossed" over from spiritual death
to spiritual life (been reborn). These stones which were
placed "in the lodging (resting) place" represent Christians as
the "living stones"—we are in Christ (1 Peter 2:5); we have
"entered into God's rest" (Hebrews 4:3-11). Centuries later,
John the Baptist prophesied by the Jordan, "I say to you that
God is able from *these* stones to *raise up children* to
Abraham" (Luke 3:4). He may have pointed to those same
stones because "It is not the children of [Abraham's] flesh
who are children of God, but the children of the promise are
regarded as descendants" (Romans 9:8). That's us!

After the crossing, God said, "... 'Because the waters of the Jordan were cut off before the ark of the covenant of the Lord; when it crossed the Jordan, the waters of the Jordan were cut off.' So these stones shall become a memorial to the sons of Israel forever" (Joshua 4:7). New creatures in Christ are such a living memorial (2 Corinthians 3:13), a testimony to God's grace.

⟶ We Are a Monument to Christ's Glory

"And it came about when the priests who carried the ark of the covenant of the Lord had come up from the middle of the Jordan, and the soles of the priests' feet were lifted up to the dry ground, that the waters of the Jordan returned to their place, and went over all its banks as before" (Joshua 4:18). Death River resumes its flow, representing Adam's spirit-offspring who continue their descent toward everlasting death, many of them oblivious to God's great rescue operation through Jesus Christ. The 12 stones that are buried in Death River depict our old spiritual identity in Adam and are "there to this day." They're a prophecy of your old identity that was eliminated in Jesus at Calvary (Romans 6:6).

Folks, if you disagree with this interpretation, what is your view? What is God's reason for manipulating all of the stones? Why *two* sets of stones? Why bury half of them in Death River? Why not just select one group of 12 stones for the obelisk? There is a deeper symbolic meaning here than building a memorial, gang. This whole scenario of stopping Death River at a city named Adam of all things, taking God's people across Death River at flood stage via a miracle through a man whose name is the Hebrew for *Jesus*, is a foreshadowing of the events of our salvation.

Life in the Promised Land

Israel is getting a new beginning with God (Joshua 5:9), and two dramatic changes occurred in His provision:

- Although God is going to continue to defeat Israel's enemies *for* them, *they will play a proactive role* in the battles. Passivity is not the plan. Although the nation will continue to see God at work *for* them, a new emphasis will be added. They will experience God working *through* them. God will be doing the work, but they will not sit passively in the bleachers.

- Although God will supply their needs for food, Israel will no longer passively collect their daily supply at sunrise. They will *participate* in its production.

This is the sample wherein God introduces an increased *intimacy* to His people. We are the culmination of this miracle in that the Holy Spirit of Christ actually indwells us as life. We live "in vital union" with God in suits of clay and can now enjoy an intimate relationship with Him.

Some Christians mistakenly assume that trusting Christ as life means passivity, which is more in keeping with Israel's wilderness experience. They were put on the shelf out there. The Spirit-filled (controlled) life in the promised land, however, was an *active, participatory* life. Battles were to be fought. Choices were to be made. Responsibilities were to be carried out. Orders were to be followed. In the same way, Christ through you will express an *active* life of *agape* service to others beginning in your home.

Lazy Flesh

Entering into God's rest as spoken of in Hebrews 3:18-19 is not a life of daydreaming while lying under the vine eating grapes. An able-bodied Christian who indulges himself all day becomes a frustrated, unhappy person. If we wish to experience God's rest, we must get with God's program. Jesus said, "Look at the birds of the air, that they do not sow, neither do they reap, nor gather into barns, and ye your heavenly Father feeds them" (Matthew 6:26). But as someone pointed out, you never see a robin lying on its back with its bill open waiting for worms to fall out of the sky. God's rest is an *active* resting, troops. Jesus speaks of it as a "yoke," which is an instrument of labor and service: "Take My yoke upon you, and learn from Me, for I am gentle and humble in heart; and you shall find *rest* for your souls. For My yoke is *easy*, and My load is *light*" (Matthew 11:29-30).

Joshua Did Not Fight the Battle of Jericho

A few observations regarding the battle of Jericho are in order.

> Now it came about when all the kings of the Amorites who were beyond the Jordan to the west, and all the kings of the Canaanites who were by the sea, heard how the Lord had dried up the waters of the Jordan before the sons of Israel until they had crossed, that their hearts melted, and there was no spirit in them any longer, because of the sons of Israel (Joshua 5:1).

God "put the fear of God" in these guys. I mean He just downloaded a big burst of it onto their hard drives. They never knew what hit them. His next step was to assemble a bunch of green Israeli troops who had never lifted a sword in battle in their lives. Not exactly a rangers unit, gang. Can't you see these guys looking at their weapons and one man asking which end you hold? Next God featured priests and trumpets as *the* major players in the battle. God is big on bands and choirs during wars. He loves the pregame pageantry. His instructions to the choir were to keep quiet till circle number 13 was completed.

345

After the final trip the band played, the choir shouted, and the walls fell flat. They charged in and wiped out the enemy. God had demonstrated a method of fighting that these people had never experienced. This battle was won just like the Jordan River had been crossed. God did it. Joshua *didn't* fight the battle of Jericho as the song says. *God* fought it *for* Joshua. The Israelites, however, were active; they were blowing trumpets and swinging swords. But God did it all *for* them. *He* knocked the walls down. *He* put the fear into the enemy. *He* was at work in the sword warfare, swinging, parrying, thrusting. This is a sample to whet our appetite on our side of the cross. The Christian life is to be experienced by letting Jesus Christ, the only One who could ever live it, manifest it through us.

Presumption

God instructed Israel not to plunder Jericho. He let them plunder other cities, but not this one. This was a test which gave them the opportunity to obey or disobey. These folks were relatively ignorant of God's ways because their parents had dropped the discipleship ball. God was having to break in new players and acquaint them with His ways. They had to learn obedience in the face of temptation. A lord of the ring named Achan thought it would be good to recycle some of that Jericho gold into a shoe box under the floor of his tent, so he did.

The next city on the itinerary was Ai, so they sent some spies to check it out. Their report read as follows: "No sweat. We don't even need to bother God with this one. We've got the hang of it now. We're on a roll. We could see their knees knocking. We can take these guys with one arm tied behind us. Send in the second team. No need to pray and ask God for marching orders. We know what to do; we're fast learners." They *presumed* that God's blessing would be on them. No preparation. No warm-ups. Hey, they didn't even hold band practice. They stayed home and sent the pep band. And Ai kicked them all the way to the bottom of the mountain like an avalanche. Folks, that's a wake-up call for us. These men paid a high price for us to learn from their mistakes. Are you listenin'?

Mercy, mercy, mercy! What happened? Why didn't God do His part? The Bible says that they fell on their faces and prayed. *Now* they "felt led" to pray (*after* they got "whupped up on")! Joshua prayed, "God, why [did You] ever bring this people over the Jordan, only to deliver us into the hand of the Amorites, to destroy us? If only we had been willing to dwell beyond the Jordan!" (Joshua 7:7). Joshua, bless his heart, was ready to go back across the river to the great circle route! There were no enemies back there. Life was so much simpler. Man, I can identify with that! Sometimes we get discouraged when we're plowing new ground. And the elders felt just like Joshua did. They accompanied his prayer by throwing dust in the air. (They were big on throwing dust back then, too, which the wives must have just *loved*.)

Then God told them what the problem was. There was rebellion against His authority among the troops. Achan's sin was exposed, and he and his family were blotted out. This penalty may seem harsh, but God was demonstrating the intensity of His hatred for sin. When He ultimately paid for man's sins, He could have done so by throwing salt over His left shoulder, because He makes the rules. But no, He and Jesus agreed to pay a horrendous price for our forgiveness. That act demonstrates how much God *hates* sin as well as how much He *loves* sinner-men. Achan blew it big time. It's a shame he chose to be Exhibit A. Had he delayed his gratification he could have shared in Ai's spoils later (Joshua 8:2). That's a tough way to get your name in the Bible.

New Strategy

God is now ready to teach the Israelites that He has strategies for working *through them*. These battles are samples of how we are to live. The thing that excites God is *relationship* with us, and one of the ways this can be fostered is through a joint effort in reaching a goal. We must, however, remember that it's His life through us, by faith, which is carrying the ball and bearing the burden. This way He gets both the glory for "perceived" successes and assumes the responsibility for "perceived" failures. (It's understood that I'm not teaching we can goof off and then blame Christ for the result.) This is why the Spirit-controlled life is referred to as "God's rest." I label those results as "perceived," because God's perception often varies from ours. He's more concerned with our *method* of living (Christ as life) than with the *results* of our actions (Romans 15:18).

The Flesh Loves a Piece of the Action

— The next target was a city called Gibeon, which was only six and a half miles from Ai. The word was out in the area that Israel was on a roll and, as stated earlier, God had put a supernatural fear of Himself in all of His enemies in Canaan (Joshua 5:1). So, the Gibeonites came up with a creative alternative to being run through by Israeli swords. If you can't lick 'em, join 'em. They dressed like envoys who had traveled so far that their clothes and sandals were trail-worn. They rode donkeys with worn-out blankets and saddlebags, carried dry, moldy bread, and straggled into the Israeli camp looking like death warmed over.

They said to Joshua, "We are your servants."

"Who are you, and where do you come from?" asked Joshua.

". . . Your servants have come from a very far country because of the fame of the Lord your God; for we have heard the report of Him and all that He did in Egypt, and all that He did to the two kings of the Amorites . . . So our elders and all the inhabitants of our country spoke to us, saying, ' ... Go say to them, "We are your servants ... make a covenant with us" ' " (Joshua 9:8-11).

Let's not be too hard on Joshua and the Israelites for falling for this line. Remember, their dads probably didn't spin many tales to their kids about life with God that began with "I remember the time . . ." So Joshua and Israel entered into a covenant with these envoys (Joshua 9:15). Obviously, it was a mistake to covenant with God's enemies. The Bible says, "[They] did not ask for the counsel of the Lord" (Joshua 9:14). Independence was at work again.

Three days after they had signed the contract with Gibeon, they discovered the truth. These liars lived six miles away and had been marked by the Commander-in-Chief for elimination, but Israel had brought them under the protection of their umbrella! Now Israel was about to make their second mistake. Instead of repenting and trusting *God* to straighten out the mess they had gotten themselves into, they recalled that "they had sworn to them by the Lord" (verse 18), so they stuck by mistake number one. Two wrongs never make a right, but it was live-and-learn time in the promised land. So Joshua assigned the Gibeonites to cut wood and haul water. How do you suppose the typical Israelite responded to not having to haul water and cut firewood every day? I would guess that it wasn't long before they began to praise God that *He* had sent the Gibeonites to them as His special gift. Ain't God gooood!

Folks, the Gibeonites are a sample of your flesh. The power of sin will work on your mind to manipulate, reason, argue, present logical evidence, etc., as to why you'll be better off to accommodate your flesh than declare it crucified. This is especially true if you've got "effective" flesh. But because Israel accommodated the flesh, *Gibeon ultimately divided the two kingdoms of Judah and Israel,* which led to factions and, ultimately, to destruction.

Avoid This Tasty Morsel

You talk about a sample! When you seek peaceful coexistence with your flesh, it moves you into the slow lane on God's plan for your spiritual maturation. If you continue to do so, the flesh will establish a spiritual stronghold—it will get a *strong hold* on you. If you do not know how to trust Christ to allow Him to break the grip that such a stronghold has on you, it can ultimately rob you of your victory.[4] It will punch the "hold" button on your telephone. You'll sit there and "blink" for the rest of your life unless you choose to crucify your love affair with your flesh. *Don't taste this sample!* Don't fool around with it. Your personal "Gibeonite" may have a sweet covering that gives the appearance of harmlessness or even enhancement, but it has a bitter center. Flesh is flesh no matter how you dress it up in its Sunday best. We are to learn from Israel's mistakes. If we treat such accounts as merely interesting stories of quaint, ignorant, ancient people, God will let us reinvent the wheel. A wise kid in school will clean up his act when the kid next to him gets punished.

I remember "Sam," a student of mine when I was a university professor in Oklahoma. He was a sensitive Christian whom God had saved from the drug culture. He attended our home Bible study and felt compassion for his old friends. That's good! But in his case, my counsel was to wait until he had become more seasoned in Christ before sharing his faith with them.

Soon afterward he went back home and got with the old gang. He told me later that he was surprised to discover that a couple of them had also come to Christ. They told him that through smoking pot they were having marvelous experiences with the Lord. They described the euphoria and encouraged him to join them for a meditation session. He did, and when I moved from there three years later, he was deeper than ever into the drug culture. Folks, tripping out on drugs was Sam's flesh pattern, and he fell for the lie that his old ways would actually enhance his walk with Christ. It was destroying him. Please don't be one of the folks who write me telling me that they should have heeded this warning, but they thought they could "handle" their flesh. You cannot. No man can. That's Christ's job! Partial obedience is disobedience. Give it up.

A Decision

I am praying that as you read this book, the Holy Spirit is nudging you to sell out to God's claims on you. We all start out much like Pinocchio, who rejected Geppetto's love, hopped off the carpenter's bench where the puppeteer had created him, declared his independence, and split. Have you repented of your declaration of personal independence from *your* Creator? I know you don't understand all the ramifications of my feeble attempts to explain God's plans for you. Neither do I. But you understand enough to know whether or not your desire is to claim yourself dead to what you were and begin to live as the new creation in Christ which you are.

If so, I would like to suggest something that I believe will be a meaningful experience for you. Go to a private spot out-of-doors. Select a small stick about one inch long and pencil-thin, plus a small white stone about the diameter of a quarter. Prayerfully picture yourself by the Jordan River at flood stage, sitting on the wrong bank, looking over the raging torrent toward *your* promised land (claiming your identity in Christ and Christ as life). Watch Jesus moving toward the river carrying His cross. As you begin to pray, picture the river as having dried up and Jesus as hanging on the cross between earth and heaven. Think, *I was crucified in Christ on that cross* as you scratch out a small grave in the soil and bury the stick, signifying your death as the guilty sinner you were in Adam. (The stick will decay and disappear, which is what happened to your old identity.)

Now picture Christ along with the new you resurrecting from the tomb as you pick up the white rock and begin walking out of the dry bed into the promised land. As you stare at that white stone in your hand, think, *I am now the righteousness of God in Christ. I am forgiven, holy, a "pure virgin" (2 Corinthians 11:2), beloved, treasured, and acceptable to God. Christ is now my very life.* Now begin to praise Him. Marvel at His worthiness of your praise. Don't hurry. Spend time with Him. Trust Him to make this a profound, unforgettable moment for you, Keep your rock as a memorial of God's grace to you—this special day that you claimed your identity in Christ. Write the date on it. Place it where it will serve as a daily reminder of this glorious event in your life. See it as one of those 12 stones. What a God He is! There has never been and will never be anyone like Him.

> I am the Lord of justice and of righteousness whose love is steadfast; and ... I love to be this way (Jeremiah 9:24b TLB).

> I am the Lord, and there is no other; besides Me there is no God. *I* will gird you ... that men may know from the rising to the setting of the sun that there is no one besides Me. I am the Lord, and there is no other (Isaiah 45:5-6).

God said that and He cannot lie. Pick up your trumpet and your sword, and start marching around your problems. "The battle is the *Lord's.*"

18 THAT THEY ARE THE BELOVED BRIDE OF JESUS

— CHRISTY LOVED HER FIANCÉ desperately. Even though she agreed that the idea of marrying Jay was a dream come true, she felt like such a yucky bride and it all seemed so far into the future that she never spent time savoring their relationship. Her emotions seemed almost to scream at her that Jay would never develop a *sincere* affection toward her. How could he? After all, *she* knew herself! And she knew that the more he got to know her, the less enchanted with her he would become. When she did the math on this, she could not feel comfortable around him. It was better when they were in a group, but anytime it was just the two of them, these same old feelings reared their ugly head.

Jay had a way of looking right into her mind, like he was reading her thoughts—and, believe it, she had some pretty ungodly thoughts. And her *history!* Ugh! Even though she loved him, she felt uncomfortable when she was with him. Strange though it seemed, it was like she loved him more when they were apart than when they were alone together. Sometimes she would fantasize herself as a ravishing beauty whirling around the ballroom floor in Jay's arms. Oh, it would be such a marvelous dream-come-true if she were like Cinderella! But alas, that's only a fairy story. She knew in her heart that she could never ever measure up to being the beloved wife that Jay deserved. She was just so ordinary. Mirrors and actions don't lie! She felt like such a klutz around him; she could never think of things to say. To make matters worse, Jay was a brilliant conversationalist. What she would give if only she could be changed into a beautiful princess—someone else that he could be proud of. What must it be like to be a woman who actually likes herself! Under *those* circumstances she might learn to be more comfortable around Jay. Sigh. It all seemed so hopeless.

Christy is a pseudonym for Christian; Jay is the first letter in Jesus. This anecdote describes the inhibitions some of us feel about establishing a warm, intimate relationship with our Bridegroom, Jesus Christ. We hold Him at arm's length due to our perception of our own "unloveliness." Our emotions are so strongly programmed with these *feelings* that we find it difficult to open up, to reach out and experience intimate warmth with Christ. I call this emotional barrier a "stuck feeler." On a 1 to 10 scale, Christy *feels* unlovable at the 8, 9, or 10 level—even on her *best* days!

Your New, True Identity

I cannot overly stress how critical it is to believe that God wishes all Christians would understand and appropriate their true identity in Christ. God wishes you, as a Christian, would understand that your new identity is more than His having erased your name from the debit side of His ledger and moved it into the asset column. It's not a mere paper transaction. In order for God to write your name in the Lamb's book of life, a *miraculous transformation* must happen whereby you are instantly, radically changed:

- from an enemy of God to a friend of God.

- from a child of Satan to a child of God.

- from a citizen of the kingdom of darkness to a citizen of the kingdom of light.

- from a loser to a winner.

- from a person with no hope whatsoever of being accepted by God, to a person who is automatically, totally, 100 percent accepted by God.

- from being guilty to being forgiven.

- from being condemned to receiving a full pardon.

- from being a glitch in God's vision, to being the very apple of His eye.

- from being totally unlovely to being lovely and lovable.

- from being a commoner to being celestial royalty!

All of this and much more became your permanent identity when you became spiritually reborn in Christ. He accomplished all of this for you.[1] Now He longs to reap the *personal* benefit from such a sacrifice by having a warm, intimate relationship with you. Hear the passion of Christ through me! Christ does not have a casual, indifferent attitude toward you. Would you be only mildly interested in someone whom you had rescued and rebirthed into your own image through suffering and dying for that person? Jesus has intense *feelings* for you. He's not made of cast iron. He's not so busy with the details of running the universe that you are a mere serial number. All of those "bullets" in the previous paragraph are literal. God can't "*see* you that way" unless you *are* that way in His dictionary. Rain on how you *feel!* Your feeler has been programmed from living in enemy territory. Let God deal with your feeler in any manner He may deem best for you. That's His problem. You are fully capable of doing your part to establish an intimate relationship with Jesus by simply moving toward His outstretched arms by faith. You must believe that He tells the truth and that your stuck feeler is lying. Christy embraces none of these truths and it's robbing her of an intimate relationship with Christ.

God's Love Letter

— For most of us, two things block us from forming an intimate relationship with God: a misunderstanding of *His* identity and ignorance of *our* identity. Jesus has solved both of these problems for us. As we learned previously, when you trusted Christ as Savior and Lord, your old identity was crucified in Christ and you became a lovely new creation. You are Jesus' beloved virgin bride: "For I betrothed you to one husband, that to Christ I might present you as a pure virgin" (2 Corinthians 11:2).

The Book of Hosea portrays Israel (and many Christians) as a wanton whore who clings to her old ways of getting her God-given needs supplied via self-effort (flesh). She's not after sex with multiple partners; she's striving to get her human needs met *her old way*. The sign she wears says, "Will Sleep with You for Food and Clothing." When we trust in our own flesh, God views this as a type of adultery. That's what the Book of Hosea portrays. *Christ* is our Bridegroom; it's *His* job to supply all our needs: "God shall supply all your needs according to His riches in glory in Christ Jesus" (Philippians 4:19). That's *all* of our needs: spiritual, psychological, and physical. We're playing the harlot when we place our trust in our own flesh to satisfy a need.

Hosea is a sample of Christ, who unashamedly pursues the Christian who looks to the flesh as her source. If there are things in your life that you've got "Hands Off, God!" signs taped to, you must remove those signs. He will continue to passionately pursue you until you cast them aside and run into His embrace. His love for you drives Him to do so. He can't stand to be second best in the competition for your love. He is a jealous God—jealous to be Number One to you. This includes your spouse, your family, your talents, even yourself. None of that belongs to you, anyway. God owns it all, and Christ on the cross before you ever gave Him the time of day is all the proof you need to believe that

God is on your side and will meet *all* of your needs. Christ is your faithful Bridegroom who has eyes only for you!

Never a Bridesmaid, Always a Bride

Look at this mind-blowing passage: "And it will come about in *that* day," declares the Lord, "that you will call Me [Husband (Ishi)] and will no longer call Me [Master (Baali)]. For I will remove the names of the [idols] from [your] mouth [your false sources from which you seek to extract your need-supply—your flesh]" (Hosea 1:16-17). Once you give up all of those false sources you'll wonder why they ever held a higher place than Christ. "*I will betroth you to Me forever;* Yes, I will betroth you to Me in righteousness and in justice, in lovingkindness and in compassion, and I will betroth you to Me in faithfulness. Then you will *know* the Lord" (Hosea 2:19-20). Folks, we are experiencing "*that* day" in line two of this paragraph. Although this passage is yet future for Israel, it is reality for us. You have been betrothed to Christ in righteousness and in justice, in lovingkindness and in compassion, and faithfulness. Amazing. You are the precious, desirable fiancée of the King of the universe.

Each "Christy" must comprehend from God's Love Letter that His description of her as a new creation in Christ is reality today, *not a future hope.* Christ has broken down and removed every barrier between God and man insofar as *God* is concerned; and remember, He gets to make the rules. All man must do is come to Him on His gracious terms, and then begin walking in the *wonder* of enjoying an intimate, loving relationship with the God of the universe.

God's desire for relationship with you is not simply for *your* benefit. It's for *God's* benefit! Relationship is to be developed and enjoyed by *two* parties. Your resisting of His efforts to break down cultural, fleshly, inhibiting barriers between the two of you is painful to *Him.* None of us would want to wound Him. Quite the opposite, we are trying to do what we believe is pleasing to Him. But, gang, if we are naïvely marching along *beside* the biblical path He's marked out for us instead of *on* it, simply because it *feels* "right" to our flesh over there, we are missing out in a major way.

Imagine how you would feel if you had made such a sacrifice for your true love as Jesus has for you, and yet the object of your affection simply wouldn't receive your entire offering. He died that our intimacy with Him might begin *here*, not in heaven. He longs for your physical death to become anticipated (1 Corinthians 15:55-56), not simply because you grow weary of the hassles of earth, but because of your growing excitement about throwing yourself into His loving arms!

The book Song of Solomon portrays Christ as the Bridegroom who is madly in love with you, the bride. Don't be turned off by the sexual innuendo in that book. Great day, the Bible doesn't teach that we are in some sort of weird spiritual-sexual relationship with God! He simply uses this most intimate of human relationships as a communication vehicle through which to portray His love for us. After all, *He's* the One who *invented* sex, so if He wants to use it metaphysically to make His point, He can do so. If this bothers you, it's your flesh kicking in. The story portrays Him as passing over all of the other women. He only has eyes for *you*!

An Intimate Walk with Jesus

Here are some questions to help illustrate what I'm viewing as an intimate relationship with our Lord. Yours may differ somewhat, and that's OK.

- Do you fellowship with Jesus Christ inside your earth-suit, as opposed to speaking to Him as if He were "way up there" somewhere?

- Do you trust His Holy Spirit moment-by-moment as your Teacher and Companion?

- Do you actively believe that He's sharing with you from His Love Letter as you read it and trust Him to touch your heart?

- Do you marvel with Him at the beauty and majesty of the flora, fauna, stars, humans, etc., that He created?

- Do you laugh together at the antics of your silly dog or cat that He created for you?

- Do you chuckle together at some of the hilarious critters He created?

- Do you simply enjoy one another's company and not feel like you have to talk all the time?

- Do you sometimes laugh out loud with Him when you do something stupid?

- Do you sometimes laugh out loud with Him when He's done something special to delight you?

- Do you take walks together, drive together, dine together, etc.?

- Are you sometimes moved deeply as you sing praises to Him?

- Do you groan or perhaps cry in His arms when you're hurting?

- Do you cry at times from the sheer emotion you feel because of your love for Him?

- Do you marvel at His power during a crashing thunderstorm and maybe even shout "Way to go!" when He lets loose with a big boomer?

- Do you *receive* the tiny wildflower He planted in the crack in the parking lot as His love gift *especially for you* to tell you that He's thinking of you?

- Do you do the same when He causes your favorite songbird to sail across your lawn or makes it sing just for you?

- Do you *receive* the sunsets and sunrises which He paints as His love gifts *especially for you* to remind you that you're always on His mind?

- Do you frequently express your gratitude to Him for such special love gifts?

- Do you let Him put His arm around your shoulder and listen with compassion when you've been misunderstood?

- Do you let Him comfort you while you repent?

- Do you let Him be your primary Comforter while you grieve?

- Do you see Him as your celestial Husband and bask in His love for you?

- Do you see yourself as His selected, chosen bride, whose hand He won by dying for you?

These are a few of the ways that He and I relate to one another. As you can see, they range from the sublime to the mundane, but they all add up to an intimate relationship, as opposed to a formal handshake or a chin-up, face-into-the-wind, pat on the back.

What Is God Like?

Another imperative for enjoying an intimate relationship with God is insight into His character. What is God like? I know you love God, but do you *like* Him? You would if you knew Him as He is. Are you anxious to see what He looks like? I think most of us have a natural inclination to wonder about this. It's kind of hard to imagine relating to a puff of smoke. I suppose this is one reason people have created icons. The sadness is compounded when we see how far afield their image of God is by the visages their idols bear. Their "god" is usually scowling and bizarre. And he often extracts horrible sacrifices from his worshipers. Consider what the false god Allah ostensibly rewards: suicide bombers! Of course, all of these so-called gods are demonic (1 Corinthians 10:20).

Efforts to produce Christian images of God have not been without their negative, unbiblical inspiration. Has God revealed Himself to man so we can "get a good look" at Him? Indeed He has. God actually put a "face" on the Father, the Son, and the Holy Spirit for us so we could see what He is really like. Jesus was God. The New Testament says of Jesus, "For in Him all the fullness of Deity dwells in bodily form" (Colossians 2:9). I reiterate C. S. Lovett's observation: "Jesus was God in an earthsuit." The first evidence of this is discovered in Isaiah 9:6, which foretells of God's human manifestation in Jesus: "For a child will be born to us, a son will be given to us; and the government will rest on His shoulders; and His name will be called Wonderful Counselor, Mighty God, Eternal Father, Prince of Peace."

- *A child will be born to us*—a human baby was born to benefit all mankind.

- *A son will be given to us*—this baby was the Son of God.

- *The government will rest on His shoulders*—all authority would be given to Jesus. He will reign over the entirety of creation "forever and ever."

- *His Name will be called Wonderful Counselor*—Jesus put a "face" on the Counselor, the Holy Spirit.

- *[His Name shall be called] Mighty God*—Jesus put a "face" on God.

- *[His Name shall be called] Eternal Father*—Jesus put a "face" on the Father.

- *[His Name shall be called] Prince of Peace*—Jesus, Exemplar of Peace, will one day reign forever over a peaceful kingdom.

The man Jesus was God manifest! Consider John 14:8-9: "Philip said to Him, 'Lord, show us the Father, and it is enough for us.' Jesus said to him, 'Have I been so long with you, and yet you have not come to know Me, Philip? He who has seen Me *has seen the Father;* how can you say, "Show us the Father"?' " And again, "He is the *image of the invisible God*, the first-born of all creation" (Colossians 1:15). — "For in Him all the fullness of Deity dwells in bodily form" (Colossians 2:9). Father, Son, and Holy Spirit were all miraculously wrapped up in the human body of the Person whom we know as Jesus. If you can relate to Jesus, you automatically relate to the Father and the Holy Spirit because, even though the Father and the Holy Spirit are separate manifestations of God, they were all three in Him. I don't understand this; I just believe it because God says so. The following illustrations fall far short of an adequate explanation, but perhaps they may be helpful. I am a son to my dad, a husband to Anabel, and a father to my sons, yet I am one. A drop of water is liquid, solid, or gas depending on its temperature, yet we think of it as one. Figure 18A is my Sunday-school teacher's take on it. F equals Father; S equals Son; HS equals Holy Spirit—three facets of one God.

362

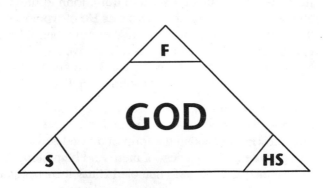

Figure 18A

Jesus: a Closer Look

It has been an edifying experience to me to string together the most lengthy descriptions of Jesus' identity as described in God's Love Letter to us. Please don't skim through these descriptions. Ask the Holy Spirit to make this a special blessing to you as you read this section meditatively.

In the beginning was the Word, and the Word was with God, and the Word *was* God. He was in the beginning with God. All things came into being through Him, and apart from Him nothing came into being that has come into being. In Him was life, and the life was the Light of men. The Light shines in the darkness, and the darkness did not comprehend it ... There was the true Light which, coming into the world, enlightens every man. He was in the world, and the world was made through Him, and the world did not know Him. He came to His own, and those who were His own did not receive Him. But as many as received Him, to them He gave the right to become children of God, even to those who believe in His name, who were born not of blood, nor of the will of the flesh, nor of the will of man, but of God. And the Word became flesh, and dwelt among us, and we beheld His glory, glory as of the only begotten

363

from the Father, full of grace and truth. John testified about Him and cried out, saying, "This was He of whom I said, 'He who comes after me has a higher rank than I, for He existed before me.' " For of His fullness we have all received, and grace upon grace.... Grace and truth were realized through Jesus Christ (John 1:1-5, 9-17).

[Christ Jesus], although He existed in the form of God, did not regard equality with God a thing to be grasped, but emptied Himself, taking the form of a bond-servant ... being made in the likeness of men. And being found in appearance as a man, He humbled Himself by becoming obedient to the point of death, even death on a cross. For this reason also, God highly exalted Him, and bestowed on Him the name which is above every name, that at the name of Jesus every knee should bow, of those who are in heaven and on earth and under the earth, and that every tongue should confess that Jesus Christ is Lord, to the glory of God the Father (Philippians 2:6-11).

He is the image of the invisible God, the firstborn of all creation. For by Him all things were created, both in the heavens and on earth, visible and invisible, whether thrones or dominions or rulers or authorities—all things have been created by Him and for Him. He is before all things, and in Him all things hold together. He is also head of the body, the church; and He is the beginning, the firstborn from the dead; so that He Himself might come to have first place in everything. For it was the Father's good pleasure for all the fullness to dwell in Him, and through Him to reconcile all things to Himself, having made peace through the blood of His cross; through Him, I say, whether things on earth or things in heaven (Colossians 1:15-20).

[God] in these last days has spoken to us in His Son, whom He appointed heir of all things, through whom also He made the world. And He is the radiance of His glory and the exact representation of His nature, and upholds all things by the word of His power. When He had made purification of sins, He sat down at the right hand of the

Majesty on high; having become as much better than the angels, as He has inherited a more excellent name than they. For to which of the angels did [God] ever say, "You are My Son, today I have begotten You"? And again, "I will be a Father to Him and He shall be a Son to Me"? And when He again brings the first-born into the world, He says, "And let all the angels of God worship Him." ... But of the Son He says, "Your throne, O God, is forever and ever, and the righteous scepter is the scepter of His kingdom. You have loved righteousness and hated lawlessness; therefore God, Your God, has anointed You with the oil of gladness above Your companions." And, "You, Lord, in the beginning laid the foundation of the earth, and the heavens are the works of Your hands; they will perish, but You remain; and they all will become old like a garment, and like a mantle You will roll them up; like a garment they will also be changed. But You are the same, and Your years will not come to an end. But to which of the angels has He ever said, "Sit at My right hand, until I make Your enemies a footstool for Your feet"? (Hebrews 1:2-13).

I saw heaven opened; and behold, a white horse, and He who sat upon it is called Faithful and True; and in righteousness He judges and wages war. And His eyes are a flame of fire, and on His head are many diadems; and He has a name written on Him which no one knows except Himself. He is clothed with a robe dipped in blood, and His name is called The Word of God. And the armies which are in heaven, clothed in fine linen, white and clean, were following Him on white horses. From His mouth comes a sharp sword, so that with it He may strike down the nations, and He will rule them with a rod of iron; and He treads the wine press of the fierce wrath of God, the Almighty. And on His robe and on His thigh He has a name written, "KING OF KINGS, AND LORD OF LORDS" (Revelation 19:11-16).

This is the *true* Christ whose Spirit indwells you. He was, but no longer is a baby in a manger. He was, but no longer is a carpenter. Jesus is not a circuit-riding country preacher on a donkey. Jesus is coming again mounted on a white charger, leading the invincible armies of heaven, and He'll be mad as a hornet at all those who have rejected Him as their Savior and Ruler. Jesus is Almighty God, who wore an earthsuit for 33 years. Jesus is God. Jesus is your Bridegroom. Jesus is your dearest Friend. Jesus is your life!

Formality

~ The number-one enemy of intimately relating to the magnificent Jesus described above is formality, according to author C. S. Lovett.[2] I agree with him. I call religious formality "having a stained-glass relationship with God." Beautiful cathedrals, choirs, orchestras, pipe organs, etc., enhance our worship experience and are wonderful—I love them. But if our sweetest moments with Christ are experienced only when accompanied by the euphoric highs produced by such ambiance, there is a serious flaw in our relationship with Jesus. What do you do when the band goes home and they turn out the lights? Someone has rightfully said that most of us never discover that Christ is all we need until Christ is all we have. But you needn't wait for that. You can begin to enjoy such intimacy right now.

Please don't take offense at what I am about to say. My intent is not to be critical of your walk with Christ, but to enhance it to His glory and to your pleasure. Many of us call God "Thee" and "Thou" and have developed a different vocabulary we use only when addressing Him. We have emulated well-meaning role models and practiced *their* method of communicating with God until words like *wouldst, givest, tarry, quicken,* etc., flow from our lips in public prayers as if they were more pleasing to God than our normal vocabulary. We say that it just sounds "right" or that it *"feels* better" to speak this way when addressing God. The fact is that we are filtering these terms through our stuck feelers that have been programmed in this world, and if our *feeler* says it *"feels* right; therefore *is* right," we claim it's God's will. Some people prefer Bibles that use formal language, thinking, *Now that sounds like a Bible ought to sound!* My friend, what I am about to say is not human opinion. We know for a fact that such formality is not inspired by the Holy Spirit because *such language does not occur in the Hebrew and Greek texts.* Why didn't God make provision for such formality if it pleases Him? It's not in the canon.

The King James Version is written in the ancient English of 1611 England. Gang, that's over three and a half centuries ago! If you had a choice between a morning paper that was printed in such a format and its competitor that used modern vocabulary, which paper would you subscribe to? Of course. Since the English of 1611 is not in our normal vein, it becomes a hurdle we must overcome to establish the intimate relationship with Jesus that He desires. Building a relationship with Jesus through stiff, formal media is somewhat like shaking hands with your spouse. It's just not natural. It doesn't have the easy flow that God wishes Christians would develop with Him. The New King James translation has corrected this problem. I recommend it as well as the New American Standard translation as study Bibles.

Familiarity

Enjoying an "easy-flowing," intimate relationship with God, on the other hand, does not mean that He wants us to address Him with nicknames as "The Man Upstairs," "The Guy in the Sky," etc. Though God did assume human form, He is not a human. He is God, and His Love Letter insists that He be treated with respect. The episodes in the Old Testament where His wrath is demonstrated against His people who failed to understand this are intended for *our* benefit—a word to the wise.

Remember when Israel was transporting the ark which they had recaptured from the Philistines? No common Israelite was permitted to touch or look into the ark, because unregenerate (unholy) man may not touch or look upon God. But as you may recall, "Uzzah reached out toward the ark of God and took hold of it, for the oxen nearly upset it. And the anger of the Lord burned against Uzzah, and God struck him down there *for his irreverence*; and he died there by the ark of God" (2 Samuel 6:6-7). Uzzah's name means "strength." He was used to intervening with his strength in situations that called for action. But God never needs man's strength or help. Uzzah made a crucial mistake. In his haste to save the day, he disrespected God's holiness. God took him out. That's another tough way to get your name in the Bible. The lesson we are to learn? God is not to be treated like He's just "one of the boys" or Someone who needs our puny help.

The Philistines doubtless trampled all over God's holiness when the ark was in *their* possession, yet He didn't strike them dead on the spot. But they were not God's people. He was not seeking to reveal Himself to nations other than Israel at that time. God is holy, and we are to treat Him as the holy God that He is.

Intimacy

Between the ditch of formality and, across the road, that of a "chummy," disrespectful familiarity with God, there lies the balance that I am calling intimacy with God. Let's return to the matter of biblical translation and see how certain other translations besides the King James Version can inadvertently erect barriers which are hurdles to establishing intimacy with God.

— I wish a tone of voice could be adequately imparted via the printed word so you could discern that I am not angry at the translators. I am not pounding my computer keyboard with righteous indignation. My intent is not to criticize the King James Version or the New American Standard translations of the Bible. The New American Standard is my favorite study Bible; at this writing, I believe it and the New King James to be the most accurate English translations available. Rather, I'm simply pointing out that when the most accurate translating techniques at our disposal are implemented, we see that the evidence falls on the side of intimacy with God, not formality, hands down.

Never Say *Abba*

The Hebrew word *Abba* is a term of endearment still used by Israelis when addressing their fathers. Although there is no accurate English translation for *Abba*, its counterpart would be *Dad, Papa, Daddy*—terms of respectful endearment in our culture. God in His Love Letter says, "And because you are sons, God has sent forth the Spirit of His Son into our hearts, crying, 'Abba! Father' " (Galatians 4:6 NASB). We sing "Abba, Father" in church, but many Christians don't know what *Abba* means. Is God pleased that we sing a foreign word to Him that has no meaning to us? No. Is God pleased that this foreign word be retained in our Bibles? No. He plainly says, "Call Me *Dad*" (from Romans 8:15). Folks, this is *God's* will! I call out to translators, praise leaders, and pastors. Lead people into intimacy with God, explaining the reason for doing so. Drop the *Abba* term and use something like *Dad* or *Papa*. It's God's will we're dealing with here. There is no biblically justifiable reason why we should cave in to cultural customs or stuck feelers that block us from intimacy with our heavenly Dad. You will doubtless take some heat on this, but calling Him *Dad* is *His* idea, not mine. I wouldn't dare take such a step on my own, but I dare not fail to take such a step simply because I fear reprisal from the formality flock. I do not write from a liberated-'60s mentality. The Holy Spirit *"cries out"* inside of each new creature in Christ to call Him by warm, intimate terms of endearment (Romans 8:15; Galatians 4:6).

My friends were on a bus in Jerusalem and saw a little boy spin around in his dad's lap, stand up, grab him by his beard with both hands, gaze lovingly into his eyes with nose-to-nose contact, and jabber, "*Abba, Abba.*" This is what *Abba* means! The Father *longs* for this kind of relationship with you. His Holy Spirit within you "cries out" for this. Why not choose right now to say, "Rain on my stuck feeler, the 'religiously correct' culture, and on you, devil; my Father says He wants me to begin respectfully calling Him *Dad*, and you can rail at me all you want to, but my decision is made." And then throw yourself into your heavenly Dad's arms. Call Him Dad or Daddy or Papa—whatever respectful, intimate term fits you best.

Is Jesus a Formal Person?

An indication of Jesus' touchability is the way that He distanced Himself from the stuffy religious traditions of His day. By treating women with respect, He caused many a religious stuffed shirt to knit his brow in scorn. Rather than joining the self-appointed stoning squad, He showed compassion toward the woman who was caught in adultery. He walked across Samaria, which was a religious taboo; the elitist religious crowd took the long way around rather than soil themselves by crossing the railroad tracks. He even drank from the cup of a Samaritan woman and treated her and her friends as people who were valuable enough to spend a few days with. I don't recall His ever doing this with the high priest. Spending time with this "tainted" woman would have blown the formal, stuffy, pompous religious leaders away. He openly defied and castigated their hypocrisy; He went out of His way to heal lepers who were social outcasts. He even stayed in their homes (Mark 14:3). Jesus brought His own drum to the party. But *He was never resistant or rebellious as a statement against authority,* such as might be the case with some modern media or rock stars. His actions were always for the glory of God and in *agape* love toward man.

Did Jesus Talk Like an Oxford Grad?

Another indication that Jesus was not "hung up" on formality is evident in the language He used. As a common carpenter with no formal education, He spoke Jewish Aramaic, which was the language of the commoner of His day, and probably Greek as well because this was the universal language. When we are in the presence of an intellectual giant, we usually try to polish up our linguistic foot a bit before putting it forward, right? We want this person to realize that we didn't ride into town on a watermelon truck. Saul of Tarsus was such an intellectual—an industrial-strength Pharisee. This guy was their top gun. I can imagine the local mothers wearing God's ears out with their prayers for Saul to choose their daughter as a wife; or the Pharisees laughing about Saul's latest one-liner barb in debating the Scriptures as he notched another Sadducee's scalp on the handle of his six-shooter. Saul was a winner. He spoke Latin, Greek, Hebrew, and Aramaic, was a rabbi at age 30, and was tutored by Gamaliel, the intellectual giant of his day. As such, he would have probably used his most polished language. It was all a part of his *shtick*. After all, he had to stay unspotted so he would be fit to occupy his place of honor on the Sabbath.

— After Jesus had ascended, He decided it was time to ring Saul's doorbell. Saul specialized in chaining up rebel Christians and teaching 'em a little respect. You've gotta love it when a smart aleck gets his comeuppance, and Saul was about to get his. Had I been the ascended, multilingual Jesus, I would have blown this pompous blowhard away with my vocabulary. I would have made Saul's tutor

Gamaliel sound like Ned in the First Reader. OK, Jesus, sic 'im! Let's see You do Your stuff.

Acts 26:14 tells us what happened: "When we had all fallen to the ground, I heard a voice saying to me in the Hebrew dialect, 'Saul, Saul, why are you persecuting Me?'" *Hebrew dialect* means "Jewish Aramaic," the language of the common people. This means that Jesus did not try to impress this highly educated intellectual with His IQ of infinity. *He spoke to Saul using the same language of the common man that He had used while He was a human.* Amazing! The glorified, awesome, magnificent Head of the church, Savior of mankind, King of the universe *still talks like a Jewish carpenter.* Our formal language doesn't impress Him.

Jesus' Love for His Virgin Bride

Your heavenly Father is tender, compassionate, merciful, and approachable. He's your Dad! Jesus broke down every barrier between Himself and you, between the Father and you, between the Holy Spirit and you. Anytime you feel like it, you can breeze right past His secretary, walk through His office door, run across the carpet, and throw your arms around His neck. He'll drop whatever He's working on to welcome such intimacy. He's got all the time in the world for you. You're the apple of His eye. Oh, dear Christian, the awesomeness of this truth! Does God have to let a house fall on us to demonstrate that Jesus is kind, gracious and, above all, approachable, even touchable?

I implore you to lay aside every hindrance of your imagination or emotions that the power of sin is using to block you from embracing Him as the Bridegroom He is to you. "I am jealous for you with a godly jealousy; for I betrothed you to one *husband,* so that to Christ I might present you as a *pure virgin.* But I am afraid that as the serpent deceived Eve by his craftiness, your *minds* will be *led astray from the simplicity and purity of devotion* to Christ" (2 Corinthians 11:2-3).

Jesus doesn't talk like a Shakespearean actor, as the media portray Him. And I doubt that He looks like the sad-eyed, pasty-faced image that the old masters portrayed Him to be in their paintings, well-meaning though they may have been. He's not stiff and formal. He doesn't desire a "stiff-upper-lip, firm-handshake, jaw-set-into-the-wind" relationship with you. You are His beloved bride!

Do you see how God's Word described you in the paragraph above—a virgin bride, loved and cherished by your Bridegroom? You're a pure virgin! If you do not agree with this, then according to this verse your *mind* has been "led astray from the simplicity and purity of devotion to Christ" by Satan. He has you embracing a view of yourself and your relationship to Jesus which differs from God's view of new creatures in Christ.

I May Know You Better Than You Know Yourself

You say, "Oh, Bill, if you only *knew* me. You don't know how much sin is in my life, a lot of it since I've been saved." Stop that! You're repeating words that the power of sin is putting into your mind. I *do* know you! I'm not addressing your performance; Christ through you can remedy that. I'm addressing your *identity*—the identity that Christ produced. If you're having difficulty receiving His acceptance, the problem is that *you* don't know who you are. *I* know what God says about you. *You*, on the other hand, are focusing on your *past*, your *feelings*, your *behavior*, your *thought-life*, your *earthsuit*, etc. Focus on what *God* says about you. You have been cleansed. You are a virgin bride, loved and cherished by your Bridegroom (2 Corinthians 11:2). Anabel developed a powerful object lesson which God has used to set many Christians free from their past. Take a beautiful piece of stemware from your cabinet and let it represent you. Moisten some soil until it becomes mud. Now as you enumerate the experiences you're ashamed of, which make you feel dirty and inhibit you from seeing yourself as pure and holy, smear mud over the stemware till it looks as dirty as you feel. Take a good look at that filthy goblet. That's what God once saw.

Now plunge the goblet into a pan of hot, soapy water and wash it thoroughly while you set your mind on God's having washed you both inside and out through Christ until you are now spotless! When the goblet is clean, rinse it and polish it with a clean, dry cloth while you meditate upon the *fact* that you are literally a pure virgin bride. Now praise Him for such marvelous grace. Only God can accomplish such a miracle! Praise Him! The issue is not whether you committed these sins as a Christian or as a lost person, but that God *has cleansed you* both now and forever! God did all of this in Christ. He gets to make the rules. You are desirable and lovely. Go on—dash into the arms that have been waiting for you all these years. This is the way you begin to build a relationship with Him. And by the way, don't forget your dancing shoes.

Godspeed to you, my dear relative in Christ. I could be mistaken, but as I write this, I sense that God is no longer enrolling Christians in a 40-year maturity plan. I don't predict dates, but I believe time is short. Be practicing your jumping jacks (1 Thessalonians 4:15-18). You and I have an unimaginably mind-blowing eternity awaiting us. My continual prayer as I put this manuscript together has been, "Lord, please use these truths to enable your people to better bring honor to Your reputation by the way they live." As the truth begins to liberate you, ask Him to show you other pilgrims who have moved over into the slow lane with their engines smoking, who would be eternally grateful to God if you would teach them how He can turn what they see as their lemon into lemonade. I'm having a great time doing it. I'll anticipate meeting you at the end of the freeway. And here's something neat to remember: There's no toll booth awaiting us there. Jesus paid it all.

I love you,
Bill

Dr. Bill Gillham is a former professor of psychology at Southeastern Oklahoma State University. He and his wife, Anabel, have spoken worldwide through Lifetime Guarantee Ministries of Fort Worth, Texas, and host the nationally syndicated radio program "Lifetime Guarantee." The Gillhams have three married sons and one son, Mason, who is with the Lord.

If you've enjoyed the trip along God's freeway, I believe you'll like my book *Lifetime Guarantee*, which extrapolates some of the truths in this book. You ladies would also be blessed by Anabel's *The Confident Woman*, which carries the same message from the woman's view. Our book *He Said, She Said* (Harvest House) applies the teachings in this book to marriage. We also have audio albums and an outstanding video series, "The Life," which is suitable for either group or individual study (study manual available).

Visit our web site at **www.lifetime.org,** or call 1-888-395-LIFE for information about our ministry.

NOTES

CHAPTER 3

1. See our book on marriage: Bill and Anabel Gillham, *He Said, She Said* (Eugene, OR: Harvest House, 1995).

2. See Gillham and Gillham, *He Said, She Said.*

CHAPTER 4

1. This revelation came to my coworker Joyce Ray through the birth of her grandson.

2. William R. Newell, *Romans Verse by Verse* (Chicago: Moody Press, 1938), pp. 212-213.

3. A. W. Tozer, *Renewed Day by Day* (Harrisburg, PA: Christian Publications, Inc., 1980), January 5.

4. D. Martyn Lloyd-Jones, *Romans, Exposition of Chapter 6* (Grand Rapids, MI: Zondervan Publishing House, 1972), p. 65.

CHAPTER 5

1. These references clearly do not refer to our physical body.

2. See my book *Lifetime Guarantee* (Eugene, OR: Harvest House, 1987) for a thorough treatment of this topic.

3. C. I. Scofield, *The New Scofield Reference Bible* (Oxford University Press, 1967), p. 1191.

CHAPTER 6

1. With apology to the original author for borrowing this illustration. I was unable to identify the source.

2. Thomas Nelson, 1952.

3. Call 1-888-395-LIFE or reach us on the internet at www.lifetime.org for a list of our materials, containing a more detailed explanation of how to apply these truths.

Chapter 8

1. *An Expository Dictionary of New Testament Words* (Thomas Nelson Publishers) by W. E. Vine is an easy tool for such interpretation.

2. If you rated your love with numbers *below* ten and you wish to get some clarification by speaking with one of our staff members, call 1-817-737-6688. We want to serve you if we can.

3. If you base your salvation on a *feeling* you once had, but have lived like the rest of the world ever since, you never give Jesus a second thought, and God's hand of discipline is absent, I'm very skeptical about your salvation. It's not my intention to give anyone such as this a false assurance of salvation.

4. W. E. Vine, *An Expository Dictionary of New Testament Words* (Thomas Nelson, 1952), p. 970.

Chapter 9

1. See Henry Halley, *Halley's Bible Handbook* (Zondervan, 1962), p. 557; Merrill Unger, *Unger's Bible Handbook* (Moody Press, 1967), p. 656.

2. Why did Paul write the epistle to the Romans, even though he had never visited them? They had no New Testament. I believe he felt compelled to teach them *the* gospel to ensure that they had a written record to arm them against the heresies the devil had raised up (i.e., Judaizers, Antinomians, etc.).

3. I don't mean to be ugly, but some well-meaning Christians today might have gathered around Paul to bind the devil and pray that thorn away without asking the Holy Spirit if God had a higher purpose which they may have overlooked. I affirm their compassion, but fault their discernment. God may have other plans that will produce far more glorious results than we can imagine. Can you see Jesus, Paul, Peter, John, and the other Bible heroes and heroines living the lives they lived if they had never been dealt some tough cards in life, even some that seemed to be from the bottom of the deck? A steady diet of feeling good, prosperity, and protection from all troubles has *never* developed Christian character, and it never will. How could things that produce a spoiled, selfish, self-indulgent lost man produce godliness in saved folks? We are not a tomato patch, gang. God has planted an oak grove by the river of life. Adversity plays an important role in the maturation process (Romans 8:28-29).

CHAPTER 10

1. Howard and Geraldine Taylor, *Hudson Taylor's Spiritual Secret* (Chicago: Moody Press, 1932).

CHAPTER 12

1. A. W. Tozer, *The Best of A. W. Tozer* (Grand Rapids, MI: Baker Book House, 1978).

CHAPTER 13

1. My book *Lifetime Guarantee* details the steps for accomplishing this

CHAPTER 14

1. Call our office (1-888-395-LIFE) for information on how to order "Biblical Perspective on Divorce and Remarriage" by Jack Hayford.
2. Matthew 5:23-24.
3. Check out Bill and Anabel Gillham's *He Said, She Said* (Eugene, OR: Harvest House, 1995) to help you understand how to let Christ live through one another in your marriage.

CHAPTER 16

1. Paul Billheimer, *Don't Waste Your Sorrows* (Christian Literature Crusade, 1977).
2. The Bible states 46 times that Jesus *was raised* by the Father; Jesus *implied* metaphorically three times that He would raise Himself (i.e., "Destroy this temple, and in three days I will raise it up"—John 2:19).

CHAPTER 17

1. Henry H. Halley, *Halley's Bible Handbook* (Grand Rapids: Zondervan, 1978), p. 153.
2. Law can never lead us into freedom or empower us to overcome sin. The law never changes (Matthew 5:18) and much like *the law he represents,* Moses' body and even his eyesight remained vibrant until his death at age 120 (Deuteronomy 34:7). While many believe that Moses couldn't lead Israel into the promised land solely due to his disobedience (Numbers 20:8-12), the deeper reason is that the law (typified by Moses) could never take man into such grace. Only Jesus, typified by Joshua, can both save us and live the *Spirit-controlled, God-pleasing life* through us.

3. Merrill Unger, *Unger's Bible Handbook* (Moody Press, 1967), p. 158.

4. Call our office at 1-888-395-LIFE for information on Anabel Gillham's audio album *The Building Up and Tearing Down of Spiritual Strongholds.*

CHAPTER 18

1. Please don't fall into one of Satan's traps by calling this your "position in Christ." That somehow translates into a mere name tag—a label. It has the effect of diminishing the reality of your identity. This is not a label; it is *you!*

2. C. S. Lovett, *Longing to Be Loved* (Personal Christianity, 1982).

BIBLIOGRAPHY

Billheimer, Paul. *Don't Waste Your Sorrows*. Christian Literature Crusade, 1977.

Friedmann, Frank. *I Was Wrong, But God Made Me Right!* Living in Grace Publications, 10051 Siegen LN, Baton Rouge, LA, 1997 (for children ages 4-8).

George, Bob. *Classic Christianity*. Harvest House Publishers, 1989.

———. *Growing in Grace*. Harvest House Publishers, 1991.

Gillham, Anabel. *The Confident Woman*. Wolgemuth & Hyatt Publishers, 1989. Revised edition, Harvest House Publishers, 1993.

———. *A Stillness in the Storm*. Harvest House Publishers, 1995.

Gillham, Bill. *Lifetime Guarantee*. Wolgemuth & Hyatt Publishers, 1987. Revised edition, Harvest House Publishers, 1993.

Gillham, Bill and Anabel. *He Said, She Said*. Wolgemuth & Hyatt Publishers, 1989. Revised edition, Harvest House Publishers, 1995.

Lloyd-Jones, D. Martyn. *Romans—The New Man—Exposition of Chapter Six*. Zondervan Publishers, 1972.

Lovett, C. S. *Death: Graduation to Glory*. Personal Christianity, 1974.

McVey, Steve. *Grace Walk*. Harvest House Publishers, 1995.

———. *Grace Rules*. Harvest House Publishers, 1998.

Nee, Watchman. *The Normal Christian Life*. Christian Literature Crusade, 1957.

Needham, David. *Alive for the First Time*. Multnomah Press, 1995.

———. *Close to His Majesty*. Multnomah Press, 1987.

Newell, William R. *Romans Verse by Verse*. Moody Press, 1938.

Ortiz, Juan Carlos. *Living with Jesus Today*. Creation House, 1982.

Solomon, Charles. *Handbook to Happiness*. Tyndale House Publishers, 1982.

———. *The Rejection Syndrome*. Tyndale House Publishers, 1982.

———. *Counseling with the Mind of Christ*. Fleming H. Revell Company, 1977.

Taylor, Jack. *The Key to Triumphant Living*. Broadman Press, 1971.

Trumbull, Charles. *The Life That Wins*. Christian Literature Crusade, 1971.

Other Good
Harvest House Reading

Classic Christianity
Bob George

For each vibrant, fulfilled Christian, there seems to be nine who feel bogged down or burned out. In Bob George's down to earth style, *Classic Christianity* shows you the way back to authentic Christianity.

The Confident Woman
Anabel Gillham

The author spent her life trying to be the perfect wife, mother, and Christian. But her life was light-years away from her dream. *The Confident Woman* is a passionate look at the transforming power of surrender to God.

Grace Rules
Steve McVey

Is it more satisfying to live the Christian life by adhering to religious rules or by letting grace rule your life? In *Grace Rules*, Steve McVey shows how understanding the concepts of law and grace helps you walk in your identity in Christ. Even better, by discovering how Jesus' grace can consistently flow out of your life, you can experience a satisfying *and* abundant Christian life.

Grace Walk
Steve McVey

What you've always wanted in the Christian life . . . but never expected. Learn to push self-sufficiency aside and let Christ live through you. Experience the grace walk and know the spiritual fulfillment you have been striving for all along.

How to Study the Bible for Yourself
(Revised and Expanded Edition)
Tim LaHaye

The updated version of this award-winning book comes packed with more examples, more flexible study options, and up-to-date suggestions to help you experience the excitement of exploring the Bible.

Lifetime Guarantee
Bill Gillham

You've tried fixing your marriage, your children, your job. Suddenly the light dawns: It's not your problems that need fixing, it's your *life!* The key to experiencing victory in Christ lies in learning how to literally "walk in newness of life" as described in the Word. Guaranteed.

Acknowledgments

Save for extenuating circumstances—such as that of the apostle John on Patmos, or Madam Guyon, who walked out with a radiant smile after 17 years of solitary confinement for her faith; or Watchman Nee, who had a similar experience for some 20 years before being martyred in Communist China—God doesn't raise up "lone ranger" Christians.

I wish to acknowledge those who have taught me beautiful truths from God: the Holy Spirit, who inspired the writers of the Bible—for this and for His grace in revealing any truth that I may have; my wife, Anabel, for "lifing out" Christ before me; my four fine sons—Preston, my partner in ministry, CEO and president of Lifetime Guarantee Ministries; Mason, who is with the Lord; Will, whom I'll acknowledge later; and Wade, for loving and respecting Anabel and me; my three godly daughters-in-law for loving Jesus, my sons, and us; the thousands of suffering counselees who have often been tools God used to drive me deeper into Christ, seeking answers for them; and (alphabetically) Paul Billheimer, Paul Burleson, Frank Friedman, DeVerne Fromke, Bob George, Tom Grady, Joe Hubbard, D. Martyn Lloyd-Jones, Karl Kakadelis, Jay Kesler, Lee LeFebre, C. S. Lewis, Peter Lord, C. S. Lovett, Steve McVey, Mike Middleton, Watchman Nee, David Needham, William R. Newell, Carroll Ray, Jr., Chuck Solomon, Jack Taylor, and last (but not least by a long shot), the dear brothers and sisters in our office: Ken Cummins, Allen Davis, Dave Jolly, Rochelle Lentschke, Lisa McKneely, Abe Martinez, John and Marcy Moneypenny, Joyce Ray, Donna Taylor, Caryn Walker, and our associate staff. And sure as the world, I've forgotten someone who is very precious to me. Add your name here: _____.

I wish to acknowledge Harvest House Publishers President Bob Hawkins, Jr., Editorial Director Carolyn McCready, and Senior Editor Steve Miller, who laboriously scrutinized this manuscript, all the while serving as encouragers. Not many would have walked this second mile. Thank you, dear friends.

Finally, I wish to acknowledge my editor: number-three son, Will. It is common knowledge around our office that when I am seen at my word processor, the rabbits had better find a hole because they are to be chased into exhaustion! Will helped to make this manuscript say what I meant to say. Thanks, bro.

No lone ranger,
Bill